The Peppers Cookbook

The Peppers Cookbook

200 Recipes from the Pepper Lady's Kitchen

NUMBER TWO IN THE GREAT AMERICAN COOKING SERIES

JEAN ANDREWS

University of North Texas Press
Denton, Texas

Foreword by Jerry Anne DiVecchio ©2005 University of North Texas Press

Some of the recipes in this book previously appeared in
The Pepper Trail: History & Recipes from Around the World
written and illustrated by Jean Andrews ©1999 University of North Texas Press

Guacamole (Avocado Salad) reprinted by permission from
Peppers: The Domesticated Capsicums, ©1984, 1995, University of Texas Press

10 9 8 7 6 5 4 3 2 1

Permissions:
University of North Texas Press
P.O. Box 311336
Denton, TX 76203-1336

The paper used in this book meets the minimum requirements of the American National
Standard for Permanence of Paper for Printed Library Materials, z39.48.1984.
Binding materials have been chosen for durability.

Number Two in the Great American Cooking Series

Interior Design by Carol Sawyer, Rose Design

ISBN-13 978-1-57441-193-5
ISBN-10 1-57441-193-4

Library of Congress Cataloging-in-Publication Data

Andrews, Jean, 1923–
  The peppers cookbook : 200 recipes from the pepper lady's kitchen / Jean Andrews.
    p. cm.—(Number two in the great American cooking series)
  Includes bibliographical references and index.
  ISBN 1-57441-193-4 (pbk. : alk. paper)
  1. Cookery (Hot peppers) 2. Hot peppers. I. Title. II. Great American cooking series ; no. 2.
  TX803.P46A524 2005
  641.6'384—dc22
                                    2005002605

Contents

Foreword

Peppers and Jean Andrews were made for each other. Peppers are complicated and confusing. Jean is fired by curiosity and a meticulous organizer. Peppers have spread by circuitous means (birds, to explorers, to garden catalogs) and adapted to locations all over the world. Jean has tracked them fearlessly to rugged, remote, exotic destinations as well as test farms in New Mexico and California. Peppers have a muddled, mysterious history botanically and geographically. Jean is a Sherlock Holmes at heart, sleuthing and deducing to discover solutions that add to the literature. Peppers range from mellow, mild, even sweet, to explosively pungent and intensely flavored. Collectively, peppers are beautiful, cloaked in brilliant colors hued from sunrise to sunset. I might not use all these descriptors for Jean, but many apply!

Jean Andrews came to my attention twenty years ago when a particularly literate and savant garden editor rushed into my office with a large book in his hand. He was fairly bursting with enthusiasm, rattling (almost ranting) rapidly about "this amazing piece of literature on a capsicum . . . never saw anything so well done" and more. The book was Jean Andrews' *Peppers: The Domesticated Capsicums*, accurately, sensitively illustrated with opaque watercolors of peppers rendered in scientific detail—not just the pod, but the whole plant, leaf, and blossom—by the author who is also an artist. One of those original paintings now hangs in my hallway, purchased through the University of North Texas, Denton, Texas to endow worthy scholarships in art that Jean supports.

Jean's photo was on the book's back jacket. Her hair was smoothed into a chignon—as I comb my own. The picture was black and white, but I could tell she was wearing a blue cotton chambray shirt because it was identical to a favorite of my own. Her smile suggested a spirited personality and, possibly, an ironic gleam of humor. Clearly, here was a person with whom I could relate and learn from.

At the time, I was the food and wine editor for *Sunset Magazine* (1959–2001), a West coast shelter publication that recently celebrated its 106th anniversary. We considered peppers part of our culinary heritage, particularly the pungent chilies, because a huge chunk of our readership resides in what was once part of Mexico. Our editorial influence often impacted the marketplace. For example, we were instrumental in convincing growers of Bell peppers to market the more flavorful, although more perishable, ripe fruit as well as the green ones; other kinds of ripe chili peppers followed. It was also our self-assigned task to help our readers identify and use advantageously both the fresh and dried chili peppers that were steadily moving from ethnic markets into the supermarket mainstream. Much of our early information came from Southern California, the Southwest, and Mexico, primary sources of the products that we used in our tested recipes. In Sunset's *Mexican Cookbook* (first edition 1969), we codified what we knew, but the pepper picture continued to evolve and expand. Nomenclature was confusing. A fresh chili pepper, as Jean explains, and its dried counterpart often have different names. Additionally, the very spelling of the word chili (chilli, chile, and more) is a subject of debate, not only among Jean's learned associates, but on our own copy desk. On more than one occasion, phone calls and faxes flashed from my office to Jean's as I sought her support and authority to resolve chili inspired debates. And as new kinds of fresh peppers continually popped up in Latin and Southeastern Asian markets, it was Jean who helped me identify them.

Serendipitously scheduled right after the publication of *Peppers: The Domesticated Capsicums* was a food conference in California's Napa Valley wine country. I was asked to chair a panel on Latin foods for an audience that ranged from celebrities like Julia Child, food print and media journalists, cookbook authors, food scientists, chefs, food industrialists, restaurateurs, restaurant reviewers, cooking teachers . . . right on down to folks just interested in eating well. Naturally, I jumped at a reason to invite Jean to participate. She was as impressive in the flesh as she was through her writing; we've been in touch ever since.

Jean often describes her life as BC and AC, Before Chilies and After Chilies. Truly, she deserves to be called a renaissance woman. Graduated a home economist, she's knowledgeable and interested in foods, nutrition, and textiles, too. Trained as an artist and illustrator, her scientific bent brings beauty and fact into her art. As a diver and researcher, she wrote and illustrated books on seashells. Self-taught, initially, in botany and horticulture, she's written and illustrated books on wildflowers.

But it was the capsicum family that pushed Jean onto center stage, focused her scholarly abilities, and earned her a world-wide reputation as an outstanding expert on the subject of peppers. Her timing was perfect. That food conference represented a major attitude shift about food and eating. Food was news, chefs as famous as movie stars, restaurants were theatre, where to dine as much a part of a trip as the destination.

Peppers were and still are right in the middle of the excitement, and so is Jean.

While following historical pepper trails around the globe, in dusty libraries with ancient manuscripts, mountain villages in the Andes and Himalayas, and even the most chic restaurants from Paris to Bangkok to Santa Fe, Jean accumulated information about the cultures and foods that used peppers. She also gathered pepper seeds, grew the plants, studied, classified, photographed, and painted them; then she ate the fruit, identified their characteristics, and cooked with the peppers to develop recipes. Clearly, content for many a volume was piling up. Each of Jean's books on chilies brings new dimensions to a subject that is, no pun intended, HOT.

Because peppers are particularly able to adapt to growing conditions and shift personalities through breeding, the scene is constantly changing. Chilies that were once considered searingly hot have been bred to pull back their heat and let their flavor come forward. Jean's *The Pepper Lady's Pocket Pepper Primer* is a landmark volume about the physical aspects of peppers-names (common and Latin), size, color, flavor, shape, uses, sources, and genealogy. *The Pepper Trail* takes up where her first book left off.

What follows logically? This tome on cooking with peppers. It's fascinating to know why the pungency of a pepper hurts so much you want more; how capsaicin—the fuel of pepper sensations—serves us medically as fact or fiction, and how nutritious peppers are.

But best of all, it's wonderful to have this expansive collection of recipes selected by Jean that uses peppers for their unique personalities—by variety, by flavor, by color—to create delectable dishes and wonderful meals.

Jerry Anne Di Vecchio

Preface

Ask yourself—what am I doing here? If you are not a pepper fan (friend or fiend) or a "wannabe," you are probably in the wrong place, because what follows is designed for those who want to cook with peppers and to know more ways to use and enjoy them as food. This is a pepper cookbook and every recipe contains at least one type or version of that pungent pod. It is also designed for the curious cook who wants to know more about the whys and wherefores of nutritious and flavorful food preparations and their ingredients. If the reader wants to learn more about other aspects of the *Capsicum* peppers, they can be found in my *Peppers: The Domesticated Capsicums,* (University of Texas Press, Austin, 1984, revised, 1995) and its companion *The Pepper Trail* (University of North Texas Press, Denton, 1999) which won the 2001 Jane Grigson Award for scholarship presented by the International Association of Culinary Professionals. Both of these books I researched, wrote, and illustrated with my own artwork and photographs.

Those books, designed to be two volumes, will tell you more than you probably want to know about New World peppers from their discovery in 1492 by Christopher Columbus until they reached your table. The first one covers the history, biology, taxonomy, physiology, descriptions, and literature with color illustrations of thirty-four *Capsicum* cultivars, but it barely touches on the food aspect of our subject. The second is all about peppers as food and their travels from the New World to the Old World with the effects they had on the cuisines of the various cultures that adopted them. This is followed by a section of recipes, certain ones of which are included herein. A few are by some of America's outstanding chefs, while others are recipes I have collected from my extensive travels as I tracked peppers on their journey from the Americas to Spain, Africa, India, Asia, the Middle and Far East, and Europe.

This book explains what peppers are, how to prepare interesting and nutritious dishes with peppers, and provides recipes for that purpose. Besides attempting to introduce you to the foodways and tastes of the world's pepper eating cultures with their traditional dishes, the contents and recipes have been designed with several things in mind—good nutrition, ease of preparation, and flavor. I love good food! Not only to eat it but also to grow it, handle it, paint it, analyze it, smell it, preserve it, and prepare it for the table. I like to try new foods and different recipes using them. This is a very personal book, the kind I want in my kitchen. To test the recipes in this compilation, I have prepared every recipe in it—except for a few of those by chef friends. At home, my friends were invited to "Guinea pig" dinners to get their opinions of new dishes I had selected and prepared.

I am not a professional food person; however, on several occasions I have served as a paid consultant to several major American food companies, the Nestle Corp. for one, and magazines such as *Southern Living* in Alabama and Sunset *Magazine* in California, that wanted their staffs to know how to use peppers. Also I have lectured on the subject of peppers in more places than I can name, including the Smithsonian, and the Schlesinger Library at Harvard. I was invited to write "Chilli Peppers" for *The Cambridge World History of Food* published in 2000 by

Cambridge University Press, and "Chili Peppers" in *The Encyclopedia of Food and Culture* published in 2002 by Charles Scribner's Son. Also, I was chosen by the Texas State Agriculture Department to be in *Who's Who in Food and Wine in Texas* and was one of three nominated to be "Grand Dame" of Les Dames de Escofier, an organization of female food professionals. My undergraduate degree is in Home Economics, and I am a Certified Home Economist with an almost manic interest in good nutrition. I have endowed Visiting Professorships in Human Nutrition and Economic Botany at The University of Texas at Austin. That University's College of Natural Science saw fit to name me to their Hall of Honor—but what I do best is ASK QUESTIONS.

In this book I want to share with you some of the answers I have found to my food and cooking questions. It has been designed with the curious cook in mind. Not only one with curiosity but also one who likes to cook and wants to know more about what they cook, what they cook with, the tools they use, how to serve it, its cultural background, and nutritional value.

Some of the 200 recipes included have been in my other books but they are all worth repeating because they fill a certain niche that can hardly be improved on— especially the traditional sauces and condiments, most of which have been collected from around the world. This book is designed to go on the kitchen counter, not the coffee table. Take it there and ENJOY! Don't be afraid to put your own twist on a recipe. Taste as you go. BLT's are the sign of a good cook (that is Bites, Licks, and Tastes— not Bacon, Lettuce and Tomato), just watch the amounts.

Please forgive any Texas bias you might find in these pages, but I am a fifth generation Texan who comes from a long line of Texas women who were excellent cooks. Buried in Texas soil are two of my great-great grandmothers, two great grandmothers, a wonderful grandmother who let me spend a lot of time helping, watching, and tasting in her kitchen where she prepared goodies known all over town for their excellence, and an auntie and mother who inherited her food preparation skills. It is in their memory I dedicate this cookbook. I hope that you, your family, and friends will enjoy using it.

PART I

WHAT IS A PEPPER?

LOOK AT ME! CULTIVAR DESCRIPTIONS

PEPPERS ON YOUR PLATE

What is a Pepper?

How do you account for the popularity of the pepper pod—neither pepper nor a pod? It is the fruit of the genus *Capsicum,* which was named and defined by J. P. Tournefort in 1700, yet is still a rather mixed-up group of plants. Not just the Spanish name *pimiento* is cause for argument but the defining characteristics of that genus are still being debated. However, there are some things on which all agree. To begin with, a *Capsicum* pepper is not related to its namesake, black pepper, which is the seed of a woody vine native to India, *Piper nigrum.*

Origin and Discovery

The confusion originated over five-hundred years ago with Christopher Columbus, whose quest for black pepper and other spices, under the auspices of the crowned heads of Spain, caused him to sail to the west from the Spanish Canary Islands in his attempt to reach the East Indian Archipelago and India from whence spices came. If successful, the new route would have broken the Moslem monopoly of the spice trade. When he arrived at the Islands of the Caribbean he was so certain he had reached his goal that he called the islands the Indies, the natives Indians, and their pungent, red spice *pimiento* after the *pimienta* for which he was searching. Later other Spanish explorers added to the confusion when they also called a second unrelated indigenous American spice *pimienta,* or pepper. It was allspice, *Pimenta dioica,* in the myrtle family.

Before the discovery of the Americas Europeans had also used another pungent spice known as Guinea or ginnie pepper, *Aframomum melegueta,* which came from Guinea in West Africa. It was known as "grains of paradise" or melegueta pepper which, along with its kin, cardamom, is a member of the ginger family. Soon after the Spanish Discovery the Portuguese acquired the new tropical, pungent, "pimento" from the "New World" and introduced it to their tropical west African bases where it flourished. The natives, who were already accustomed to pungent spices, fell in love with the new, fiery *Capsicum* pods. In 1535, the Portuguese first brought those capsicums to Brazil with their African slaves, who couldn't eat without them. The new pungent spice had not only largely supplanted the native melegueta pepper but also adopted its common name—"Ginnie" pepper. These elongate cayenne type chili peppers or "Ginnie" peppers were the capsicums the Portuguese introduced to India and the Far East from their African outposts.

If it is not related to the black pepper of India, then just what is a *Capsicum*? The genus *Capsicum* is a member of the plant family Solanaceae along with potatoes, tobacco, petunias, the deadly night shade, and others. Thousands of years ago, some tropical Amerindians domesticated a wild, native *Capsicum* into a wide variety of plants with fiery fruits that grow from sea level to an altitude of ten thousand feet but are killed by frost. The original capsicums were perennial herbaceous to woody shrubs native to the American tropics. Today, breeders have developed annual varieties that can be grown in areas subject to freezes.

There is still no agreement among scholars as to its exact place of origin—either somewhere in central Bolivia or southwestern Brazil. Some capsicums had been carried by birds, their natural means of dispersal, to other parts of

South and Central America long before humans migrated across the Bering Strait to America, and before human migration reached Mesoamerica (Middle or Central America). That indigenous spice had also been carried by birds and native Americans from Mesoamerica to the Caribbean long before the Columbian Connection began in 1492. The pre-Columbian natives had also domesticated the four or five species of capsicums that are cultivated today, and no new species have been developed since that time.

All species of wild capsicums have certain common characteristics: small, pungent, red fruits that may be round, elongate, or conical and are attached to the plant in an erect position. The seeds of the deciduous fruits are dispersed by birds that are not affected by the pungency. Wild *Capsicum* flowers have a stigma-bearing style that extends beyond the anthers to facilitate pollination by insects. Domesticated cultivars have short styles that promote self-pollination. When humans began to cultivate the Capsicum plants they, unconsciously or perhaps even consciously, selected seed from those fruits more difficult to remove from the calyx so that birds could not pluck them, thereby remaining attached until harvest. They also found that capsicums, which hung down and were hidden among the leaves, were more difficult for hungry birds to collect. Consequently, pendent fruit became more desirable, and today most domesticated capsicums have pendent fruit instead of erect. As larger and larger fruits were selected, the size and weight increased, which caused the capsicums to become pendent. The fruit, the most valued part of the plant to humans, was changed through the grower's selection for the desired characteristics. All mild and sweet capsicums are the result of selection because all wild capsicums are pungent—mouth warming. This pungency results from the presence of a group of closely related alkaloid compounds and is unique in the vegetable kingdom.

Origin and Use of Name

When Columbus first came upon capsicums the Arawaks, who had come to the West Indies from South America, called their South American pepper *axí*, which the Spanish transliterated to *ají* (*ajé, agí*). That language is extinct now, and so are the Arawaks. Today, that name is applied to the pungent varieties in only a few places in the Caribbean along with much of South America. However, *uchu* and *huayca* are ancient native American words still used for capsicums by some Amerindian groups in the Andean area. A different *Capsicum* species arrived from Mesoamerica without a native name. The Spanish called fruits of both species *pimiento* or *pimientón* in the Caribbean Islands (depending on the size) after *pimienta* or East Indian black pepper. Those Spanish names traveled with the new plant to Spain but not to all parts of Europe; it is called *piment* in France, *peperone* in Italy, and *paprika* by the Balkan Slavic people.

In 1518, when the Spanish conquerors came to Mexico, they heard the Nahuatl speaking natives calling their fiery spice by a Nahuatl name that sounded like "chee-yee." A half century later, when the Spanish botanist Francisco Hernandez arrived in 1570, he wrote that Nahuatl name as *chilli*, giving it the Spanish spelling using a "*ll*" which sounds like "y"—hence, *chilli*. The term chilli did not appear in print until 1651 when his work was first published. Later the Spanish "*ll*" sound as a "y" reverted to the sound of a single "*l*" (el) in Spanish.

The Nahuatl stem *chil* refers to the *chilli* plant. It also means "red." To the generic word *chilli,* the term that described the particular *chilli* cultivar was added (e.g., *Tonalchilli* = chilli of the sun or summer, *Chiltecpin* = flea chilli). In Mexico today, the Spanish word *chile,* which was derived from *chilli,* refers to both pungent and sweet types and is used in combination with and placed before a descriptive adjective, such as *chile colorado* (red chilli) or a word that indicates the place of origin, such as *chile poblano* (chilli from Pueblo). The same variety can have different names in different geographic regions, in various stages of maturity, or in the dried state. Consequently, the names of capsicums in Mexico can be very confusing.

The Portuguese language uses *pimenta* for capsicums and qualifies the various types—*Pimenta-da-caiena,* cayenne pepper; *Pimenta-da-malagueta,* red pepper; *Pimenta-da-reino* or *-da rabo,* black pepper; *Pimenta-da-jamaica,* allspice; while *pimentão* is pimento, red pepper or just pepper. *Ají* and *chile* are not found in a Portuguese dictionary, nor did they carry those words with them in their travels.

It is likely that the current *Capsicum* names were first carried to the Eastern part of the world by the Dutch. After that the English were probably responsible for their movement because in Australia, India, Indonesia, and Thailand *chilli* (*chillies*) or sometimes *chilly,* is commonly used by English speakers for the pungent types, while the mild ones are called capsicums. However, until very recently only mild varieties were to be had in Australia, while Indonesians and Thais don't yet consume sweet capsicums so they have no word for them. Each Far Eastern language has its own word for chillies—*prik* in Thai and *mirch* in Hindi, to name but two.

The United States is where the most confusion exists. Here we find both the anglicized spelling, chilli (chillies) or chili (chilies) and the Spanish *chile* (chiles) used by some for the pungent fruits of the *Capsicum* plant, while chili (minus one *l*) is also used as a short form in *chili con carne,* a variously concocted mixture of meat and chillies. *The Oxford English Dictionary* gives chilli as the primary usage, calling chile and chili variants. *Webster's New International Dictionary* prefers chili followed by the Spanish *chile* and the Nahuatl *chilli.* In the American Southwest, the Spanish *chile* refers to the long green/red chilli that is/was first known as the Anaheim or the long green/red chilli, but is called the 'New Mexican Chile' by the locals. New Mexicans even had the name entered in the *Congressional Record*

of November 3, 1983 (misidentified as C. *frutescens* instead of C. *annuum* var. *annuum*). In an English speaking country it seems incongruous to choose the Spanish *chile* over the anglicized chili, or chilli. It would be so much less confusing if they were called what they are—*Capsicum,* but getting Americans to call all peppers capsicums would be like getting us to use the metric system.

Not because one name is right and another is wrong, but for the sake of consistency and clarity, in this book *Capsicum* or pepper will be used for the fruit of the *Capsicum* plant. When used in singular form it is capitalized and in italics—*Capsicum.* When plural, it is lower case and without italics—capsicums. The pungent types will be chilli or chili pepper. Chili pepper is the most common usage in American scientific papers. Chili with one *l* is the spicy meat dish, and pimento is the sweet, thick-fleshed, heart-shaped red *Capsicum.* If *chile* in italics is used, it will refer to a native Mexican cultivar or, without italics, to the long green/red 'New Mexican Chile,' which is a registered cultivar. Whenever possible the name of the specific fruit type/group or cultivar name will be used. It is hoped that the reader will follow suit, thereby helping to stabilize the troublesome situation.

The important thing to keep in mind is that each variety has its own character and if another variety is substituted, the flavor of the dish will be changed. Therefore it is essential that not only the specific *Capsicum* but also its specific form (fresh, dried, canned, pickled, etc.) be used and not just hot pepper or green pepper. Studying the illustrated cultivar descriptions starting on page 11 will make this easier.

Nutritional Information

Capsicums are not only good, they are good for you. Nutritionally, capsicums are a dietary plus. They contain more vitamin A than any other food plant; they are also an excellent source of vitamin C and the B vitamins. One jalapeño contains more vitamin A and C than three medium-size oranges. Capsicums also contain significant amounts of magnesium, iron, thiamine, riboflavin, and niacin. Even though chili peppers are not eaten in large quantities, small amounts are important where traditional diets provide only marginal vitamins. In *Peppers,* I give a detailed account of the nutritional value of capsicums along with the story of their use by the Hungarian scientist Albert Szent-Györgyi in his discovery of vitamin C (see fig. 1).

I Gram Uncooked	Vit. A (ICUS)	Vit. C (MG.S)
Bell pepper	50	1.20
Fresh orange	2.24	.538
Carrot	30.5	.35
Potato	.375	.016
Tomato	8.49	.22

Figure I

Vitamin C is a very unstable nutrient. It is readily destroyed through exposure to oxygen in the air, by drying, by heating, and it is soluble in water. In other words, cooking is very damaging to it. Keep cut or peeled capsicums well covered to prevent contact with oxygen. Don't permit them to stand in water for more than one hour. Nevertheless, cooked and canned green capsicums retain considerable vitamin C. Because vitamin C diminishes with maturity, green capsicums are higher in vitamin C than ripe red capsicums. Vitamin A is just the opposite because it increases as the fruit matures and dries. Also, oxygen exposure does not destroy vitamin A, and it is quite stable during the cooking and preservation process.

Pepper seed, like all seed, have some protein and fat (oil), although they are primarily carbohydrate. There is also a little manganese and copper, but otherwise they add little nutritionally. In Anglo-America they are traditionally removed, but in other countries removal is seldom customary—especially in the small chili peppers. Removing seed from fresh green or red chili peppers reduces the pungency to some extent because the seed absorb capsaicin (CAPS) from the placental wall where they are attached. Pepper seed that are large when mature (for example ancho and 'New Mexican Chile' types) become woody in texture when dry. Some find that texture undesirable; however, others grind them up to give a nutty flavor to sauces (for example *chile cascabel*). Higher grades of paprika and pepper flakes have had the seeds and veins removed before grinding. Whether you leave the seed in or remove them is strictly a matter of personal preference having little effect on nutritional value.

Weight conscious readers may be pleased to learn that studies have found that eating capsicums and a few other pungent spices cause the metabolic rate to increase. This diet-induced thermic effect requires six grams of chillies or a very pungent chili pepper sauce (for example Tabasco Pepper Sauce®) combined with three grams of prepared mustard to burn off an average of forty-five calories in three hours. Prepare the pungent mixture and put it in a small jar with a screw-lid. Take a teaspoonful about thirty minutes before each meal—you'll get used to it.

Scientific studies in recent years reported the nutritional and medical attributes of capsicums. During this time the public's nutritional awareness has increased. Our daily vocabulary now includes terms like low-calorie, low-cholesterol, complex carbohydrates, high-fiber, low-sodium, unsaturated oils, and low-fat, and food growers and processors have responded to public demand by providing for these nutritional requirements (see fig. 2). An educated change in traditional American food-style is vital to good health. Capsicums are in line with these food restrictions and at the same time their distinctive flavor adds zest to an

Name of Food Capsicum annumm	Amount in Edible Portions of Common Measures	K. Calories	Protein (gm)	Fat (gm)	Carbohydrates (gm)	Fiber (gm)	Calcium (mg)	Phosphorus (mg)	Iron (mg)	Zinc (mg)	Manganese (mg)	Potassium (mg)	Ascorbic Acid (Vit. C) (mg)	Thiamin (mg)	Niacin (mg)	B_6 (mg)	Follacin (mcg)	Vit. A (IU)
Peppers, Sweet, Raw Green and Red	1/2 C chopped = 50 g	12	0.43	0.23	19.76	0.60	3.0	11.0	0.63	0.09	0.07	98.0	64.0	0.043	0.275	0.610	8.4	265.0
Peppers, Chilli, Raw Green and Red	1/2 C chopped = 75 g	30	1.50	0.05	7.10	1.35	13.0	34.0	0.90	0.23	0.178	255.0	181.9	0.068	0.713	0.209	17.5	578.0
Paprika	1 teaspoon = 2.1 g	6	0.31	0.27	1.17	0.44	4.0	7.0	0.50	0.08	—	49.0	1.49	0.014	0.322	—	—	1273.0
Cayenne Pepper	1 teaspoon = 1.8 g	6	0.22	0.31	1.02	0.45	3.0	5.0	0.14	0.05	3.0	36.0	1.38	0.006	0.159	—	—	249.0
Jalapeño, Canned Solids and liquid	1/2 C chopped = 68 g	17	0.54	0.41	3.33	1.56	18.0	12.0	1.90	0.13	—	92.0	8.8	0.02	0.340	—	—	1156.0
New Mexican Chile Canned	1/2 C chopped = 68 g	17	0.61	0.07	4.45	0.82	5.0	12.0	0.34	—	—	—	46.2	0.014	0.549	—	—	415.0

Source: U.S. Department of Agriculture 1976. *Composition of Foods: Spices.* USDA Agricultural Handbook No. 8-2 Washington, D.C.: Government Printing Office, Superintendent of Documents.

Figure 2

otherwise bland, creamless, fatless, starchless, saltless, sugarless meal. Capsicums are a real health food!

Capsaicin (CAPS), The Pungent Principle

Vitamins and fiber are not the reason people eat chili peppers; they eat them because they are pungent, which causes a sharp stinging or burning effect. Take away the vitamins and the fiber and people would still eat chili peppers, but take away the capsaicin (CAPS) and they don't want them. Capsicums are the only plant in the world that has capsaicin, hence the name. It is a unique group of mouth-warming amide-type alkaloids containing a small vanilloid structural component that is responsible for the stinging or burning sensation associated with capsicums by acting directly on the pain receptors in the mouth and throat. This vanilloid element is present in other pungent plants used for spices such as ginger and black pepper. For some time capsaicin was believed to contain only one active pungent principle but more recently, studies have added other compounds to form a pungent group of which capsaicin is the most important part. Three of these capsaicinoid components cause the sensation of "rapid bite" at the back of the palate and throat, and two others cause a long, low-intensity bite on the tongue and midpalate. Differences in the proportions of these compounds may account for the characteristic "burns" of the different *Capsicum* cultivars. In both sweet and pungent capsicums, the major part of the organs secreting these pungent alkaloids is localized in the placenta to which the seeds are attached along with dissepiment (ribs or veins), which is the part of the placenta that divides the interior cavity into sections or lobes (see fig. 3). The seeds contain only a low concentration of CAPS.

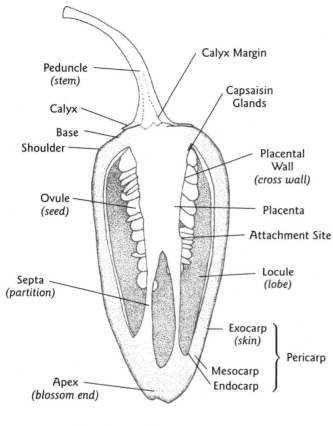

Peduncle *(stem)*

Calyx

Base

Shoulder

Calyx Margin

Capsaisin Glands

Placental Wall *(cross wall)*

Ovule *(seed)*

Placenta

Attachment Site

Septa *(partition)*

Locule *(lobe)*

Exocarp *(skin)*

Apex *(blossom end)*

Mesocarp

Endocarp

Pericarp

Figure 3
Cross Section of a Pepper

The response to some additives in food used at optimal levels is their perception in the mouth as a warm, mouth-watering quality, which is commonly referred to as hot, stinging, irritating, sharp, caustic, acrid, biting, or burning. V. S. Govindarajan, a sensory analyst and *Capsicum* authority from India, insists that this response should be defined by the term "pungency," rather than those other less desirable connotations routinely used. He also suggests that pungency be given the status of a gustatory characteristic of food—as are sweet, sour, bitter, saline, astringent, or alkaline. I try to use "pungent" in

place of temperature descriptors such as "hot" or "burning," but long-standing habit interferes as it does when I try to use meters instead of yards.

The CAPS content is influenced by the growing conditions of the plant, the age of the fruit, and could possibly be variety-specific. The amount of CAPS is increased by dry, stressful conditions. The CAPS content begins to increase in the fruit about the eleventh day after inception, becoming detectable when the fruit is about four weeks old. It reaches its peak just before maturity, then drops somewhat in the ripening stage. Sun-drying usually reduces the capsaicin content, the highest retention being obtained when the fruits are air-dried, with minimum exposure to sunlight.

CAPS keeps most animals from eating peppers; however, birds do not have pain receptors sensitive to that pungent principle. Consequently, they are the principal natural dispersal agent of capsicums. A bird's digestive tract softens the seed without significant damage, which promotes germination. Many small animals cannot see red, but the red color attracts birds to the ripe fruit.

Capsaicin (CAPS) is hard to detect by chemical tests. It has virtually no odor or flavor but a drop of a solution containing one part in one-hundred-thousand causes a persistent burning on the tongue. CAPS is eight times more pungent than the piperine in black pepper, but unlike black pepper, which inhibits all tastes, CAPS only obstructs the perception of sour and bitter; it does not impair our discernment of other gustatory characteristics of food. In the kitchen, one should taste a tiny portion to estimate the pungency and adjust usage accordingly. A simple scale of one to ten has been used in this book to rate the pungency of the various cultivars described herein.

CAPS activates the defensive and digestive systems by acting as an irritant to the oral and gastrointestinal membranes. That irritation increases the flow of saliva and gastric acids. Eating CAPS also causes the neck, face, and front of the chest to sweat in a reflexive response to the burning in the mouth.

There are several ways to put out the fire. CAPS is not soluble in water. No amount of water will wash it away; however, cool water will give temporary relief by changing the surface temperature. In 1984, I discovered that the addition of a small amount of chlorine or ammonia ionized the CAPS compound, changing it into a soluble salt (Andrews 1984, 127). This works miracles on your hands, but, of course, you can't drink chlorine or ammonia. However, as are many organic compounds, CAPS is soluble in alcohol. Again this works on the skin but caution must be noted when you drink it. For your burning mouth, try using cheap vodka as a mouthwash—gargle then spit it out—great for the designated driver.

Oral burning can also be relieved by lipoproteins, such as casein that remove CAPS in a manner similar to the action of a detergent, thereby breaking the bond the CAPS had formed with pain receptors in your mouth. Milk and yogurt are readily available sources of casein. It is the casein, not the fat, in milk that does the job; therefore, butter and cheese will not have the same effect. CAPS or the burning sensation produced by it is proving to be a non-habit-forming alternative to the addictive drugs used to control pain. Already this treatment is being used to deal with the pain associated with shingles, rheumatoid arthritis, and phantom-limb pain.

Aroma, Flavor, and Color

Each pepper cultivar—serrano, jalapeño, habanero, cubanelle, etc.—has a distinctive flavor. The flavor compound of capsicums is located in the outer wall (pericarp); very little is found in the placenta and cross wall, essentially none in the seeds (see fig. 3). Color and flavor go hand in hand because the flavor principle appears to be associated with the carotenoid pigment: strong color and strong flavor are linked. For example, the red or colored Bell Peppers are far superior in flavor to the less expensive, unripe greens. Being able to recognize the differences in flavors of the various cultivars is most important in cooking. Using a different variety can completely change the character of a dish. An ancho or a guajillo cannot be substituted for a cayenne without a noticeable difference.

Color is the most compelling element in a painting and it is also an important component in foods as well. Even if you don't eat capsicums, their use as garnishes can enhance the total appearance of your dish or table. The carotenoid pigments responsible for the color in capsicums make them commercially important as natural dyes in food and drug products throughout the world. Red capsanthin, the most important pigment, is not found in immature green capsicums but develops with maturity. Green capsicums are simply gathered before they are fully ripe. Unripe capsicums have better keeping quality and are less difficult to transport than ripe ones; consequently, they are more available and less expensive in the market. The distinctive *Capsicum* flavors develop only as the fruit ripens, reaching its peak at maturity.

Taste and smell are separate perceptions. Americans are learning to appreciate aroma in capsicums as Asians and Africans have long done. The fragrance is produced by several aroma compounds. The taste buds on the tongue can discern certain flavors at dilutions up to one part in two million but odors can be detected at a dilution of one part in one billion. The more delicate flavors of foods are recognized as aromas in the nasal cavity adjacent to the mouth. Compare the aroma of a jalapeño with that of habanero and you will recognize the specific odor of each immediately.

Why Chili Pepper Lovers Love Chili Peppers

What is it about a fruit that makes one-quarter of the adults on the earth eat it every day in spite of the fact that nature designed it to be pungent (burn) in order to protect it? The burning effect produced by CAPS is a principal reason for liking capsicums. The initially negative feeling becomes positive. Regular consumption of chili pepper has a slight desensitizing effect, good news for the chili pepper lover who craves the burn. Liking to eat chili peppers is definitely an acquired taste unique to human mammals. Young children do not care for them.

What is a *Capsicum?* An old dictionary of "Aztequismos" defined *chile* as "*el miembro viril*" or virile member. However, since this book concerns food and why we like to eat capsicums as a food, I'll not go into the medical or physiological aspects that concern responses to such sensations as its aphrodisiac potential, opponent-endorphin responses, and benign masochism. If you want to know more about endorphin-stimulating capsaicins, look at my *Peppers.*

Look at Me! Cultivar Descriptions

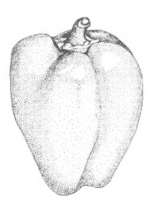

Descriptions of Peppers Used in the Recipes

Unless noted otherwise, the peppers you will be using in the recipes in this book are *Capsicum annuum* var. *annuum* Linné. In certain varieties of Mexican peppers the fresh and dried forms have different names. A simple scale of one to ten has been used to rate the pungency of each cultivar. Use the high rated ones with caution.

Banana Pepper and Hungarian Wax

C. annuum var. *annuum* Linné, 1753

COLOR: Pale yellow-green to yellow, maturing to bright red

SHAPE: Elongated cylinder, tapering to a point. Wax-type

SIZE: 5½ to 6 inches long by 1½ inches wide

PUNGENCY: Sweet: 0. Hot: 5

SUBSTITUTES: 'Cubanelle' for sweet; 'Caloro,' 'Santa Fe Grande' for pungent

OTHER NAMES: 'Sweet Banana,' 'Hungarian Yellow Wax'

USES:

Fresh: in salads, as garnishes, stuffed (as is done in celery), in vegetable dishes and stews, fried. Pickled: as garnishes, in salads, on sandwiches, as a condiment

SOURCES:

Fresh: Home garden, farmer's markets

Dried: Not used dried

Processed: Pickled banana peppers available in food stores

Seeds: Most seed suppliers. Available cultivars: 'Early Sweet Banana,' 'Giant Yellow Banana,' 'Hungarian yellow wax,' 'Long Sweet Yellow'

Bell Pepper

C. annuum var. *annuum* Linné, 1753

COLOR: Green to red, orange, yellow, brown, or purple

SHAPE: Blocky. A few cultivars, such as the tomato-shaped 'Sunnybrook' or the long, narrow 'Ruby King,' do not conform. Bell-type

SIZE: 4 to 6 inches long by 3½ to 4 inches wide
PUNGENCY: Sweet: 0, except for 'Mexi-bell': 3 to 5
SUBSTITUTES: Banana, 'Cubanelle,' pimento peppers
OTHER NAMES: Capsicums, mango, *morrón, pimentón,*
    or any one of the hundreds of hybrid cultivar names
USES: Stuffed (parboiled 2 to 3 minutes first), fried, in
    casseroles, vegetable dishes, salads, garnishes, relishes,
    soups, crudités, sauces
SOURCES:
    Fresh: Food stores, farmer's markets, home garden
    Dried: Bell Peppers are not dried whole. Dehydrated
        flakes can be found in the spice section of
        food stores
    Processed: Ripe red ones are canned as a pale
        substitute for pimento. A flavorful, slightly pungent,
        tapered variety (name undetermined) grown in
        Eastern Europe and the Balkans is recently available
        roasted, peeled, and canned as "roasted red pepper
    Seeds: There is a multitude of cultivars in any seed
        catalog. Popular cultivars: 'Ace Hybrid,' 'Argo,' 'Big
        Bertha,' 'Cal Wonder,' 'Klondike bell,' 'Ma belle,'
        'Oriole,' 'Staddon's Select,' 'Yolo Wonder'

Cayenne

C. annuum var. *annuum* Linné, 1753

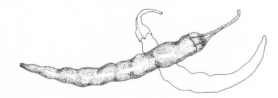

COLOR: Dark green to red; new yellow and orange
SHAPE: Elongate cylinder, wrinkled, curved;
    Cayenne-type
SIZE: 5 to 6 inches long by ½ to ¾ inches wide
PUNGENCY: Hot to very hot: 7 to 8

SUBSTITUTES: Jalapeño, serrano, Thai
OTHER NAMES: A pepper of the elongate cayenne-
    type was one of, if not the first, capsicums introduced
    to the Far East. It has become the most common type
    of *Capsicum* grown in the world with different names
    in every country
USES: Commonly used powdered or dry in Creole and
    Cajun dishes, Indian, Indonesian, Thai, Pakistani,
    Hunan, and Sichuan cooking. In meat and vegetable
    dishes, salad dressings, and as a table spice
SOURCES:
    Fresh: Farmer's markets, home gardens, and some
        food stores
    Dried: In any ethnic or supermarket spice section,
        powdered or whole
    Processed: Powdered in the spice section of almost any
        food store; used in some pepper sauces; used in
        some Cajun seasonings
    Seeds: Most seed suppliers carry one or more varieties.
        Available cultivars: 'Cayenne Langer,' 'Cayenne Large
        Red Thick,' 'Cayenne Pickling,' 'Golden Cayenne,'
        'Hades Hot,' 'Hot Portugal,' 'Japanese Fuschin,'
        'Jaune Long,' 'Long Red,' 'Long Slim,' 'Mammoth
        Cayenne,' 'Ring of Fire'

Cherry

C. annuum var. *annuum* Linné, 1753

COLOR: Medium green to red
SHAPE: Oblate. Cherry-type
SIZE: ¾ to 1 inches long by 1¼ to 1½ inches wide

PUNGENCY: Sweet or hot: 0 to 4
SUBSTITUTES: Any pickled pepper
OTHER NAMES: Hot cherry, Hungarian cherry, sweet cherry
USES: Pickles, relishes, jams, salads, garnishes, condiments
SOURCES:
Fresh: Home gardens, farmer's markets
Dried: Not used dried
Processed: Pickle section in food markets
Seeds: Most seed suppliers have at least one cultivar. Available cultivars: 'Bird's Eye,' 'Cerise,' 'Cherry Jubilee,' 'Cherry Sweet,' 'Christmas Cherry,' 'Super Sweet,' 'Red Giant,' 'Tom Thumb'

Chile de Árbol

C. annuum var. *annuum* Linné, 1753

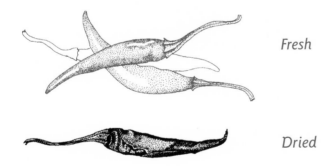

Fresh

Dried

COLOR:
Fresh: Green to red
Dried: Bright red
SHAPE: Elongate conical, narrow shoulders; pointed apex. Cayenne-type
SIZE: 3 inches long by ⅜ inches wide
PUNGENCY: Hot: 7
SUBSTITUTES: Cayenne, chiltepín, japonés, dried Thai
OTHER NAMES: *Alfilerillo, bravo, cola de rata, cuauhchilli,* ginnie pepper, *pico de pájaro*

USES: Primarily dried, in table sauces
SOURCES:
Fresh: Seldom used fresh; home gardens in the United States
Dried: Found packaged in the spice section of many supermarkets and ethnic food stores
Processed: Not processed
Seeds: Catalogs of specialty seed companies; from packaged dried fruits

Chiltepín (Chiltecpín)

C. annuum var. *glabriusculum* (Dunal, 1852) Heiser & Pickersgill, 1975

COLOR:
Fresh: Green to red, some nearly black; glossy
Dried: Brownish red
SHAPE: Ovoid
SIZE: ¼ inch long by ¾ inch diameter
PUNGENCY: Very hot: 10+
SUBSTITUTES: Really nothing, but try cayenne pepper, Thai peppers, 'Tabasco' peppers, (not the sauce)
OTHER NAMES: *Amash, amomo,* bird, *bravo, chilillo, chilipiquin, chilpaya, chilpequin, chiltipiquín, del monte, huarahuao, malagueta, max, piquén, piquin,* to name but a few
USES: Fresh or dried they are mashed together with anything on your plate; table sauces; seasoning meats, vegetables, soups, and stews. Soak peppers in a little hot water; allow to sit, mash, then use the water for seasoning

SOURCES:

Fresh: In the lower part of the Southwest, grows wild in backyards, fencerows, anywhere birds stop; in the rest of the country, found in some markets

Dried: Ethnic food markets, Native Seeds. SEARCH (3950 W. New York Dr., Tucson, AZ 85745), home gardens

Processed: Some pickled in the Southwest; erratic availability in markets

Seeds: Native Seeds. SEARCH; specialty seed houses, friends in the Southwest. They are slow to germinate

'Cubanelle'
C. annuum var. *annuum* Linné, 1753

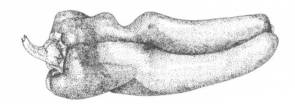

COLOR: Pale yellow-green, to orange, to red; at times all those colors at once; glossy

SHAPE: Elongated cylinder, undulating; sunken apex. Cuban or ethnic-type

SIZE: 6 inches long by 2¼ inches wide

PUNGENCY: Sweet: 0

SUBSTITUTES: Red, yellow, or orange Bell Pepper (green, if hard pressed); banana; 'Szegedi' or any sweet ethnic-type

OTHER NAMES: Italian Pepper

USES: Always used fresh: fried, in salads; as a vegetable, stuffed, in any recipe calling for a Bell Pepper

SOURCES:

Fresh: Home gardens, farmer's markets, some ethnic food stores on the East Coast

Dried: Cannot be air-dried; perhaps can be dehydrated as you would Bell Peppers

Processed: Not processed

Seeds: Commercially available but you may need to search the catalogs; Available cultivars: 'Biscayne,' 'Cubanelle,' 'Cubanelle PS'

Guajillo, dried; Mirasol, fresh
C. annuum var. *annuum* Linné, 1753

Mirasol

Guajillo

COLOR:

Fresh: Green to red to brownish red

Dried: Translucent reddish brown

SHAPE: Elongate conical; pointed apex. Cayenne-type

SIZE: 3 to 5 inches long by ½ to 1¼ inches wide, very variable

PUNGENCY: Hot: 4 to 5

SUBSTITUTES:

Fresh: serrano, jalapeño, Thai

Dried: *cascabel,* 'New Mexican Chile'

OTHER NAMES:

Fresh: *Miracielo*

Dried: *Cascabel, puya, pullia, puya, travieso, trompa,* perhaps *costeño* and *chilhuacle*

USES:

Fresh: In table sauces, used like the serrano

Dried: In sauces, seasonings, for color

SOURCES:

Fresh: Not yet readily available in markets in the United States; home gardens or Latin American specialty stores

Dried: Primarily in the Southwest or in ethnic food stores

Processed: Not processed

Seeds: Catalogs of specialty seed catalogs. Available cultivars: 'La Blanca 74,' 'Loreto 74,' 'Real Mirasol'

Habanero

C. chinense Jacquin, 1776

COLOR: Green to yellow-orange, or orange, or orange-red

SHAPE: Round to oblong, undulating; pointed apex. Habaneros-type

SIZE: 1 to 2 inches long by 1 to 2 inches wide

PUNGENCY: Very, very hot: 10+

SUBSTITUTES: Nothing can match its flavor and aroma, but try five jalapeños for each Habanero, or one dátil, one Scotch bonnet, or one rocoto

OTHER NAMES: Congo, bonda man Jacques, bonnie, ginnie, Guinea pepper, *pimenta do chiero, siete caldos,* Scotch bonnet, and *pimienta do cheiro* in Brazil

USES: In table sauces, cooked sauces, as a seasoning

SOURCES:

Fresh: Some markets on the East Coast catering to Caribbean people, home gardens; increasingly in supermarkets and specialty food stores

Dried: Will not dry well on the bush. The dried ones being sold have only the heat, the flavor that distinguishes the fresh Habaneros is all gone

Processed: Bottled sauces, canned; in specialty shops and some supermarkets

Seeds: Catalogs of some specialty seed companies, not easily found. In 2004, Texas A&M University released a new mild Habanero developed by Kevin Crosby, PhD, plant geneticist

Jalapeño

C. annuum var. *annuum* Linné, 1753

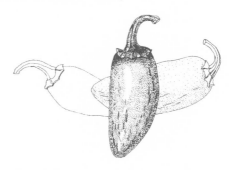

COLOR: Bright to deep blackish green; matures red

SHAPE: Cylindrical; blunt apex. Jalapeño-type

SIZE: 3 inches long by 1 ½ inches wide

PUNGENCY: Hot to very hot, according to season, soil conditions, state of maturity: 5

SUBSTITUTES: 'Caloro,' 'Caribe,' 'Fresno,' 'Santa Fe Grande,' serrano,

OTHER NAMES: *Acorchado, bola, bolita, candelaria, cuaresmeño, de agua, gorda, huachinango, jarocho, mora, morita*

USES: In condiments, sauces, soups, stews, meat and vegetable dishes, appetizers, desserts, as garnishes

SOURCES:

Fresh: Most supermarkets (it's becoming more readily available throughout the United States), although some commercial growers in the Southwest raise jalapeños, most are imported from Mexico; home gardens

Dried: Will not air dry, must be smoked. Any smoked pepper is called a *chipotle* and when *chipotles* are canned with vinegar they are *adobado* (pickled). Ripe, red, jalapeños are the most commonly smoked variety

Processed: Canned sliced or whole, pickled (*en escabeche*), prepared with other canned and frozen foods; in cheeses, sauces, candies

Seeds: Most seed suppliers will have at least one cultivar. Available cultivars: 'Early Jalapeño,' 'Espinalteco,' 'Jalapa,' 'Jalapeño M,' 'Jaloro,' 'Jarocho,' 'Jumbo Jal,' 'Mitla,' 'Papaloapan,' 'Rayado,' 'San Andres,' 'TAM Mild-1'

Long Green/Red Chile (Anaheim)

C. annuum var. *annuum* Linné, 1753

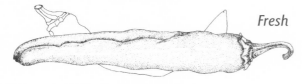

Fresh

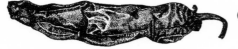

Chile Colorado (dried)

COLOR:
Fresh: Bright green to red
Dried: Brownish red
SHAPE: Elongate, flattened, tapering to a blunt point. Long Green/Red Chile/Anaheim-type
SIZE: 7 to 10 inches long by 1¾ to 2 inches wide
PUNGENCY: Mild to hot, depending on cultivar: 1 to 4
SUBSTITUTES: Poblano for fresh, ancho or guajillo for dried

OTHER NAMES: Anaheim, California long green chile, *chilacate, chile college, chile colorado, chile de ristra, chile verde,* 'Chimayo,' 'Hatch,' 'New Mexican Chile,' 'New Mexico No. 9,' *pasado,* and many other cultivars. Packaged dried peppers often incorrectly labeled *guajillo*

USES: Stuffed (*relleno*), in soups, stews, sauces, casseroles, fried, as a garnish, in souffles, etc., as well as for decoration

SOURCES:
Fresh: Most food stores in the Southwest; becoming available nationwide
Dried: Same as fresh
Processed: In the spice section of food markets; sold as pizza pepper; red pepper flakes; powdered (as paprika and used in chili powder). Canned green chiles, whole or chopped.
Seeds: Seed suppliers have cultivars such as: 'Anaheim,' 'Anaheim M,' 'Big Jim,' 'California, 'Chimayo, 'Colorado,' 'Coronado,' 'Eclipse,' 'Española Improved,' 'Long Green/Red Chile,' 'NM No. 9,' 'NuMex,' 'R-Naky,' 'Red Chile,' 'Sandia,' 'Sunrise,' 'Sunset,' 'TAM Mild Chile,' etc.

Pasilla, dried; Chilaca, fresh

C. annuum var. *annuum* Linné

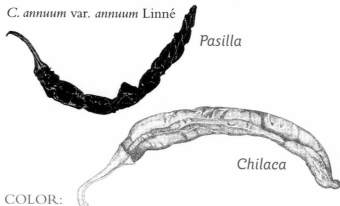

Pasilla

Chilaca

COLOR:
Fresh: Dark blackish green ripening to dark brown
Dried: A warm black

SHAPE: Elongate, flattened, irregular, wrinkled; pointed
apex. 'New Mexican Chile'/Anaheim-type
SIZE: 6 to 12 inches long by ¾ to 1¾ inches wide
PUNGENCY: Medium to hot: 3 to 4
SUBSTITUTES:
Fresh: Poblano
Dried: 'Long Green/Red Chile,' 'New Mexican Chile,'
poblano-mulato
OTHER NAMES:
Dried: *Chile Negro*/black chile, *chile de Mexico, chile para
deshebrar, quernillo, pasa, prieto*
USES:
Fresh: in sauces and as a vegetable after charring
and peeling
Dried: in table sauces, as a garnish and condiment
in soups, and is essential to *mole* and other
cooked sauces
SOURCES:
Fresh: Probably not found outside Mexico;
home gardens
Dried: Many supermarkets in the Southwest; some
ethnic food stores
Processed: Not processed
Seeds: Catalogs of specialty seed houses. Available
cultivars: 'Apaseo' and 'Pabellón 1'

'Pepperoncini'

C. annuum var. *annuum* Linné, 1753

COLOR: Green to red
SHAPE: Elongated cylinder, pointed apex, wrinkled.
'New Mexican Chile'/Anaheim-type

SIZE: 3 to 5 inches long by ¾ inches wide at shoulder
PUNGENCY: Sweet to mild: 0 to 1
SUBSTITUTES: 'Golden Greek' or any pickled pepper
OTHER NAMES: None
USES: Green fruit pickled with salads
SOURCES:
Fresh: Home gardens, farmer's markets
Dried: Not dried
Processed: Pickled, in most food stores
Seeds: Most large seed company catalogs, specialty
seed suppliers. Available cultivars: 'Golden Greek,'
'Pepperoncini'

Pimento

C. annuum var. *annuum* Linné, 1753

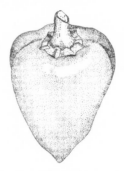

COLOR: Green to red; glossy
SHAPE: Conical, pointed apex, often heart-shaped.
Pimento-type
SIZE: 4½ inches long by 3½ inches wide at shoulder
PUNGENCY: Sweet: 0
SUBSTITUTES: Red Bell Pepper, tomato pepper
OTHER NAMES: Pimiento
USES:
Fresh: in salads, or in any recipe calling for Bell Pepper;
canned, in casseroles, cheese spreads, garnishes,
to stuff olives. Substitute: roasted and peeled red
peppers (canned and imported)

SOURCES:

Fresh: Home gardens, farmer's markets, occasionally in food markets

Dried: Not dried

Processed: Canned, common in supermarkets

Seeds: Catalogs of most large seed companies. Available cultivars: 'Bighart,' 'Canada Cheese,' 'Mississippi Nemaheart,' 'Perfection,' 'Pimiento Select,' 'Pimiento-L,' 'Sunnybrook,' 'Truhart Perfection,' 'Truhart, Perfection-D,' 'Yellow Cheese'

Poblano, fresh; Ancho and/or Mulato, dried

C. annuum var. *annuum* Linné 1753

COLOR: Dark green; matures red or brown

SHAPE: Tapered to a blunt point; wrinkled. Ancho-type

SIZE: 4 inches long by 2½ inches wide

PUNGENCY: Mild to hot: 3

SUBSTITUTES:

Fresh: Long Green/Red Chile, 'Mexi-bell,' 'New Mexican Chile'/Anaheim Chile

OTHER NAMES: *Ancho, chile para rellenar, joto, mulato, pasilla*

USES: Stuffed or *relleno*, strips or *rajas*, in soups and sauces. Roast, seed, and peel before using

SOURCES:

Fresh: Food stores throughout the Southwest. More food stores in other parts of the country are carrying it in the imported produce section

Dried: Ancho, brown and mulato, brownish-black

Processed: Not processed

Seeds: Specialty seed suppliers. Poblano does not always produce typical fruit in the United States, except in the area around Oxnard, California. Available cultivars: 'Ancho,' 'Ancho Esmeralda,' 'Chorro,' 'Miahuateco,' 'Mulato Roque,' 'Verdeño'

Ancho (dried)

C. annuum var. *annuum* Linné

COLOR: Dark brown, brick red after soaking

SHAPE: Flattened, wrinkled. Ancho-type

SIZE: 4 inches long by 2½ inches wide

PUNGENCY: Mild to rather hot: 3 to 4

SUBSTITUTES: Long Green/Red Chile, Mulato, 'New Mexican Chile,' *pasilla*

OTHER NAMES: Chile Colorado (in Texas), *mulato, pasilla*

USES: In sauces for enchiladas, chili con carne, adobados (meat prepared with a sour seasoning paste is *adobado*), commercial chili powders

SOURCES:

Fresh: See: poblano (previous entry)

Dried: Most food stores in the Southwest, ethnic specialty stores

Processed: Sold as chili powder in spice section

Seeds: Specialty seed suppliers. Available cultivars: 'Chorro,' 'Esmeralda,' 'Flor de Pabellon,' 'Verdeño'

Mulato (Dried)

C. annuum var. *annuum* Linné, 1753

COLOR: Dark brown
SHAPE: Flattened, wrinkled. Ancho-type
SIZE: 4 inches long by 2½ inches wide
PUNGENCY: Mild to hot: 3 to 4
SUBSTITUTES: Ancho, *pasilla*
OTHER NAMES: Ancho, *pasilla*
USES: In sauces like *mole poblano*
SOURCES:
Fresh: Poblano
Dried: Imported from Mexico, sold in food stores throughout the Southwest, usually in mixed lots with ancho
Processed: Canned mole sauce is now available where Mexican products are sold
Seeds: A few specialty seed suppliers carry it, but the poblano/mulato does not usually produce typical fruit when grown in the United States. Available cultivars: 'Mulato V-2, 'Roque'

Rocoto
C. pubescens Ruiz & Pavon, 1797

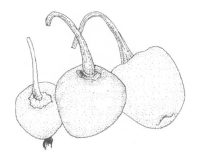

COLOR: Green to golden yellow or red
SHAPE: Globose to oblate
SIZE: 1½ to 2 inches long by 1½ to 2 inches wide
PUNGENCY: Very, very, very hot: 10+
SUBSTITUTES: Nothing really, but try 1½ to 2 habaneros or 6 to 8 jalapeños for 1 rocoto

OTHER NAMES: *Caballo* (Guatemala and bordering Chiapas, Mexico), *canario, manzana,* and *perón* in Mexico; in Costa Rica it is *manzana* but more often jalapeño
USES: In table sauces, as a seasoning, stuffed, in vegetable and meat dishes
SOURCES:
Fresh: Not readily available in the United States
Dried: Not dried
Processed: Not available
Seeds: Perhaps a specialty seed catalog

Serrano
C. annuum var. *annuum* Linné, 1753

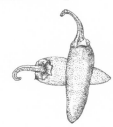

COLOR: Green to red, glossy
SHAPE: Elongated cylinder; blunt apex. Serrano-type
SIZE: 2¼ inches long by ½ inches wide
PUNGENCY: Hot to very hot: 6 to 8
SUBSTITUTES: Chiltepín, 'Fresno,' jalapeño, Thai
OTHER NAMES: *Balín, chile verde, cora, serannito, típico*
USES: In table sauces, guacamole, relishes, vegetable dishes, as a seasoning or garnish
SOURCES:
Fresh: Most food markets, but less common than the jalapeño; home gardens, farmer's markets
Dried: Does not dry well. The dried japonés are not dried serranos
Processed: Mexican pickled (*escabeche*) serranos are occasionally found in specialty stores

Seeds: Catalogs of most large seed houses and specialty seed companies. Available cultivars: 'Altimira,' 'Cuauhtemoc,' 'Cotaxtla Cónico,' 'Cotaxtla Gordo,' 'Cotaxtla Típico,' 'Huasteco 74,' 'Panuco,' 'Serrano Chili,' 'Tampiqueño'

'Tabasco'

C. frutescens Linné, 1753

COLOR: Pale yellow-green to yellow to orange to red
SHAPE: Elongate cylinder; pointed apex. Tabasco-type
SIZE: 1 to 1½ inches long by ¼ to ⅜ inches wide
PUNGENCY: Very hot: 10
SUBSTITUTES: Chiltepín, 'Cascabella,' 'Louisiana Sport' 'Mississippi Sport,' Thai

OTHER NAMES: None
USES: In sauces, as a seasoning
SOURCES:
Fresh: Home garden. Not often used fresh
Dried: Not dried
Processed: Pepper sauces made with 'Tabasco' peppers abound, occasionally pickled whole peppers are available in food stores
Seeds: Specialty seed catalogs, a few major seed catalogs. The seed you get will probably be 'Greenleaf Tabasco'

Peppers on Your Plate

Selection and Use

Before cooking with or eating *capsicum* peppers you should familiarize yourself with the methods for selecting, preparing, and handling them—and take the time to follow instructions. Peppers are expensive, you don't want to waste them, but most of all, DON'T GET BURNED. When working with chili peppers, wear protective gloves if preparing more than one or two of them. Work in a well-ventilated area—the fumes are tear-jerkers. Do not put your hands in your eyes, or any bodily orifice for that matter. If you get too much on your hands, wash them in one part household chlorine bleach to five parts water. Do this at the start—don't wait until you are burning beyond relief. Repeat if necessary; it really works! An ammonia solution of the same proportions will also work, but it smells worse. When making relish or anything requiring quite a few chili peppers, I keep a small bowl of the chlorine solution by the sink to dip my hands in as needed, a practice born of sad experience.

Keep any peeled and cut vitamin C rich peppers well-covered because that vitamin is destroyed by contact with oxygen. According to food scientist Harold McGee (1990,64), the only plastic food wrap that does not let in too much oxygen is polyvinylidene chloride (Saran Wrap®). Press all the air out before sealing (see Fresh Storage P. 22).

Capsicums are a fruit that is used like a vegetable. Chili pepper *aficionados* will either grow their peppers or buy them in a supermarket, ethnic food market, or farmer's market. By whatever means they are come by, you should be aware of a few points when selecting peppers. Capsicums of any type can be picked when they are green or when a fully mature red, though they can also mature to orange, yellow, purple, or brown—depending on the variety. Both the compounds that furnish the flavor (see P. 9) and the pungency (see P. 7) of peppers do not develop immediately, rather increasing gradually with maturity. Consequently, the immature fruits are less pungent and less flavorful than the fully mature ones. This accounts for a jalapeño chipotle being so much hotter than the familiar green jalapeño because only fully mature red fruits of any chili pepper are smoked to create chipotles, and the pungent capsaicin and the flavors increase with maturity.

In your gardens choose fruits that have smooth, glossy skins and are firm to the touch. If you have to really tug to get it off the stem, it is not quite ready. These same qualities should be looked for by those who must buy peppers in the marketplace. Keep in mind that peppers originated in the tropical Americas. Except for green (unripe) Bell Peppers and certain new cultivars, which have been bred to grow in some temperate areas year round, tropical peppers are a seasonal crop, and the best selection will be in the summer and fall. In the store you are often met with a bin of peppers that are wrinkled has-beens. In that case, all you can do is pick around for those with the fewest wrinkles. Buy peppers in season, when they are bright, shiny, and crisp, then freeze for later use (see Freezing P. 24).

Dried

Not all peppers air-dry or sun-dry satisfactorily. Those that dry well have skins thinner than the succulent ones such as Bell Pepper, jalapeño, serrano, 'Santa Fe Grande,' 'Fresno,' and many sweet ethnic varieties. If possible, select dried peppers that are not packaged because you can choose the better ones. Look for clean, insect-free peppers (tiny holes in the skin are made by insects that also make powdery dust), that are still pliable, not brittle. The skin should have no light-colored blotches or transparent spots. Many packaged dry chili peppers are tagged with incorrect names. Pay no attention to those labels but do look at the size, shape, and color and determine the variety for yourself after studying the descriptions and illustrations herein.

Storage

Fresh. If you are not going to use the peppers immediately, they may be stored in the refrigerator for four or more weeks by wiping fresh pods with a clean, dry, cloth, then placing them in an airtight container or a tightly sealed heavy zip-lock plastic bag. Draw out all the air with a straw or tube. Place the tightly closed container in the refrigerator (optimum temperature 45° to 46°F). Each time you use peppers from the container, dry the unused pods, return them to the dry bag, then remove the air and reseal—a home vacuum-packer would be ideal, but expensive. Every six days remove the container from the refrigerator and allow the peppers to come to room temperature, dry them, return to container, remove air, and seal. This is a method of storage that I discovered while working with peppers. If you cannot store them this way and are not going to use them within a week, it is best to freeze them and use them for cooking.

If peppers are to be shipped, kept out of the refrigerator, or if you don't have time to withdraw the air, put them in a paper sack. NEVER put them directly into an air filled plastic bag before packaging them, for they will spoil rapidly.

Dried. Dried peppers will keep almost indefinitely if stored properly. Make certain they are dry and put them in tightly closed, heavy plastic bags or jars of glass or plastic in a cool, dry place, preferably the refrigerator or freezer. Check them from time to time to be certain they are not deteriorating or beginning to mold. Mildew will usually start on the inside where the seed attach to the placenta (see fig. 3). Peppers with traces of mildew should be disposed of right away. Remember, only thin walled/skinned peppers will air-dry satisfactorily.

How to Use Fresh Peppers

The best way to use peppers is right off the bush; unfortunately that is seldom possible. How ever you acquire them, they will need to be washed, stemmed, deveined, and seeded before they are chopped or otherwise utilized in a favorite dish. All this business of roasting and peeling peppers before you cook with them is enough to scare away most novice pepper cooks. The only fresh peppers that really need to be skinned are the poblano and the longer, tough-skinned 'New Mexican Chile'—whichever of its cultivars you may be using—and even that ritual can be forsaken with certain of its cultivars if the recipe calls for chopped, minced, or puréed chili peppers; experiment with one pod first. However, this blistering and peeling is all part of the pepper mystique. Pepper buffs just like to get right in there with their charismatic pods. Canned roasted red peppers from the Balkans have come on the market rather recently.

The large Bell Pepper, 'Cubanelle,' poblano, and others of these types should be parboiled or blanched for two to three minutes before they are used whole for stuffing if the filling is not to be cooked in the pepper shell. If you have a microwave oven put them in a covered microwave safe container with a couple of tablespoons of water and microwave them for a minute or two on high, depending on the size and quantity. Either way, care must be exerted to not cook them to the point that they cannot hold their shape. As soon as they are removed from the heat, plunge the peppers into cold or iced water to stop the cooking.

Small chili peppers can be washed, stemmed, seeded, and deveined without skinning. In Mexico, India, Indonesia, and the Orient, none of those steps are followed before the fiery fruit is plopped into the pot or wok, whole or chopped. It is recommended that if you decide to clean more than one or two pods, wear plastic or rubber gloves and keep the tissue box handy. When seeding only a couple, handle them gingerly, taking care to not touch the cut surface; use a small tool to remove the seeds. I have designated the cupped end of a metal cuticle pusher for the job—try it! The principal reason for removing the "innards" of a chili is to reduce the pungency. In Mexico, peppers that have had the veins and seeds removed are called capóns, which, like a *capón* chicken, means they have been castrated. *Chipotles capons,* which require more preparation time, naturally bring a much higher price than those left intact.

Usually, if a recipe calls for a pepper to be roasted, it is not only to remove the peel but also because that charred flavor is desired. When you roast and steam them to remove the skin there is considerable risk of overcooking your peppers to the point that they become too soft to stuff or chop. This can be avoided by immediately plunging them into a container or sink filled with iced water to stop the cooking.

Like skinning a cat, there is more than one way to roast and skin a pepper. Many food stores now carry imported roasted red peppers in jars. These already roasted and peeled jarred peppers are flavorful time savers.

Peeling

Before peeling a batch of 'New Mexican Chiles' or poblanos, test one to see if the skin is so tough that all that work is necessary. If you have very fresh, young peppers and plan to grind or chop them, they may not require peeling. However, I tried the lazy way one time (and only one time) with some supermarket 'New Mexican Chiles,' cultivar unknown. I did them in the food processor without peeling. I ended up having tiny pieces of cellophane-like skin in my chopped peppers. I had to cook and strain them before I dared use them in my sauce. The 'New Mexican Chile' presents the most "skin" problems and some of its myriad cultivars are worse than others. I repeat, test one to see if yours have tough or tender skins.

Peeling peppers can be done by "blistering" or roasting the pods using one of several methods. Your choice will probably be determined by your source of heat. Don't forget to keep that little bowl of chlorine solution handy!

Blister Methods for Peeling

STEP 1: If you are leaving the pepper whole, always pierce or make a tiny slit in the pod to vent it so that it will not explode.

BURNER ROASTING. If you have a gas stove, set the flame at medium and place your peppers on the burner trivet. If the openings in the burner are too large or if you have an electric stove, place a cake rack, hardware cloth, steel cooling rack, or one of the new stove burner racks designed for stove-top grilling over it. Never let the skin of the pepper touch the electric element. For an electric stove, set the burner on high. Use kitchen tongs to rotate the pods as they start to char. Continue turning until the entire pepper is blackened and blistered. Remove as soon as they are charred to prevent cooking.

BROILER. Arrange the peppers on an aluminum foil-covered broiler pan or cookie sheet and place it 3 to 5 inches under the broiler. As in the burner method, keep turning the pods until completely charred. This method allows the peppers to cook more because the oven holds the heat. If shape and firmness are required in your peeled pepper, do not use this method; however, it is a quick way to blister a number of pods at the same time for making stews and sauces. Constant attention is required.

OVEN ROASTING. Preheat the oven to 550°F. Slice off the stem end of blocky peppers like Bell Peppers or poblanos so that the end is flat. Stand the peppers on the flat end on the oven rack or a cookie sheet so that they are not touching each other. Pierce other pepper types so they won't explode and lay them flat, without touching each other, on the rack or pan. Roast until blistered, for three to seven minutes. No turning is required, but watch closely. Immediately plunge into ice water. This method will give a crisper pepper.

NOTE: Because roasting peppers is such a chore, prepare ten or twelve large peppers, such as poblanos, at a time. Do not skin the charred peppers. Individually wrap each with plastic for ease of separation. Bag and freeze those wrapped ones you do not plan to use at once so they will be ready when needed. Leaving on the charred skin retards loss of vitamins and it comes off easily when thawed.

MISCELLANEOUS METHODS. The same principles of roasting as in the three previous methods can be used with a charcoal grill or barbecue grill; or in a heavy griddle or skillet on top of the stove. Roasting in hot oil in a saucepan is not recommended. Commercial roasters using revolving cylindrical cages set over gas flames have become commonplace in New Mexico and parts of the Southwest where 'New Mexican Chiles' are sold in bulk.

STEP 2 : When the peppers are cool, begin peeling at the stem end while holding the pepper under running water. A small knife will help. Wear rubber or disposable plastic gloves to protect sensitive hands from the fierce capsaicin. Remember, for freezing, do not peel in order to retain more flavor, color, and vitamins. Don't forget the chlorine water for your hands!

STEP 3: Slit the pod; remove veins and seeds by cutting and washing. For more attractive stuffed chili peppers, leave the stems attached.

Freezing

Frozen peppers may be used in cooking for seasoning, or as stuffed peppers; they are too soft for salads. Most of the nutritive value is retained if care is taken not to expose the peeled or cut fruit to the air, as oxygen destroys vitamin C rapidly. Leave the blistered and steamed peel on the pods as long as possible to guard against this loss. When freezing pungent chili peppers, parboiling before freezing will prevent capsaicin loss.

For Long Green/Red Chiles and poblanos:

STEP 1. Blister and steam in a damp cloth but do not peel. When thawed, the skin comes off readily.

STEP 2. If space is a problem, remove the stem and seeds; otherwise, freeze the entire pod to prevent exposure to oxygen.

STEP 3. Flatten the whole pods to remove air and fold once for easy packing and handling.

STEP 4. Pack in a moisture and vapor-proof package, excluding as much air as possible. Double layers of waterproof paper between the pods will facilitate separation when peppers are needed.

For Bell Peppers and large sweet peppers:

STEP 1. Wash, core, seed, and dry the peppers. Cut in half; place the halves on a metal pan or baking sheet without touching and freeze, otherwise they will all stick together.

STEP 2. Stack the frozen halves one inside the other and pack in a moisture and vapor-proof package, excluding as much air as possible. Freeze. Use from the bag as needed.

For chili peppers (jalapeños, serranos, etc.):

STEP 1. Wash and dry the peppers. Blanch and dry. Place the whole pods on a metal pan or baking sheet and freeze.

STEP 2. Place the frozen pods in a moisture-vapor-proof package, excluding as much air as possible. Freeze. Use from the bag as needed.

How to Use Dried Peppers

Drying Peppers: There are so many varieties of dried, dehydrated, and smoked peppers available at food stores and markets that it is not worthwhile to do it yourself.

Rehydration: Anchos, pasillas, mulato, guajillos, cascabels, chipotles (smoked), and other dried peppers are usually rehydrated (plumped with water) before being used in food preparation. To do this, either place the chili peppers in a sauce pan, cover with water, bring to a boil, remove from heat and let stand for an hour; or place in a bowl and cover with boiling water and let stand for an hour. Drain the chili peppers and reserve the soaking water for use in sauces, soups, stews, etc. You can leave the chili peppers in the water for more than an hour if necessary but the longer they remain in the water, the more the flavor and

nutrients are dissolved; try not to leave them more than one hour. After they have been drained, remove the stems, seeds, and veins. Now they are ready to be used as they are, or shredded, chopped, or pureed.

Making a paste: Rinse the dried chili peppers in cold water. Remove the stem and seeds; break the pods into pieces. Soak in enough warm water to cover for thirty to forty minutes but never more than one hour. Place them in a blender with some of the soaking water and puree. Add water as needed to make the desired consistency. The paste can be cooked in hot oil with other ingredients to make a sauce. Store in a covered jar in the refrigerator until needed. For a variation use toasted chili peppers.

In some remote Indian villages in Mexico the traditional law governing the way a woman who has been accused of adultery is punished is still practiced. A cruel and humiliating treatment is imposed on her. She is held down by other women who force a burning chile paste into her genitals. (*Corpus Christi Caller-Times,* February 9, 2004).

Toasting chili peppers: Rinse the dried chili peppers under cold running water and pat dry. Heat a heavy skillet over medium-high heat until a drop of water will sizzle. Place a few chili peppers in the skillet; toast until just fragrant, turning frequently to avoid scorching. Large types such as the ancho should be pliable; if not, soak them in a bowl of boiling water for a few minutes. Remove the seeds and veins from the larger types, but this is not necessary for small chili peppers. Rehydrate the toasted chili peppers as directed previously.

Another option is to rinse and dry the chili peppers, then fry them in ½ to 1-inch of hot oil in a skillet over high heat until aromatic and puffy. Drain on paper toweling and proceed as above.

Making a powder: Dried peppers can also be made into a powder by removing the stems, seeds, and veins and grinding four to six pods at a time in a blender until pulverized. Sift and regrind the larger pieces. Store in a covered container in the refrigerator and use when the recipe calls for powdered red pepper or chili powder. One tablespoon is equal to one dried ancho, mulato, and pasilla or two 'New Mexican Chiles.' One-eighth teaspoon of ground dried chili peppers like cayenne can be substituted for one chiltepín, chile de árbol, or japonés.

Ingredients and Terms

An uncontested claim could be made that no other cultivated plant has such a multiplicity of fruit types with such diverse uses over such an expanse of the world as does Capsicum. I call them the seashells of the plant kingdom. The publication of my *Peppers: The Domesticated Capsicums* in December of 1984 coincided with an increase in the acceptance of the pretty, pungent pod—and that popularity has continued to grow. I'm delighted, and so are the burgeoning number of producers of peppers and pepper products.

Peppers have many uses as comestibles—as vegetable, spice, and condiment—and the list is growing. Let's look at a few of the types of products found on the shelves of the supermarket. The important attributes valued in *Capsicum* products are: color, pungency level, and aroma. Within these types of pepper products are so many variations and brands that it would not be possible to include them all.

Prepared Pepper Products

(Condiments and pepper preparations)

ACHAAR (AĆHAR). A pickled, oily Indian condiment, often, but not necessarily, very hot. Limes, lemons, mangoes, ginger, eggplant, and other things might be used to make an aćhar, but the decisive ingredient is chili pepper.

It is served with curries. Contrary to the origin of the word *achaar/aćhar* given in the first edition of my book *Peppers* (1984, 5), *achaar* is Persian, not Portuguese, and it does not mean "chili." The word, and probably the pickle, came to India early in the sixteenth century with the Moguls from the northwest at the same time the Portuguese entered the southwest coast bringing the hot element—chilies. The pickles and peppers met and melded on the sub-continent to become *achaar,* the favored hot pickle in India. It can be bought in Indian food stores or gourmet food shops.

ADOBO. Spanish for pickle sauce commonly used for pickling meats; also a dry marinade for meats made by pureeing together peppers—pungent and/or sweet—garlic, salt, pepper, spices, and lime juice or vinegar. Meat is rubbed with the adobo and allowed to sit for several hours or overnight, then it becomes *adobado* (pickled/ preserved) and is ready to cook. *Adobo* sauce originated in pre-Columbian Mexico and moved on with the Manilla Galleon to the Philippines where only the name remains the same. Empty the contents of a can of chipotle adobo into a blender and pureé. Place in a covered container and refrigerate. Add to mayonnaise, marmalades, sauces, etc. as desired.

AJVAR. A spread, dip, or relish used as an accompaniment to grilled meat, cheeses, sandwiches, as an appetizer, or on anything. It is traditionally made of the long, red, mildly pungent Balkan peppers or with eggplant. Bottled relish can be found in Mediterranean, Middle Eastern or Balkan food stores (ZerGut is one brand) and is becoming more common in grocery stores (see Recipe P. 148).

ALEPPO/SANLIURFA PEPPER. This is the name of a pepper product, not a pepper type. Called by the names of ancient cities only about 100 miles apart in Turkey (Urfa or Sanliurfa) and Syria (Aleppo or Halab) where this pepper is commonly grown and prepared. The fully ripe, red, chili peppers are cut in half lengthwise and the placenta, seeds, and veins carefully removed. The halves are placed with the cut side up on plastic that has been spread on the ground in the full sun. They remain there, uncovered, for one day. That night, they are covered with plastic. After that, the plastic is removed from over the peppers at night and the peppers are recovered during the day until they are dry. The clean, dried peppers are ground, then mixed (kneaded) with a just enough olive oil to be absorbed. This product, produced in the Middle East, is made from a very flavorful, mildly pungent, small (1 to 2-inch) cone-shaped *Capsicum annum* var. *annuum* pepper that was bred in the area of southeastern Turkey near Urfa (Sanliurfa) and northern Syria around Aleppo (Halab). As yet it is a pepper type unnamed by American pepper breeders and is not grown commercially in the United States where the ground product is usually called by the name Aleppo Pepper, for the ancient spice road city in northern Syria near the border with Turkey. Very flavorful; mildly pungent. In those areas it is usually sold in bulk in marketplaces and served in small bowls on every table. It can be found in Middle Eastern food stores in the United States. I bought it at one in Boston. If not found, ask for it to be stocked. Use it on everything, including cantaloupe and melons. Paprika, Cayenne, and Crushed Red Pepper are no substitutes. It is habit forming! I have grown it from a few seeds found in the product. Order from the Phoenicia Grocery located at 12116 Westheimer in Houston, Texas, 77077. Telephone: (281) 558-8225; or call Penzeys Spices (800) 741-7787. The method of preparation was explained to me by Dr. Davut Keles, Alata Horticultural Research Institute, Erdemili, Mersin, Turkey.

CAYENNE PEPPER. A ground product made from small peppers that contain large amounts of capsaicin. It is not obligatory to make this seasoning from cayenne-type peppers, although it may contain some, along with African, Mexican, and Louisiana chili peppers. The name cayenne is derived from *Kyan,* the word for pepper in Tupi, an Indian language of northern Brazil and the Amazon basin. The powder ranges in color from orange-red to a deep red; as a result it is sometimes labeled simply "red pepper," a term the American Spice Trade Association considers to be inappropriate. After the Cayenne pepper arrived in Louisiana it became typical of Cajun and Creole cuisines.

CHILI OIL. A seasoning oil made with pulverized dried red chili peppers. Make your own by heating ½ cup vegetable oil in a small skillet over medium heat; add 4 teaspoons ground cayenne pepper, ground dried red 'New Mexican Chiles,' hot paprika, or ground dried small red chili peppers. Remove from the heat and carefully add ½ cup hot water while guarding against spattering. Simmer over medium heat for ten minutes, then cool. After the oil rises to the top, skim it off and put it in a tightly sealed jar. Discard the chili sediment. Use when a recipe calls for chilly oil, chili/chili oil, Chinese chili/chili oil, etc.

CHILI POWDER. (Note the one *l* with *i* at the end.) Dried pods of milder cultivars such as 'New Mexican Chile' and/or Ancho are principal ingredients of this blend of several peppers and other spices—oregano, cumin, cayenne, garlic powder, paprika. It was first produced commercially in 1892 by Willie Gebhardt, a German Texan in New Braunfels, Texas, to be used in making chili con carne. A popular brand still bears his name.

Purists would never use a commercially prepared chili powder in their chili pot. Warning: commercial chili powder cannot be substituted for ground Ancho, Mulato, or Pasilla if the recipe calls for them because other spices in that product would alter the recipe.

CHILI/CHILE POWDER OR PEPPER. Only ground red chili peppers (one or more types) are used. It is NEVER a blend of ground peppers and other spices, as is chili powder made for chili con carne. They can not be interchanged. Some chili powders are finely ground, others may be coarse, while others have seed ground with the flesh. Pungency is dependent on the types of peppers used. Powdered chili would be a more appropriate name.

CHILI/CHILI SAUCE. Commercial chili sauces contain little or no chili peppers. They are seasoned crushed tomato catsups with tomato seeds, onion, garlic, sugar, vinegar, spices, and perhaps a little chili pepper. Usually more textured than catsup, this sauce is one of a breed of sauces and catsup developed from chutneys and pickles when English cooks found the liquid in the pickle bottle more interesting than the pickled vegetable. Many manufacturers have dropped it.

CHINESE PEPPER MIX. A freshly ground mixture of whole black, white, and Sichuan peppercorns (*Zanthoxylem piperitum*) that have been roasted in a dry skillet over medium heat until fragrant before grinding.

CHIPOTLE. A smoked pepper. Any thick-walled chili pepper that is dried by smoking as it will not air dry. The jalapeño is the variety most commonly dried by this method. A chipotle is not a variety of pepper.

CHIPOTLE ADOBADO. Smoked peppers that have been pickled (see *adobo* at beginning of this section).

CHUTNEY. The principal type of this delightful Indian accompaniment to curries and meats usually has as its basis two fruits or two vegetables or a fruit and a vegetable, plus onions, tamarind, ginger, garlic, and chili peppers cooked with vinegar, sugar, and salt. Many of these are "put up" as you would preserves; however, today we are enjoying many innovative uncooked, fresh, chutneys. Create your own combination!

CREMA MEXICANA OR CREMA CENTRO AMERICANA. Sour cream, but not the type made in the United States. It is a very rich, thick cream used on tortillas as you would butter on many other things, as a topping for green enchiladas, beans, desserts, in fruit soups—you name it. It is very tempting to take a spoon and just eat it out of the jar. It can be bought in Mexican and Central American food stores in the United States such as the Fiesta Food Stores. In Costa Rica and Panama it is called *natilla,* the first cream of milk.

CRUSHED RED PEPPER. The acceptance of this product has grown in recent years along with the fame of pizza. The long red 'New Mexican Chile' is the primary, although not necessarily the only, pepper variety dried and crushed, including the seeds, to be used in this product. It is often called pizza pepper or *pepperoni rosa*.

CURRY POWDER. This condiment originated in India from *garam masala,* freshly ground dry spices, (see Masalas, P. 29) and spread to other areas under Indian influence. It is used to prepare a variety of sauces (curries) to be mixed with meat, seafood, and/or vegetables and served with rice and condiments. Since the eighteenth century, when English interest in and occupation of India began in earnest, curry powder has been used in Great Britain and Europe. A standardized, prepared curry powder does not exist in India, and what we buy here is a poor substitute for a freshly ground batch of spices. In the home of the curry, combinations of spices are ground with peppers specifically for the dish being prepared. It might consist of as few as five or as many as fifty ingredients.

The pungency of curry powder depends on the amount of chili pepper used. Commercially prepared curry powders are made by grinding slightly roasted chili peppers to a powder and mixing that powder with ground turmeric for the yellow color, then adding coriander along with other spices, that may be one or more of the following: allspice, anise, bay leaves, caraway, cardamom, celery seed, cinnamon, cloves, dill, fennel, fenugreek, garlic, ginger, mace, mustard, nutmeg, pepper (white and black), poppy seeds, saffron, mint, cubeb berries, sumac seeds, juniper berries, zeodary root, and salt. After my extensive travels in the curry belt, I can only say, again, that the product on our food market shelves pales by comparison to the freshly ground spices.

Get a spice mill, mortar and pestle, or electric blender and try the mixes on page 198. Store in the refrigerator with air removed and tightly closed.

FISH SAUCE (NAM PLA). Southeast Asian sauce made from layering fresh anchovies and brine. Used as the Chinese use soy sauce. No substitute. Buy in Oriental food store.

FIVE-SPICE POWDER. A blend of various spices including fennel, Sichuan pepper, cloves, cinnamon, and anise; used for chicken, fish, and marinades. No substitute. Buy in Oriental food stores.

GARAM MASALA. A blend of dried spices that have been roasted just before they are ground into a fine powder by a *masalchi* (the person who grinds) and used sparingly toward the end of cooking a dish, or sprinkled over the cooked food as a garnish. There are as many versions as there are chefs. Make it yourself (see P. 198).

HARISSA. The Maghreb—Tunisia, Algeria, Morocco—in north Africa is the home of this fiery blend of dried red chili peppers, lemon juice, olive oil, garlic, salt, and spices.

Harissa paste both flavors and colors such dishes as its traditional companion *couscous,* a steamed grain dish. Look for it in specialty or ethnic food stores or make it yourself (see P. 152).

HOISIN SAUCE. A thick, spicy, sweet, dark brownish-red Chinese condiment made of soybean flour, garlic, chili peppers, ginger, and sugar. Used in stir-fried dishes, on mu shu pork, and in Chinese barbecue sauce. It is sold in cans or bottles at Oriental food stores, and will keep for months in a tightly closed jar in the refrigerator. There is no substitute.

NAM PRIK. Thai hot sauce is a very hot mixture of ground shrimp, garlic, sugar, and dried red chili peppers mixed with lime juice, fish sauce, and chopped Thai or serrano peppers. Used on chicken or grilled meats. Look for it in Oriental food stores. No substitute.

PAPRIKA. No single cultivar of pepper is used to make paprika. Paprika is a ground product prepared of the highly colored, mild red fruits of one or more cultivars of *Capsicum annuum* var. *annuum,* and it is used to season and color food. Sweet paprika is primarily the flesh with more than half of the seeds removed, while hot paprika contains seeds, veins, calyces, and stalks, depending on the grade. *Paprika* is also the name by which all peppers are known in the Balkans. Pungent Hungarian paprika is prepared from a long cayenne-type pepper they call "spice paprika" and is somewhat pungent, while Spanish and Moroccan paprikas are prepared from a milder, tomato-shaped pepper. Paprika is produced in Bulgaria, Czechoslovakia, Yugoslavia, Hungary, Spain, Portugal, Morocco, Chile, and in the United States—Arizona and California.

PEPPER JELLY. Not long ago pepper jelly could only be found at the county fair or those other places where ladies brought in their jams and jellies to sell, but now many varieties of it can be found in every large food market. Most of it is made with a combination of Bell Peppers and a chili pepper, such as jalapeño, or habanero. It is eaten as an accompaniment to meat and poultry, as mint jelly is with lamb, and it is nice in a roasted acorn squash half, or over cream cheese on a cracker for the snack tray. Perk up an old fashioned jelly roll cake with pepper jelly (see P. 195).

PEPPER SAUCE (BOTTLED). In 1992, on the shelf of a supermarket in a Texas city of two-hundred and fifty-thousand, I counted at least forty different pepper sauces. Six or seven years before that there would have been six to ten. Today, I don't have time to count them all. No matter how many you may find, there are two basic types of pepper sauce:

1. Those that use whole fruits of very hot varieties preserved in vinegar or brine. These are used to douse cooked vegetables, especially greens. The liquid can be replenished with more vinegar or brine (this can be done several times).
2. Mashed or puréed chili peppers that either have or have not been allowed to ferment that are then used as is or mixed with vinegar and spices.

These sauces are generally put up in small bottles designed to dispense the fiery liquid one drop at a time. "Shots" of hot pepper sauce are added with caution to stews, eggs, soups, oysters, and Bloody Marys, to mention a few. Although Tabasco Brand Pepper Sauce® (made by McIlhenny & Co.) has almost become generic for the second type of pepper sauce, its makers are justifiably vehement in their insistence that the others are not THE "Tabasco Sauce," and that there is but one original fermented sauce made of Tabasco peppers and it is to be known as Tabasco Brand Pepper Sauce® not simply Tabasco sauce. I regularly get announcements of new pepper sauces made from all kinds of chili peppers—

dátils, jalapeños, habaneros—in many styles: Malaysian, Thai, Jamaican, Yucatecan. Try them until you find one you like, or design your own.

Tabasco Brand Pepper Sauce® is made from a pepper mash that is packed into fifty-gallon Kentucky white oak barrels, covered, layered with salt, and allowed to ferment for three years. At that time the mash is filtered, homogenized, diluted one to three with vinegar, and bottled in the world-famous bottle with its cherished trademark. McIlhenny & Co. now makes several other pepper sauces including their Tabasco Garlic Sauce and Tabasco Chipotle Sauce.

Vinegar or sherry pepper sauce is a simple favorite. Fill a sterile bottle with whatever small chili peppers you might have—chiltepines, tabasco, sports, Thais, 'Floral Gems'—then fill the bottle with a good vinegar, tequila, or sherry. Let it sit for several weeks before using and refill when necessary. Use on vegetables, eggs, soups, or what have you.

PICKLED AND PROCESSED PRODUCTS. Today you cannot keep up with the growing array of pepper products appearing in our food markets. Pepper processors are hard put to keep up with the increasing popularity of the captivating *Capsicum*. We now have canned peppers, pickled peppers, sauces, dips, cheeses, vegetables with chili peppers, chili-flavored potato chips, chili con queso soup, hot corn chips, candy, jellies, stuffed olives—the list goes on and on. A commonly used Spanish term for "pickled" is *en escabeche*. These products are used in place of fresh or dried chili peppers to add zip to any recipe or to prepare traditional dishes requiring them. Pickle processors like to use little bite-size chili peppers to eliminate the danger of "spurting" that may occur when biting into a large pickled pod. Many an unwary bystander has been temporarily blinded when a careless *aficionado* put the bite on a pickled jalapeño. Sliced *"nacho"* style jalapeños are handy to use. To make sweet nacho slices, add 1½ Tbs. of Splenda® artificial sweetener to the opened jar, shake and let sit for a day or two.

Do not confuse *escabeche,* a thin, vinegar pickling medium, with the *adobo* style of pickling that is done with a much thicker type of pickling sauce.

PEELED AND CANNED PIMENTO PEPPERS (PIMENTO/ PIMIENTO). The spelling pimento was adopted from pimiento by early producers of the canned peppers of that sweet variety. They are used in pimento cheese and many other dishes for flavor and color. Pimento canning was a rather large industry in the southern United States but today very few canneries still operate. Fresh red Bell Peppers from Holland, now grown here, and imported canned, roasted red peppers have all but replaced pimentos.

PIRI PIRI. The dried red piri-piri pepper is called *jindugo* in former Portuguese Africa. It is sold in Portugal in two sizes, the tiny 1-inch long type that is like the Brazilian malagueta pepper (probably *Capsicum frutescens,* not to be confused with melegueta pepper or "grains of paradise" from Africa's west coast) and a larger variety, about three inches long. Both are extremely hot. Many Portuguese and African households simply put the whole, stemmed, dried red peppers in a glass jar, filling it about a third full of peppers then topping it off with olive oil. The sauce is left to mature for a week or so.

RED PEPPER POWDER AND FLAKES. (See entries for Aleppo pepper, crushed red pepper, chilli/chili/chile powder and cayenne pepper).

ROASTED RED PEPPERS. (Not pimento peppers). A long, pointed, wide-shouldered, red, mildly pungent, ethnic pepper of the type grown in the Balkans and Turkey is roasted and peeled and bottled whole, sliced, or chopped. It can be used when roasted Bell Peppers are called for in salads, on sandwiches, in cooking, as a condiment, or where added flavor and color are desired. Use in place of the less flavorful pimento. Most are imported but can be found in local groceries and specialty food stores. Not only tasty but labor saving.

SALSA PICANTE OR MEXICAN HOT SAUCE. The standard Mexican table sauce can be purchased in bottles in any food market. This once humble preparation made fresh daily by every Mexican homemaker, is a mixture of chopped tomatoes, onions, and chili peppers with a few herbs— mainly cilantro, garlic, some salt, sometimes a little vinegar or lime, and a pinch of sugar. Picante sauce, *salsa picante,* or *salsa cruda* are used as a dip for toasted tortilla chips (*tostadas*), in and on Mexican dishes, as well as on eggs, tacos, and hamburgers. The market for this *salsa* is growing at a rate of fifteen to twenty percent annually, and it now outsells catsup. There are literally hundreds of variations of *salsa picante. Pico de gallo* (rooster's beak) is a name occasionally given to this hot sauce; however, the original Mexican dish by that name is more like a salad made with *jícama,* oranges, onions, and a dash of powdered red pepper or chopped serranos (see Sauces P. 142).

SATAY (SATÉ) SAUCE. An Indonesian sauce, that can be bought in Oriental food stores or gourmet shops; made of chili peppers and peanuts ground with lemon grass, shrimp paste, lemons, coconut milk, sugar, and salt; to be used on grilled meat. No substitute.

SAMBAL. Any kind of fiery-hot or spicy relish or condiment served with food. Of Malaysian/Indonesian origin, the burning sambals are found wherever that influence is felt. The basis is always chili peppers plus a range of such ingredients as garlic, shallots, shrimp paste, tomatoes, tamarind, and even peanut butter. East African sambals, which accompany curried dishes, are mixtures of vegetables, such as cucumbers or carrots, with chili peppers. Southern India is known for a coconut sambal. Many are often in the form of a paste or a thick sauce that varies in degree of pungency. Some are sour, while others are sweet. They can be likened to the *salsa picante* of Mexico and some are virtually the same as *salsa cruda* (uncooked). At most, they are made fresh daily in small amounts; however, for a sambal fan in a hurry, a reasonable facsimile can be bought in bottles like American catsup in Oriental food stores and some supermarkets.

During a houseboat trip lasting several days on a river in Kalimantan (Borneo) the native cooks let me prepare the fresh sambal for each meal. They are quite simple (see Recipe P. 153).

SMOKED PEPPERS. (see Chipotle P. 28).

SOFRITO. A traditional Spanish seasoning mixture of onions, garlic, capsicums—sweet and/or pungent—herbs, annatto, and sometimes ham, sautéed in olive oil or lard. Canned sofrito is now available.

WHOLE PEPPERS, DRIED. There are numerous types of chili peppers sold in bulk or in packages as dried whole pods. The varieties most commonly sold in this manner are the long red 'New Mexican Chile,' *pasilla, mulato, ancho, cascabel, guajillo, de árbol, japonés, chiltepín/pequin, catarina,* and others.

WHOLE PEPPERS, FRESH. In the United States and Canada the peppers most easily found commercially are the various Bell Pepper types, long green/red 'New Mexican Chile,' and the yellow wax types. Some of the Mexican favorites found in markets in the United States on a fairly regular basis are jalapeño, serrano, and poblano. In ethnic food stores varieties favored by the ethnic group served there are often found. These are used fresh as vegetables, in sauces, and as seasoning.

MISCELLANEOUS. In 1984 I wrote about jalapeño lollipops, jalapeño jelly beans, olives stuffed with jalapeños, "armadillo eggs" (deep-fried jalapeños stuffed with Italian sausage dressing), and the "Martinez" (martini made with jalapeño stuffed olives). Now the list could go on and on because chili peppers are put in almost anything you can think of, and as we travel more, our earth gets smaller and our tastes broader. To such old standbys as Jamaican Pickapeppa sauce, which is similar to Worcestershire sauce but pungent, can be added sauces from all parts of the world. Now on the market are new imports like mandram, a West Indian stomachic made of ground chiltepínes, cucumber, shallots, chives or onions, and lime or lemon juice; the Arabic *ras el hanout,* a mixture of spices—black pepper, chili, turmeric, lavender, etc.—used in Moroccan dishes. If you go to various ethnic food shops and poke around for new things, you will find others too numerous to mention, but you can be certain they will have one thing in common—they are HOT!

Ingredients

Many of the recipes included in this book have had foreign inspiration or sources; hence the ingredients are often exotic, with names that vary from country to country. I have included their scientific names because they are in Latin and remain constant the world over. Those names can be used in scientific reference books for further information.

ACHIOTE/ANNATTO. *Bixa orellana.* Achiote is the Spanish and annatto the English name for a beautiful, small, pink-flowered, tropical tree, native to the West Indies; the fruit looks like bright red castor bean pods. The seeds are a powerful coloring agent, used to color foods more than to flavor them. The seed itself is not eaten, but boiled in oil and then strained. The colored oil or oily paste takes the seed's name. Little pots used to make and store Achiote are called *achoteras.* They are designed to strain seeds from oil while seeds stay inside to be used several times (make one with a tuna can). Look for seed or preparations of it in supermarket spice sections or Latin American and Indian food stores. Substitute turmeric.

Pre-Columbian Amerindians living in the tropics used powdered Bixa to paint their bodies. Sometimes Eurasians substitute achiote for henna (*Lawsonia inermis*) as a dye stuff.

ALEPPO PEPPER. *Capsicum annuum* var. *annum* (see P. 26).

AVOCADO. *Persea americana.* In Mexico it is called aguacate after *ahuacatl,* a Nahuatl word meaning testicle in reference to the shape. In South America it is *palta.* Also referred to in Mexico as "poor man's butter." Sometimes known as alligator pear this buttery, high calorie, vitamin rich fruit turns dark when exposed to oxygen but can be protected with citrus juice, prepared citric acid, vinegar, and/or by excluding oxygen with closely wrapped plastic wrap (Saran Wrap® is most effective). To peel easily, cut the fruit in half, take a tablespoon and insert it just under the skin and scoop the entire avocado half out of its shell in one motion. No substitute.

BULGAR WHEAT OR CRACKED WHEAT. *Triticum* spp. Made by steaming and drying wheat kernels, then cracking them. Large size used for pilaf; medium, for cereal; fine, for tabbouleh. High in protein. Rather long cooking time is required. Substitute for rice or couscous.

CANOLA OR RAPESEED OIL. *Brassica rapus.* Name is elision of "Canada oil" from the rape plant, a relative of mustard plant. Lowest in saturated fat of all oils and second highest in mono-unsaturated fat after olive oil. Substitute for any cooking oil or salad oil.

CARDAMOM. *Elettaria cardamomum.* Very aromatic seed from a member of ginger family; native to India. Has not gained real acceptance in America, but is an Asian, Arabic, and Scandinavian favorite. Do not buy powdered form. Get small gray-green pods, remove seeds; grind your own. Or use whole pods as in India, but be sure not to eat the pods. Made expensive by very specialized growing requirements—a little goes a long way. Store tightly closed in refrigerator or freeze. No substitute.

CILANTRO. *Coriandrum sativum.* Although native to eastern Mediterranean it is sometimes called Chinese parsley, culantro, or coriander. Both leaves (cilantro, fresh coriander) and dried seeds are eaten. Roots occasionally used in Indonesia. Gaining popularity because it is a component of many Mexican, North African, and Oriental dishes. Does not keep well; however, an herb keeper (www.SolutionsCatalog.com) that holds water keeps herbs fresh for a week or more. Otherwise, put stems in water, cover, keep in refrigerator for two to three days. Supermarket cilantro occasionally has roots in place, however, home gardens only dependable source. Substitute parsley for color but not for flavor. Many people can't stand the flavor of cilantro.

CITRUS FRUITS. *Citrus* spp. All belong to same species of temperate trees with shiny evergreen leaves; cannot withstand severe freezing. Species was thought to have arisen in southeast Asia but most cultivated species are native to India. Fruits are botanically berries with a leathery skin that gives off an aromatic odor when fruit is peeled, bruised, or grated. Fruits of all are high in Vitamin C, that prevents scurvy. When cut fruit or juice is exposed to oxygen in air Vitamin C is quickly destroyed. Keep well covered. Oranges are most used citrus for both flesh and juice. Citrons and lemons are usually only used for juice; however lemons are exploited for secondary purposes. Limes were introduced to Europe by Arabs around twelfth century. Cultivation in New World began in seventeenth century. Soon a correlation between eating fresh fruits and absence of scurvy was recognized. British sailors were ordered to drink a daily ration of lime juice, hence they were called "limeys." Grapefruit originated from a cross occurring in West Indies before 1750. Tangerines or Mandarin oranges were first cultivated in China.

COCONUT AND COCONUT MILK. *Cocos nucifera.* Coconut palms probably native to Indo-Pacific; dispersed over oceans by currents before 1492. Coconut meat, eaten in pieces or grated, is oil-rich layer of mature endosperm found on inside of seed coat. Liquid found in fresh coconut, called coconut water, is drunk as a refreshing beverage in tropics but it is not coconut milk. Coconut "milk" is man-made by soaking grated coconut meat in hot water, squeezing out the liquid, as follows: Place 1 cup of grated coconut to 4 cups of boiling water in blender; blend for 1 or 2 minutes. Strain through mesh or cheese cloth. Store in refrigerator or freeze if not to be used in a day or two; keeps one to two weeks. Use same coconut meat to make two batches; second will not be quite as rich as first. Feed remaining coconut to birds.

CORIANDER. Another name for Cilantro. (See this section).

CORN. *Zea mays.* Is only major cereal grain domesticated in New World. First domesticated in highlands of Mexico at least 7,000 years ago. Cultivation spread both north and south. Called corn by Europeans who used the word "corn" for all edible grains. It does not have same nutritional value as other whole grains. Because it has no gluten, it can only be used for flat breads. It can be grown in both tropical and temperate climates; converts carbohydrates and water into foodstuffs more efficiently than any modern cereal grain. The six major varieties are: pod, dent, flint, popcorn, flour corn, sweet corn. It is deficient in amino acids, tryptophane, lysine, and low in protein. (See corn meal below and masa in this section). Hominy is made when whole corn kernels are soaked in a solution of lye, boiled, and the outer skin is removed. When hominy is dried and ground it becomes grits.

CORN MEAL. *Zea mays.* Meal made of ground, dried yellow, white, or blue corn kernels; used for quick breads, puddings; in mid-sixteenth century it replaced sorghum or millet to make polenta. Europeans accepted maize immediately but used it in the traditional way other grains were used, without nixtamalization (see Masa in this section). As a consequence, many maize-dependent cultures suffer dietary deficiencies such as pellagra (i.e. some southern sections of the United States). Try using part corn meal and part quinoa flour. Blue corn meal, from grinding dry kernels of blue-colored corn, is favored by Hopi Indians of Arizona; available in southwestern supermarkets, or order from Native Seeds/SEARCH, 526 N. 4th Ave., Tucson, AZ 85705.

COUSCOUS. *Triticum* spp. A semolina/durum wheat product, either whole or bleached, (see P. 76 and 78) made into very tiny (1–3 mm) balls or granules of un-kneaded flour dough, then dried. Traditionally made from freshly ground whole grain but also made of barley, bran, millet, or corn which are more nutritious than white rice, pasta, or bleached wheat flour. Dry granules are steamed and served as you would pasta or rice, either hot or cold. It has long been a staple food in North African countries. From there its popularity spread throughout the south and east Mediterranean, to Middle East and more recently to Europe and the Americas. Use it in recipes calling for white rice.

CREME FRAICHE. A thickened, nutty flavored matured cream, not sour cream. To make it: stir 1 tablespoon of buttermilk into 1 cup of whipping cream and heat until lukewarm. Remove from the heat, loosely cover; allow to stand at room temperature until thickened, eight to thirty-six hours, depending on temperature of room. Store, covered, in refrigerator for up to two weeks.

CUMIN (COMINO). *Cuminum cyminum.* The flat, oval, brown seeds of this eastern Mediterranean and Egyptian annual herb of the parsley family look like caraway or fennel seeds; very different in flavor. Essential to Thai, Indian, Middle Eastern, North African, Mexican, and southwestern United States cooking. Often toasted before using. No substitute.

EPAZOTE. *Chenopodium ambrosioides.* From the Nahuatl *epazotl*, it is an annual herb with deeply serrated leaves and a strong, camphor-like odor that is native to Mexico and Central America. A few chopped leaves of this almost weed-like plant give character to squash, black-eyed peas, and other vegetable dishes. Several sprigs added to a pot of beans are said to alleviate the problem of flatulence. It works! Use fresh or dried. Store easily dried leaves in a tightly closed jar. Purchase it in Latin American food markets or grow your own, but be careful—it is like a weed and will take over your herb bed. Grow it in a flower pot to keep it from spreading. Seed may be labeled *pazote* (saltwort) or Jerusalem Oak Pazote. No substitute.

FAGARA. *Zanthoxylum armatum* and/or *Z. planispinum.* Peppery seeds play role of black pepper in China. Look for them in an Oriental food store. Substitute black peppercorns.

FLOURS. *Triticum* spp. and others. (see P. 76).

FRUCTOSE. (See entry for sugars).

GALANGAL. *Allpinia galangal.* Siamese ginger. A ginger-like root from Southeast Asia. Used in Thai and Indonesian cooking. Buy in Oriental food stores. Substitute fresh ginger.

GARLIC. *Allium sativum.* The most powerfully flavored member of the lily family. Leeks, onions, and shallots are also members. It may have originated in Central Asia or the Mediterranean region. It was used by the Egyptian, Greeks, and Romans; introduced to New World by Spaniards. A mineral rich food esteemed for both its culinary and medicinal qualities. Although favored in Mediterranean cuisine, its many varieties have virtually conquered the world.

HOJA SANTA. *Piper auritum.* "Holy leaf" is same genus as black pepper. A tropical plant I have seen growing wild in Mexico and Costa Rica. It will take over a garden if allowed to do so. Its large leaves have an anise-like flavor that is imparted to foods. Mexicans add it to soups, stews, or line tamale shucks with it, and wrap them around fish or chicken before cooking. Lush plant is easy to grow in the warmer areas of the United States; requires a lot of room.

GINGER. *Zingiber officinale.* The spice commonly called ginger is actually a rhizome. The "root" of this tropical, Southeast Asian native is indispensable in Oriental cookery. Select plump, smooth roots, scrape off thin skin, place roots in a jar, fill with sherry wine, cover; store in refrigerator. It keeps for weeks. Do not freeze. It is also preserved in syrup or candied and coated in sugar to be used as is or chopped and sprinkled over desserts. Most super markets and all Oriental food stores sell both fresh and preserved ginger. Oriental Ginger is Galangal or Kha. There is no substitute.

JÍCAMA. (hick-a-ma) *Pachyrhizus erosus.* Jícama is the large, turnip-like, brown-skinned root of a native Mexican legume with a crunchy, slightly sweet white interior that does not discolor. Best used fresh, for crispness is lessened when cooked, but is good braised or in stir-fry. Store in the refrigerator for up to two weeks. More and more supermarkets carry this in their special vegetable section. Select firm roots. Substitute peeled and seeded cucumber.

LACTOSE. A sugar found in no other food except the milk of all animals. It accounts for about half of the calories in milk. All sugars must be broken down before being absorbed and used in the body. Lactase, the lactose-breaking enzyme, reaches its highest level in humans shortly after birth, then declines, because most mammals never encounter lactose again after weaning. When lactose reaches the colon intact it produces carbon dioxide gas causing distress. Few adult humans can tolerate more lactose than that in a pint of milk per day. Cheese, yogurt, and other cultured foods are virtually lactose free because fermenting bacteria use it as fuel. Human lactose tolerance beyond nursing stage is a rather recent adaptation. Although humans have drunk mother's milk since time began, cows, goats, and sheep have been milked for only a few thousand years.

LEEKS. *Allium ampeloprasum.* Member of lily family that originated in Near East in ancient times before going to Europe and South America. Leaf blades are little different from bulb; consequently a substantial portion of leaves are eaten. More commonly used in Asia and South America than in the United States where it would be used more if not so expensive. Wonderful in soups, stir-fry, braised, grilled, pureed, or poached. Use dark greens in soups; wash thoroughly before using.

LEMON GRASS. *Cymbopogone citratus.* A fairly tall, clumping grass. Bulbous, white base and leaves essential to Thai, Vietnamese, and Indonesian cuisine; probably native to that area. Easy to grow, but a hard freeze kills it. Grow it, or try an Oriental food store, or substitute lemon peel.

LENTIL. *Lens culinaris.* First cultivated in Middle East more than eight or nine thousand years ago. Lentil use spread around the Mediterranean. Named for flattened shape of the seed, this legume has a lens shape. Among legumes, only carob and peanuts have more protein; lentils are not high in fiber. Called dal, it is used extensively in India. It cooks quickly. Cook a half cup of dried lentils; purée cooked lentils and their liquid in a blender; use to enrich other bean dishes and soups. Eating brown rice, corn, durum wheat, or whole wheat along with legumes not only adds variety but also makes a complete protein source.

MAKRUT LIME. *Citrus hystrix.* Substitute juice from fresh limes for the juice together with any citrus leaf for the leaves of this Asian citrus. Oriental food stores may have leaves if you don't live where citrus trees grow.

MANGO. *Mangifera indica.* Fruit of a large tropical tree native to India. It is eaten both ripe or green, raw or cooked, dried or made into preserves and chutneys. There are many varieties of this aromatic fruit—some good, some stringy. Juice may cause problems to the skin of some people who are hypersensitive to the irritants in the sap. Precaution: use one knife to peel fruit, and a clean knife to slice flesh to avoid contaminating it with the resin in peel. Most supermarkets have mangos, at least part of the year. Select rather firm, partially ripe fruit, blushed with red or yellow on a taut skin. Smell the stem end to make certain it has not begun to ferment. Substitute fresh peaches.

MANIOC. (Cassava, Khoai Mi, Manihot, Singkong, Yuca). *Maniot esculenta.* A tropical New World, tuberous, food plant; now an extremely important food starch of tropical lowlands in both hemispheres. Edible part is the large, tuberous root. There are two groups—sweet and bitter. The latter requires special preparation through labor intensive grating, pressure, and heating to make it safe to eat as this removes the poisonous cyanogenetic glucosides. In temperate areas it is used as food in the form of tapioca for puddings, or commercially as a starch or sizing.

MASA. *Zea mays.* Masa is made of maize, called corn by Europeans, only major domesticated cereal in New World before Columbus (see Corn in this section). Not only did pre-Columbian Indians in Mexico domesticate maize but also discovered nixtamalization. This complex process of soaking and boiling ripe grains with charcoal/wood ashes (lye) that forms an alkaline solution, makes the separation of the transparent skin (pericarp) from endosperm and allows for easier grinding. The process greatly enhances protein value. Combined with beans, treated corn-masa furnishes all the protein needed for a working male. Maize-dependent places in the world, where this process is not known, suffer from pellagra and other dietary deficiencies. Pellagra was common in the deep south of the United States before and after the Civil War when corn was usually the only grain available. Masa is basis of tortillas and tamales. Dry masa is becoming more readily available. Now produced by Quaker Oats®. Try using it instead of corn meal or mix it half and half in recipes calling for corn meal. It is wonderful for breading or flouring (dredging food with flour or crumbs before frying) in place of the usual flour or corn meal.

MELBA TOAST. This crisp, dried bread can be bought in packages but is expensive. Prepare your own by buying baguette loaves or bagels; slice less than ½-inch thick, or save left over bread and cut it into small squares or rounds no thicker than ½-inch. Place thin slices on an ungreased cookie sheet; put into a 200°F oven. After thirty minutes, turn oven off and go to bed. Next morning remove crisp melba toast from oven; place it in zip lock plastic bags. Use as canapes with ajvar, (see P. 26) in Andalusian gaspacho, to thicken soups and sauces, or use like crackers with soups and salads. It will keep for a long time.

MENNONITE CHEESE. A white farm cheese made by Mennonites, members of a Protestant religious group founded in the sixteenth century. Substitute a white farmer's cheese, white cheddar, or Monterey Jack.

MEXICAN CHEESES. Until second voyage of Columbus people of the Americas had no dairy animals. Domesticated Andean llamas were milked, but their milk was not drunk. It is thought some sort of cheese may have been made. There are now many, many cheeses in Mexico but few of them are available in food markets in the United States. *Queso fresco* (fresh) and/or *Queso blanco* (white) are mild, fresh cheeses used to crumble over the various tortilla dishes. Feta makes an adequate substitute. *Queso añejo* (aged) is a dry cheese similar to Parmesan. *Asadero* (roasting) is a cheese to be melted, like mozzarella.

MEXICAN CHOCOLATE. *Theobroma cacao.* Name for chocolate derives from two Nahuatl words, *xoco* (bitter), and *atl* (water). In pre-Columbian Mexico a chocolate drink was made with cold water, sweetened with honey, and spiced with vanilla, then beaten until foamy with a *molinillo* (a wooden beater that is twirled between the palms). Today the drink is made from small cakes of sweetened chocolate. In the United States, it can be purchased at most Latin American food stores. Substitute sweet chocolate; contains caffeine.

MUSTARD. *Sinapis alba* (white); *Brassica nigra* (black). Seed of this Mediterranean native ranks with salt and sugar as our most common spices. Records of its use date to fifth century B.C. Both ancient Greeks and Romans used it. By 42 A.D. Romans were preparing a condiment similar to the modern type. Flavor develops only when aromatic seeds are crushed and mixed with water. Many mustard preparations are available or you can prepare your own. No substitute.

MUSTARD OIL. *Brassica* spp. A yellow oil made from mustard seed—pungent when raw but sweet when heated slightly. Used in Indian cookery to prepare vegetables or fish, and for pickling. Peanut oil can be substituted. Found in Indian food stores.

NOPALES. *Opuntia engelmannii* (or similar species). New or very young green pads (these are flat stems, not leaves) of prickly pear cactus, a New World native. Ripe fruits, *tunas,* can be eaten. Many supermarkets now carry fresh *nopales* (*nopalitos* means small) in season (spring) and also canned. Look for opuntia tunas to be the next Kiwi fruit. No substitute.

ONION. *Allium cepa.* Probably originated in central or southwest Asia; eaten before recorded history. Pungent onion and its relatives, garlic (*A. sativum,*) leeks (*A. ampeloprasum,*) and chives (*A. schoenoprasum*) are not only used for flavor but also nutritionally, and medicinally. In markets in India and South America you will not find anything but red onions—in their recipes use only red onions or substitute leeks or shallots but do not use strong yellow or white onions. Leeks are used extensively instead of onions in Andean countries where red onion is "cured" or marinated. This mellowed raw onion is used in salads or as a condiment—very good. To cure: peel and finely slice the onion then rub salt into it. Let sit for at least ten minutes. Rinse several times; squeeze out water. Add lime juice. Marinate ten minutes; drain. Keep in air tight container for at least a week. Also works with white or yellow onions.

PALM SUGAR. *Coco nucifera* or *Borssaus flabellifer.* Sap of either coconut palm or sugar palm is formed into light brown cakes; used in cooking. If it cannot be found at an Oriental food store, soft brown cane sugar can be substituted.

PAPAYA. *Carica papaya.* Sometimes called papaw; large herbaceous herb growing to twenty feet tall; bears large, melon-like, green to orange fruits with pinkish orange flesh that emerge from a trunk-like stem. Native to tropical America, introduced to Philippines by Spaniards in mid-sixteenth century; from there became pantropic. Ripe fruit is commonly eaten fresh with lime or lemon; unripe fruit is never eaten raw because of latex content. Can be used in making pies, sauces, jams, and marmalades—alone or combined with pineapple. Fruit should be ripe and slightly soft. To ripen put in a paper bag in dark place. Do not chill fruit before it is ripe. Most supermarkets have papayas year round. Peaches or cantaloupe could be used in a pinch.

PASTA. Name established itself after World War II; wide range of products it refers to has a long history. Basically a product of boiled flour and water. Not thought of as a luxury food. First reference in Europe was 1279, before Marco Polo went to China and tasted noodles. Came to Americas with Spaniards. Thomas Jefferson probably introduced it to the United States when he returned from France in 1789. Massive Italian immigration in late nineteenth century popularized it. Pasta has little nutritional value unless made from coarse nodules of second break durum, a hard wheat flour called semolina, or from whole wheat flour. Production was mechanized in Naples, Italy, in 1878; manufacture began in the United States during World War I. Served plain, stuffed, in soups and broths, baked, and in many separate dishes with sauces or dressings. Read the label and choose nutritious semolina or whole wheat. (see P. 90–91 for cooking pasta).

PECANS. *Carya illinoinensis.* A temperate nut (any oily seed is commonly called a nut) borne on a large tree. Nuts are dry fruits with a hard pericarp. Embryo is edible part. Native of Mexico and southwestern United States, and is now grown extensively in the southeastern United States. Thin-shelled varieties have been developed by grafting; now over three-hundred named varieties. Pecans become an important part of regional cuisine.

PEPITAS. *Cucurbita pepo.* In Spanish fruit seeds are *pepitas*; in Latin American recipes, raw, hulled, unsalted pumpkin seeds are those referred to. Greenish in color with a nutty flavor; are ground for sauces; used toasted or plain. Will keep for several months stored in refrigerator in tightly closed containers. Protein content very high. Toasted pumpkin "pepitas" found in nut section of supermarkets. Substitute sunflower seed or pine nuts, but both have less protein.

PILÓNCILLO. A little loaf (*pilón*) of unrefined brown sugar from Mexico; can be cone, loaf, or cylinder shaped. Substitute dark brown sugar (see Sugar, this section).

PIMENTO/PIMIENTO. *Capsicum annuum* var. *annuum.* Pimentos come in various shapes (round, lobed, heart-shaped) and colors (yellow, red). First pimento peppers grown in the United States were from Spain. Large heart-shaped fruits are very aromatic. "Pimento" is name adopted by the Associated Pimento Canners of Georgia instead of Spanish *pimiento* for thick-fleshed, sweet, bright red *Capsicum* usually cored, flame peeled, and canned whole or diced; however, pimiento is still used on many products on grocers' shelves. Pimento (fresh or canned) is used as garnish, in cheese spreads and bricks, in casserole dishes, or wherever bits of color are desired in food.

PINE NUTS. *Pinus pinea* (pignoli, Mediterranean), *P. koraiensis, P. eduis* (piñon, America). Buttery flavored seeds from pine cones; have been eaten by humans at least 300,000 years. Labor-intensive seed extraction makes them expensive.

PIZZA. Idea of pizza came from Greeks who baked bread in flat rounds and added ingredients on top. First made by Raffeale Esposito in Naples, Italy, about 1830. Spread throughout Italy; little known elsewhere before World War II. Although the first American pizzeria opened in 1905, pizza was common only in Italian neighborhoods, and was popularized by returning World War II GIs. Can be made with anything from most healthy ingredients to most fattening; usually includes cheese and tomato sauce.

PORTABELLA MUSHROOM. *Agaricus* spp. Edible fungi; very, large (caps up to six inches wide), fully mature form of crimini—common, cultivated, white mushrooms. Plants have neither leaves, nor roots; live by parasitic activity; the fruit of a network of underground stems. *Agaricus* mushrooms need little cooking—excellent raw in salads. Wipe clean with damp, soft cloth. Remove meaty stems; save for stuffing, soups, or stock. Dark brown gills are edible but will darken the preparation. Scrape them off if this darkening is not desired.

POTATOES, WHITE. *Solanum tuberosum.* Native tuber of South America has been known outside the Americas for only a few hundred years following its discovery by Spaniards, who did not introduce it to Europe. Probably introduced to England by Sir Francis Drake, and moved across the channel to Europe. In Andean countries there are many varieties and colors beside white; these are just arriving in North American markets. Nutritional value of white potatoes without peel is low, primarily carbohydrate. Nutritionally comparable to white rice, white flour pasta, and white bread—that only fill you up and provide fuel for energy or calories, in the form of starch.

STARCHY POTATOES: Russets (Idaho or baking potatoes); thick, brown paper-like skin and white flesh. Fluffy, dry texture suitable for frying, baking, mashing.

ALL-PURPOSE POTOATOES: Texture of many thin-skinned varieties is between starchy and waxy. Mature thin-skinned white potatoes hold their shape well when cooked; creamy when mashed. Thin-skinned yellow-flesh 'Yellow Finns,' and 'Yukon Golds' have dense, creamy texture suitable for roasting and mashing.

WAXY POTATOES: New potatoes (any potato harvested before maturity) and round red potatoes have firm, smooth, texture that makes them suitable for boiling, roasting, and steaming; they turn gummy and slick when puréed or mashed. More nutritious due to lower glycemic index (GI) than other potatoes.

Keep potatoes in cool (50°F is ideal), dark, well ventilated place. If refrigerated, starch will turn to sugar, affecting color and flavor when cooked.

POTATOES, SWEET. *Ipomoea batatas.* A pre-Columbian Andean root crop; how it reached Old World unknown. No kin to white potatoes or yams; in the same genus as morning glories. Often mistakenly called yams that are genus *Dioscorea.* In the 1930s growers developed several very sweet, orange-fleshed varieties marketed as yams—very confusing! Numerous varieties; all with high moisture and sugar content.

QUINOA. (keen-wha) *Chenopodium quinoa.* Fruit of highly variable quinoa is not a typical cereal but is an annual, broad-leafed herb three to six feet tall, with fruit grown in clusters. Each fruit encloses a seed. Dried seed resemble grains; taste similar to rice. A native of South American Andes where it and potatoes were important during Inca Empire. In contrast to most edible crops it grows at high elevations. Among all grains it ranks first in iron and third in protein content. Its protein is equal to milk. Cooks quickly; can be made into flour for flat breads. Use in stews and soups instead of rice or couscous. Leaves can be eaten as a green vegetable. Found in specialty or health food stores; becoming readily available. The new quinoa flour can be substituted for masa or corn meal or mixed with them. Try quinoa in any recipe calling for rice or couscous.

RICE. *Oryza sativa.* Domesticated at least nine-thousand years ago in Asia. Considered the world's most important crop because more people eat it. It is eighty percent starch, an excellent supply of muscular energy. Modern milling procedures to produce polished or white rice removes the coating of fiber-rich bran and B-group vitamins, causing profound negative nutritional changes; do not use it. Use unmilled brown rice, basmati, long grain white, converted rice (Uncle Ben's®), or wild rice, *Zizania palustris* & *Z. texana* (wild rice cultivation began only in 1959) or another grain such as bulgar, quinoa, couscous made with semolina, or barley.

Types:

Short-grain white: almost round when uncooked; sticky when cooked.

Medium-grain white: all purpose; slightly stickier than long-grain when cooked.

Long-grain white: stays separate when cooked.

Arborio: grains have a white dot in center; creamy when cooked but firm in center; use for risotto.

Aromatic: long-grain, delicately flavored and slightly fragrant; Basmati & Jasmine.

Brown: less processed than white; retains bran layer producing nutty flavor, brown color; fiber.

Wild: not a rice; it is a seed of an aquatic grass; nutritious.

RICE VINEGAR. *Oryza sativa.* A light amber, red, or dark black colored condiment or flavoring agent made from rice. Light type is used in sweet-and-sour dishes, black is used to darken color of sauces; red type is used mainly as a dip for meats and vegetables. Buy it at Oriental food stores; it will keep indefinitely. There is no substitute.

RICE WINE. *Oryza sativa. Shaosing,* China's most popular wine comes in white or yellow. The sherry-like yellow is made of yellow rice; warm before drinking from tiny cups. In cooking, substitute Japanese *sake,* dry sherry, or gin; never cream or cooking sherry. The clear, vodka-like white wine from north China is not used as flavoring but rather to neutralize strong odor. Purchase at Oriental food or liquor stores.

ROMA TOMATOES. (see Tomatoes).

SESAME. *Sesamum indicum.* Flat, white seed from a herbaceous annual. Ground for oil in some cultures since a few thousand years before Christ. This non-pungent, nutty flavored oil, used for seasoning, not cooking, is consumed at or near principal areas of production—Africa, India, China, and Middle East. Whole seed used in cooking and baking are tastier when toasted. Sprinkle seed on bread and cakes, over rice or other cooked foods, in salads and salad dressings, use to dredge meat, fish, or poultry before cooking. Grind to make a paste—tahini (see below). Sesame will keep almost indefinitely in refrigerator if frozen to kill possible insect larvae before storage. Best found in Oriental and Middle Eastern food stores. No substitute.

SICHUAN PEPPERCORNS. *Zanthoxylum piperitum.* Not kin to either black pepper or capsicums. It is the small red-brown seeds from prickly ash trees; available in Oriental food stores. Substitute black peppercorns.

SOY BEAN. *Glycine maximus.* One of world's major staple foods. Remarkably nutritious bean; more protein than any other plant, also rich in oil for cooking. Originated in the Orient; cultivated in China by the third millennium B.C. After World War II it aroused interest in America. Not as palatable as table beans. They have become a major farm product. Most of the crop is processed and transformed into altered products: TOFU or bean curd, SOY SAUCE, SOY MILK, SOYA KAAS (cream cheese style), MISO, other fermented products. Soy products are becoming more common.

STAR ANISE. *Illicium verum.* Licorice-like flavor of seed of this small Chinese evergreen tree is rather new to American cooks. Entirely different botanically from anise (*Pimpinella anisum*). Look in Oriental food stores. No substitute.

SUGARS. Sugars are rudimentary carbohydrates. Granulated sugar is sucrose from sugar cane (*Saccharum officinarum*) probably native to New Guinea, or European beets (*Beta vulgaris*). Glucose is sugar found in fruits and vegetables; fructose is major component of honey and corn syrup. Crystalline fructose is more refined and less natural than sucrose. Fructose must be used in its natural form to be a "healthy" substitute for sucrose. When only small amounts are called for, Splenda® may be substituted.

TABBOULEH. (see P. 64).

TAHINI. An oily cream paste similar to peanut butter, extracted from sesame seeds. Used as is or incorporated in savory dips such as hummus, baba ghanoush or in making sweet halva or sauces. Ethnic food stores. No substitute. (see Sesame this section).

TAMALES. Seasoned masa mixed with lard; spread on corn husks (shucks) or banana leaves; steamed. May be unfilled or filled with a variety of seasoned fillings; rolled with ends folded. "Shuck" is removed before eating. Can be found canned (a very poor substitute, often wrapped in flavorless paper) and frozen in most supermarkets. Fresh in southwestern supermarkets or Latin American food stores. In Texas almost everyone has a favorite local "tamale lady" to make them for special occasions—a Christmas Eve tradition in south Texas. (see Corn Meal, this section).

TAMARIND. *Tamarindus indica.* Tropical tree of India; produces large brown bean pod. Seeds inside brittle shell are enclosed in a sticky, brown pulp with a tart flavor. In India the pulp is an integral part of chutneys and sauces. It gives Worcestershire sauce its characteristic flavor. Soak dried pulp in enough lukewarm water to cover until soft—twenty-five to thirty minutes. Squeeze until pulp dissolves in water; strain to remove seeds and fibers. A rather salty, bottled tamarind paste is available in Indian food stores. In the Southwest, dried pods are frequently available in supermarkets. Dilute paste with water to prepare juice or reserve soaking water to use when tamarind juice is called for. Substitute dried apricots mixed with Worcestershire sauce.

TAMARILLO. *Cyphomandra betacea.* In same family as tomato. "Tree Tomato" is egg-shaped, red or golden fruit of a small tropical tree from Andean South America with skin similar to a pomegranate. It can be substituted for tomatoes in sauces and salsas or stewed with honey or sugar and a little cinnamon for a desert. Ecuadorians use it for their *Salsa Ají*. Delightful! Substitute Roma tomatoes and a little fresh lime juice.

TOMATILLOS. *Physalis ixocarpa.* Small Mexican, green husk "tomatoes"; not real tomatoes but related to the Cape gooseberry, *Ribes* sp. Their tartness adds distinction to many Mexican style dishes and sauces but should not be limited to those. Try tomatillo sauces on pasta, chicken, fish, quinoa, rice, or experiment. Select firm, unblemished fruit; remove husks before using. Fresh tomatillos can be found in Southwestern supermarkets; canned ones available most places. Drain canned ones before using. Green tomatoes can be substituted.

TOMATO. *Lycopersicon esculentum.* A new world Solanaceous plant; came to Old World after 1521 conquest of Mexico. Superstitions kept it from being accepted into European cuisines until the seventeenth century. Actually, it was not eaten in Italy until the nineteenth century. Introduced to Virginia via Bermuda in seventeenth century; not accepted as a food until early nineteenth century. Best source of *lycopene,* a cancer-fighting antioxidant. Cooking and sun-drying tomatoes increases lycopene. Americans eat many tomatoes, both raw and cooked, and they are ranked high in the United States as a good source of vitamins A and C. Roma tomatoes are small, cylindrical, Italian-type tomatoes used for cooking and sauces. It has fewer seeds and less juice than regular tomatoes. Excellent for sauces and sun or oven drying. In my travels I have noticed that Roma tomatoes have almost entirely replaced other types of tomatoes in markets of Third World Countries in both hemispheres. They still have not taken over the Balkans, northern Pakistan, and other nearby countries that were at one time a part of the USSR, but they probably will.

To select: Vine ripened, fragrant, deeply colored, heavy for their size, and give slightly when gently squeezed. According to Texas A&M University, once the fruit has blushed (begun to turn red) on the bush it will continue to fully ripen to full flavor when picked; however, if picked green, flavor will not develop even though it turns red.

To peel: dip into boiling water for a few seconds; remove with a slotted spoon; immediately place in iced water to stop cooking. Skin will readily pull off.

To store: Do not store tomatoes in refrigerator. Refrigeration makes flesh mealy and kills flavor. Those overripe can be frozen to be used in cooking.

TORTILLA. An unleavened, thin, flat, round bread made of corn masa or wheat flour. Basis of Mexican, Southwestern, and Tex-Mex cookery. Those made with wheat flour are handy substitutes for typical flat breads of India and Middle East. Available in bread and/or refrigerator section of many supermarkets. Essential for enchiladas and tacos. No substitute. (see Masa, this section).

TURMERIC. *Curcuma domestica.* An Asian member of ginger family. Its rhizomes are dried and ground producing a deep yellow powder containing curcumin. It is ubiquitous in India where it is used to flavor nearly every dish and as a food preservative and dye. In the United States it is mainly known in curry powder. Alzheimer's disease is virtually unknown in India where everyone eats turmeric. Curcumin has antioxidant and anti-inflammatory effects. Alzheimer's studies at the University of California at Los Angeles were conducted with anti-inflammatory synthetic drugs and studies with natural curcumin. Curcumin studies verified a relationship of anti-inflammatory drugs and Alzheimer's. Try adding it to dried beans, soups, sauces, etc. The flavor grows on you. No substitute.

VINEGAR. Vinegar or "sour wine" has been used "forever" as a flavoring and preserving agent. It makes itself, but the best vinegar is made by a controlled process. To insure that the right bacteria are present to produce the best vinegar, add vinegar from a previous batch to the wine to be fermented. This "starter," which forms on fermenting vinegar, should contain "mother of vinegar," a jelly-like scum filled with living bacteria. Balsamic vinegar is made from "must," not from wine; aged for decades. Malt vinegar is made from an unhopped type of beer and its flavor is not recommended for salads. Cider vinegar is made from apples. There are many types of vinegars; all may have added flavors such as herbs, chili peppers, and fruits. (see Rice Vinegar, this section).

WALNUTS. *Juglans* spp. True nuts are a dry fruit with a single seed, hard pericarp, and a husk-like covering partially enclosing fruit. Walnuts, chestnuts, filberts, and pecans are true nuts—peanuts and almonds are not. Impressive studies have shown that nuts have great health benefits. Small amounts should be part of your daily diet—an ounce or two a day will do, otherwise high caloric (160–190 calories per ounce) and fat (14 to 19 grams per ounce) content causes weight gain. Although walnuts top the list, strong taste is unpleasant to many. Blanching, then toasting is an easy way to get rid of it. Buy several pounds of shelled walnuts. Preheat oven to 250°F. To blanch, fill a large sauce pan or soup pot with enough water to submerge nuts. Bring water to a rolling boil; add nuts; quickly return water to boiling. Boil for no more than one minute. Pour nuts into a colander; wash under cold water; drain. Spread nuts on a clean cup towel; pat dry. Spread nuts in a flat cake pan of a size that they are not much more than ½-inch deep. Place pan in oven; after ten minutes, turn oven off; go to bed. Next morning remove crisp nuts from pan; place in a container that can be tightly closed. These will keep for some time if well closed after each time some are removed.

WILD RICE. *Zizania aquatica.* Not related to common rice. This New World species was used by Native Americans but never domesticated by them. It grows as eight to twelve feet tall reeds in water and marshes; very sensitive to changes of depth and water quality. Expensive due to difficulty of growing and harvesting. Among "grains," it and quinoa have highest protein content.

YAMS. *Discorea* spp. World's second most important starchy tuber or root. Different species are native to Africa, Asia, and South America; each domesticated independently. D. *rotundata* of Africa is the most common. Grown both for eating and ceremony; can weigh up to 122 pounds. Although sweet potatoes are often called yams they are NOT related. True yams are generally used to make a fine, easily digested, powdered starch.

YOGURT. A fermented milk food originating in Asia. Came to western Europe in the twentieth century from Turkey via the Balkans, hence Turkish name; to the United States in the late 1950s. Fermentation converts lactose or milk sugar in milk to lactic acid, giving yogurt its characteristic sour taste and making it a great milk substitute for lactose intolerant consumers. Made from many different milks—cow, goat, sheep, camel, mare, water buffalo, yak. Casein in yogurt curbs burning sensation caused by capsaicin in chili peppers. Yogurt sauces such as raita (see P. 63) are usually served with peppery dishes in India, Near East, and Balkans.

To make dripped yogurt cheese:

Use 1 quart (2 pounds) plain nonfat yogurt (do not use yogurt with gelatin).

1. Set a strainer or colander over a deep pan or bowl, supporting it so base of strainer is at least 2 inches above pan bottom.
2. Line strainer with two layers of cheesecloth or a clean piece of muslin or linen. Dump 1 quart plain, nonfat yogurt into cloth. Enclose strainer and pan with plastic wrap to keep airtight.
3. Chill at least twenty-four hours or up to four days, pouring off whey, the liquid that separates from the cheese, as it accumulates. Shorter draining produces a moister cheese and more volume. Longer draining produces a thicker cheese and less volume.

4. Scrape yogurt cheese from cloth and use, or store airtight up to nine days from when draining began. Drain off any whey that accumulates. Use in recipes calling for cream cheese or similar cheese. Very low calorie.

Cooking Notes

The cooking notes are few in number because most kitchens have a standard cookbook like *The Joy of Cooking,* which can serve as a reference. Notes included here are for your convenience because they have been used frequently in the directions for the recipes.

AL DENTE. To be firm to the tooth or to have a little bite. Cooked until tender but retaining a agreeable firmness.

BASE. Use instead of bouillon cubes. For example, Chicken Base.

BLANCH. Plunge food into boiling water; cook until softened, or partially or fully cooked. To do this in a microwave, place vegetables in a recommended microwave-safe container, add a few tablespoons of water, cover; microwave on high up to five minutes, depending on quantity; stir. If needed, repeat. Very important to plunge into ice water to stop cooking.

BROWN FLOUR. Use to thicken, enhance color, and add flavor to gravies. Put 1 cup of flour in a heavy, dry skillet over very low direct heat. Stir constantly until golden brown. Do not let it get too dark because it will become bitter and lose its thickening power. Store in a tightly cover jar in refrigerator or freezer.

For sauce: In a sauce pan over a low fire, melt 2 tablespoons butter; stir in 1 tablespoon browned flour until smooth. Gradually add about 1 cup of boiling broth, stirring constantly, until desired thickness. Season as desired.

CHOPPING HERBS. Wash and dry herbs, as moisture causes sogginess. Remove any wood-like stems; process in a food processor by pulsing on and off.

CLARIFY BUTTER. Melt chunks of butter in a small, heavy pan over low heat so that fat can be separated from solids. When foam has risen to top, remove from heat; skim off foam. Pour butter off carefully in order to leave solids in pan. Clarified butter keeps almost indefinitely when refrigerated in a tightly closed container.

DÉGLACE. To déglace a pan is to dilute the concentrated juices left in a pan in which meat, poultry, or fish have been roasted, braised, or fried. Use wine, clear soup, stock, sometimes cream, or, in a pinch, water.

DEMI-GLACE. A demi-glace (demi-glaze) is made in a sauce pan over high heat by bringing 1 quart of brown stock (see Stock, this section) to a boil over high heat; reduce heat and add 4 teaspoons of cornstarch mixed with 4 teaspoons cold water. Simmer until reduced by a half and mixture is thick enough to coat a spoon. Stir until cool to prevent separation. This will keep up to a week in refrigerator, or longer if frozen. Use in making sauces. Note: canned beef or chicken bouillon can be substituted if homemade stock is not available.

GRINDING SPICES. Whole spices and herbs may be ground in a small electric spice or coffee grinder, or by using a mortar and pestle. In order to maintain the volatile natural flavoring compounds of spice, grind only what is needed at the time. Do not over-grind. Between uses, clean grinder by grinding dry rice grains, then dispose of them.

GRINDING VEGETABLES. Ground vegetables have a distinct coarse texture as opposed to shredded or chopped vegetables that can be obtained with the coarse grind disk on an old-fashioned meat grinder (hand turned or electric) or a Brun type mixer/grinder (mine is 1970 vintage). It is almost impossible to get a comparable texture with a food processor—it will be either too coarse or too mushy.

KEEPING HERBS. Fresh herbs are expensive and very difficult to keep, that was until I discovered an herb keeper that keeps them fresh for weeks at a time. Herb Keeper #65972 at *www.SolutionsCatalog.com* or Solutions, P.O. Box 6878, Portland, OR 97228.

MICROWAVE. Use primarily for rapid heating or defrosting. Also use for quick cooking of vegetables, fruits, cereals, etc. Foods will not brown in a microwave. Always use only glass or ceramic containers. Waxed paper and paper towels can be used for covers, etc. Before using plastic containers make certain they are microwave safe. Caution: Do not use plastic bags and plastic wrap because microwaves can cause plastic molecules to migrate into food.

NON-REACTIVE CONTAINER. A glass, enamel or agate coated, stainless-steel, or any other type container that will not set up a chemical reaction with the food placed in it. Especially important when the foods are highly acidic.

PARBOIL. (see Blanch, this section).

REDUCE. To decrease the volume of a liquid by boiling, thereby concentrating the flavor.

ROASTING VEGETABLES. Place the vegetable (tomatoes, garlic, shallots, eggplant, etc.) on an aluminum foil-lined pan four to six inches under the broiler flame. Broil until the skin is evenly charred, turning as needed. Remove only badly charred skin in order to maintain desired flavor. Squeeze the garlic or shallots from their skins. Use as directed in the recipe.

An alternative method is to place the vegetables on an aluminum foil-lined pan in a preheated 550°F oven and allow to remain only until blistered, three to seven minutes, being careful not to cook. Plunge into ice water for a crisper vegetable.

ROUX. A common thickener for sauces. Julia Child and others give recipes for a savory, high fat brown, blonde, or white roux but they can be very tedious and time consuming. (see Brown Flour P. 44).

SAUTÉ. To cook and brown food in a very small amount of really hot fat, usually in an uncovered skillet. The secret is to have the fat or oil very hot, the food dry, and to sear quickly to prevent loss of juices.

STOCK. The broth from boiled bones, meat, chicken, or fish; used in preparing soups and sauces. A flavorful stock is important. When boiling a chicken or other meat, add onion, celery, peppers, garlic, carrots, bay leaves, peppercorns, and herbs. Cook over low heat until the meat is tender. For a richer stock, remove the meat, debone, then return the bones to the stock and simmer for an hour or more. Remove the meat or bones, degrease, and strain. For a clear stock, never allow the broth to boil. Veal meat and bones produce stock with a neutral flavor. For a brown stock with a more robust flavor, cook the bones in a roasting pan in a 450° oven, turning several times, until bones are golden brown on all sides. Add the browned bones to the stock pot along with the vegetables.

SWEAT. (see Wilting, this section).

TOASTING SEEDS. Place seeds—sesame (benne), cumin, pumpkin (pepita), sunflower, poppy, etc. in a flat pan and toast for about twenty minutes in a 350°F oven. Stir fre-

quently, taking care not to scorch. This can also be done in a microwave by spreading the seed in a shallow microwave container and cooking, stirring in one-half to one-minute intervals, until toasted. Toasting brings out the nutty flavor. Prepare with or without a little vegetable oil. Yet another method is in a dry skillet over low heat on a stove, using little or no oil and guarding against burning by watching carefully and stirring frequently.

WILTING. Vegetables can be wilted (or sweated) in a covered skillet with a small amount of oil, over medium heat, stirring frequently to prevent any browning. Cook them to a barely limp state. This can be done in a covered dish in the microwave without using oil, a plus for the calorie and health-conscious cook.

Substitutions for Ingredients

Sweetening, Flavoring:

1¼ cups sugar + ⅓ cup liquid = 1 cup light corn syrup or honey

3 tablespoons cocoa + 1 tablespoon butter = 1 (1-ounce) square unsweetened chocolate

⅛ teaspoon cayenne pepper = 3 to 4 drops liquid hot red pepper sauce.

Thickening:

1 tablespoon cornstarch = 2 tablespoons all-purpose flour

1 tablespoon arrowroot = 2 ½ tablespoons all-purpose flour

1 tablespoon potato flour or rice flour = 2 tablespoons all-purpose flour

2 teaspoons quick-cooking tapioca = 1 tablespoon all-purpose flour (use in soups only)

Leavening:

¼ teaspoon baking soda + ½ teaspoon cream of tartar = 1 teaspoon double-acting baking powder

¼ teaspoon baking soda + ½ cup sour milk = 1 teaspoon double-acting baking powder in liquid mixtures; reduce recipe liquid content by ½ cup

Flour:

1 cup sifted all-purpose flour minus 2 tablespoons = 1 cup sifted cake flour

1 cup sifted self-rising flour = 1 cup sifted all-purpose flour + 1¼ teaspoons baking powder and a pinch of salt; when using, substitute measure for measure for all-purpose flour, then omit baking powder and salt in recipe.

Dairy:

1 cup skim milk + 2 teaspoons melted butter = 1 cup whole milk

1 cup milk + 1 tablespoon lemon juice or white vinegar = 1 cup sour milk (let stand five to ten minutes before using)

¾ cup milk + ¼ cup melted butter = 1 cup light cream

equal part plain, low-fat yogurt = equal part whole milk in biscuits or scones

Eggs:

1 egg yolk = 1 egg (for thickening sauces, custards)

2 egg yolks + 1 tablespoon cold water = 1 egg (for baking)

1½ tablespoons stirred egg whites = 1 egg yolk

2 tablespoons stirred egg whites = 1 egg white

3 tablespoons mixed broken yolks and whites = 1 medium-sized egg

¼ cup egg substitute = 1 whole egg

Miscellaneous:

1 cup boiling water + 1 bouillon cube, 1 teaspoon meat paste, or 1 envelope instant broth mix = 1 cup broth

PART II

RECIPES

1 APPETIZERS

SALADS

SOUPS

Appetizers

(Also see Sauces and Spreads P. 141)

PICANTE BLOODY MARY

The Bloody Mary was first made in the 1920s at Harry's Bar in Paris, France, by Ferdinand Petiot. For a change try my version using tequilla.

Makes 12 Servings

- ⅓ cup fresh lime juice
- 3–5 serranos, stemmed and seeded (to taste)
- 1 bunch cilantro (fresh coriander), stemmed and chopped (reserve some sprigs for garnish)
- 1 46-ounce can picante V-8® juice
- ¾ cup tequilla or vodka, chilled
  Salt to taste

Blend first three ingredients in blender. Mix with V-8® Juice and tequilla. Strain into a pitcher; twice if necessary. Serve in a hi-ball glass over ice; salt to taste. Add a sprig of cilantro or a slice of lime for garnish.

ROASTED RED PEPPER DIP

This creamy dip can be made quickly by substituting ⅔ cup of drained, canned roasted red peppers instead of roasting the peppers yourself.

Makes 1½ Cups

- 2 medium red Bell Peppers or ⅔ cup canned/jarred roasted red peppers
- 1 teaspoon extra-virgin olive oil
- 3 garlic cloves, peeled and minced
- 1 serrano or jalapeño, seeded and minced
- 1 tablespoon balsamic vinegar
- 1 cup sour cream or nonfat plain yogurt
- 1 tablespoon fresh basil, minced
  Cayenne pepper to taste
  Salt and freshly ground black pepper

Use canned roasted red peppers or roast Bell Peppers over a gas flame or under the broiler until charred all over. Put in a plastic or paper bag and let steam for 20 minutes. Remove skins, veins, and seeds; pat dry and finely chop. In a skillet, cook garlic in oil over moderate heat until fragrant, about 30 seconds. Add roasted Bell Pepper, serrano peppers and vinegar; cook over moderately low heat, stirring, until dry, about 12 minutes. Transfer to a bowl to cool. Stir in sour cream, basil, and cayenne. Adjust seasoning. Dip can be covered and refrigerated for up to 3 days. Serve with chips, bread sticks, Melba toast or crackers.

WHITE BEAN DIP

This healthy, low fat, dip is a variation of the Ecuadorian "salsa de chocho." Chochos are big, dried lima beans. It is sort of an Andean hummus. I found it easier to use our navy beans or baby limas because each big white lima must be slipped out of its skin after soaking. They are wonderful used that way, but the procedure is tedious. Make it at least a day ahead.

Makes 2 Cups or More

Day Before:
Soak 1 cup dried navy, white, baby lima, or big lima beans overnight in water to cover. If using big limas, remove the skins after soaking (they slip off easily).

Next Day or Day Before Serving:
Drain beans; put in a large covered pan with water to cover by several inches. Bring to a boil; reduce heat; cook covered until very tender. Add boiling water as needed. Drain. Set aside.

2 tablespoons olive oil
1 cup leeks or red onion, finely chopped
2 garlic cloves, peeled and minced
1½ cups chicken broth
2 tablespoons fresh basil, minced
2 serranos, seeded and chopped; or to taste
1 teaspoon lemon juice
 Salt and freshly ground black pepper to taste

Put oil in a large sauce pan (2½ quart), over low heat, add leeks and garlic; cook until translucent. Add broth; cook another 5 minutes. Add drained beans, basil, serranos, and lemon juice; mix well. In batches, put mixture into a blender; process until smooth. Return puréed mixture to saucepan; cook over low heat, stirring, until it thickens (about like hummus or peanut butter). Remove from heat. Season with salt and pepper. Chill overnight before serving. Use as dip for raw vegetables, chips, or crackers. Keeps well covered in refrigerator for a week, or freezes well for later use.

EASY HUMMUS

Instead of using dried chickpeas (garbanzo beans) which require a lot of cooking, this uses canned white beans. Purists may consider canned chickpeas.

Makes 2 Cups

2 15-ounce cans navy beans, drained; reserve the liquid
1 cup tahini paste (see P. 41)
2 garlic cloves, peeled and mashed
3 tablespoons fresh parsley, chopped
½ teaspoon cayenne pepper or 1 teaspoon Aleppo pepper
2 tablespoons olive oil
1 lemon, juiced
 Salt and freshly ground black pepper to taste

Place beans in bowl of a food processor; process until smooth. Add remaining ingredients; process until it becomes a smooth, spreadable paste. Add reserved bean liquid as needed. Place in a shallow serving dish; sprinkle with paprika. Serve with pieces of pita bread, sliced cucumbers, or crisp crackers.

NOTE: 8 or 10 green olives added to processor makes a tasty variation.

BABA GHANOUJ, TEXAS STYLE (EGGPLANT DIP)

Another healthy, low fat dip based on a Middle Eastern favorite. You won't even know you are eating eggplant. I use a little wooden cleaver found in a souq (market) to chop the vegetable. It is like the ones I saw being used in homes throughout the Middle East and Central Asia. The texture of the dip is better than when eggplant is chopped with a knife. In lieu of that, try the edge of a wooden spoon or wooden spatula. The food processor makes it too slick. Make the day before use so the flavors meld.

Makes 2 ½ Cups

2   eggplants (about 1½ pounds each)
2   tablespoons sesame seed or tahini paste (see P. 41)
4   tablespoons olive oil
2   serranos, seeded and chopped (or more to taste)
3   garlic cloves, peeled and chopped
1   lemon, juiced
2   tablespoon fresh parsley leaves
2   tablespoon fresh mint leaves
½   teaspoon cayenne pepper, or to taste
    Salt and freshly ground black pepper to taste

Preheat oven to 450°F. Pierce eggplants in several places. Wrap them separately in aluminum foil; place on a baking sheet. Bake until soft; about 45 minutes. Unwrap and let stand until cool enough to handle. While cooling, place all other ingredients, except salt and pepper, into a blender. Process until creamy smooth. Halve eggplants lengthwise; remove all flesh, discarding seeds and skin. Coarsely chop eggplant and place in a bowl. Add creamed mixture; stir until well mixed. Season with salt and pepper to taste. Adjust other seasonings. Cover and place in refrigerator overnight to mellow. Serve at room temperature with flat bread, chips, or as a dip for vegetables. Keeps, well-covered, up to a week in the refrigerator. Eggplant does not freeze well.

NOTE: If using only 1 eggplant, use only ½ the amounts of other ingredients.

HOT ARTICHOKE DIP

This rich, creamy, warm dish sounds complicated but it is very easy. Your guests will think you have pulled out all the stops.

Makes 2 Cups

1   4-ounce can artichoke hearts (not marinated), drained well
3   tablespoons Parmesan, Asiago, or Romano cheese, shredded
2   tablespoons reduced-fat or nonfat mayonnaise
2   garlic cloves, peeled and crushed
1   teaspoon Aleppo pepper or cayenne pepper to taste
2   tablespoons roasted red pepper, chopped (use canned)
¾   cup plain low-fat yogurt
    Paprika for garnish

Preheat oven to 350°F. Place artichokes, cheese, mayonnaise, garlic, and peppers in food processor. Process until artichokes are finely chopped. Combine mixture with yogurt, stir in chopped red pepper, and spoon into small baking dish. Bake until hot, about 20 minutes. Sprinkle with paprika. Serve with toasted English muffin wedges, Melba toast, or fat-free crackers.

NOTE: If you must use marinated artichokes, add a little granulated sugar or Splenda® to offset vinegar.

CREAMY CHILE DIP

A delightfully different dip for raw or parboiled vegetables, or tostadas; or used as a stuffing for celery, banana peppers, or cherry tomatoes when served as appetizers.

Makes 1 Cup

- 6 Long Green/Red Chiles, peeled, seeds removed, chopped; or 1 (4-ounce) can, drained, chopped
- 1 8-ounce package cream cheese or dripped yogurt (see P. 44)
- 2 tablespoons milk
- 3 tablespoons green onion (scallion), finely chopped
- 4 garlic cloves, pressed
- ½ teaspoon cayenne pepper or to taste

Combine all ingredients; beat until creamy. Add more milk if necessary. Allow to sit for at least 1 hour at room temperature before serving.

TANGY CHEESE BALL

Great for parties because it can be made ahead of time, and leftovers can be remolded and frozen! A favorite from my Corpus Christi, Texas, friend, Lillian Murray, an experienced hostess, having spent many years hosting parties at conventions throughout the United States that were held by her family's insurance company.

Makes 1 Large or 2 Small Balls

- 6 ounce Roquefort or bleu cheese, at room temperature
- 10 ounce very sharp, crumbly cheddar cheese, finely grated, at room temperature
- 12 ounce cream cheese, at room temperature; or dripped plain yogurt (see P. 44)
- 1 small onion, grated
- 1 tablespoon Worcestershire sauce
- 1 teaspoon cayenne pepper, or to taste
- 1½ cup pecans, finely chopped
- 1½ cups parsley, stemmed and minced

Place cheeses in a large bowl with onion, Worcestershire, and cayenne pepper. Add ½ cup each of nuts and fresh parsley; reserve remainder. With your hands, blend all thoroughly. NO PROCESSOR! Shape into 1 large or several small balls; place each in a small bowl lined with plastic or aluminum foil. Refrigerate over night. Before serving, roll balls in a mixture of remaining parsley and pecans. Serve with unsalted or water crackers.

ZESTY SPINACH DIP

A new twist on the old favorite spinach dip. Serve with crisp, low-fat, whole grain crackers.

Makes 2½ Cups

- 1 10-ounce package frozen spinach, thawed, drained, chopped
- ½ cup red Bell Pepper or canned roasted red pepper, chopped
- ¼ cup green onions, chopped
- 2 garlic cloves, peeled and crushed
- 1 green serrano, stemmed, seeded, and minced
- ½ teaspoon hot pepper sauce, or to taste

Put all ingredients in a mixing bowl; stir until well blended. Cover; refrigerate until serving time.

ROASTED PORTABELLA MUSHROOMS WITH BASIL-RED PEPPER CREAM

Portabella mushrooms are so good! I even remove the stem and use a big cap instead of pastry for individual pizzas— much less fattening.

Makes About 24

Mushrooms:

    6 medium-size portabella mushrooms
       Olive oil to coat
       Salt and freshly ground black pepper, to taste

Basil-Red Pepper Cream

    1 cup fresh basil leaves
    ¼ cup roasted red pepper (canned), chopped
    3 tablespoons pine nuts, sunflower seed, or
       pepitas, toasted
    2 tablespoons Parmesan cheese, grated
    2 garlic cloves, peeled
    1 teaspoon Aleppo pepper or ¼ teaspoon cayenne
       pepper
       Salt and freshly ground black pepper, to taste
    ½ cup cream cheese, softened
    6 slices seven-grain or Health Nut bread,
       lightly toasted
    1 red pepper, roasted and thinly sliced for garnish.
       Use canned red pepper

Preheat oven 325°F. Prepare mushrooms by cleaning and removing gills. Lightly coat with olive oil. Season with salt and pepper. Place mushrooms on a baking pan and roast in oven for 30 minutes. Remove pan from oven and cool. Cut mushrooms into thin slices. Set aside.

Basil Cream
Place basil leaves, roasted red pepper, nuts, Parmesan cheese, garlic, and Aleppo pepper in blender. Pulse until smooth. Add salt and peppers to taste. Add cream cheese and blend until incorporated. To serve, spread the cream on toasted bread slices. Fan sliced mushrooms on top. Trim crusts. Cut each slice into squares or triangles. Garnish tops with piece of roasted red pepper.

BLEU CHEESE PUFFS

A tasty appetizer that can be prepared ahead, sealed in bags, and frozen until just before serving.

Makes About 24

    2 8-ounce packages cream cheese, low-fat will
       work or dripped yogurt
    1 cup mayonnaise, Hellmann's® recommended
       (try the light)
    1 tablespoon onion, grated
    ¼ cup fresh chives or green onion tops, minced
    1 cup bleu cheese, crumbled
    ½ teaspoon cayenne pepper
    1 loaf whole wheat or multi-grain bread,
       thinly sliced
       Paprika for garnish

In a medium bowl or a food processor, place cream cheese and mayonnaise; mix well. Stir in onion, chives, bleu cheese, and cayenne. Set aside. Remove crust from bread slices (you may prefer to leave crusts on); cut in squares, or use a small cookie cutter to cut into rounds. Spread 1 tablespoon of cheese mixture on each piece. Place filled squares on a baking sheet; cover and freeze until ready to prepare. When ready to serve, preheat oven to 350°F. Remove baking sheet from freezer and unwrap; place frozen puffs in oven. Bake 15 minutes. Garnish with paprika. Provide a spreader. Serve immediately along with Red Pepper Ajvar (see recipe P. 148). Pakistani Mango Chutney (see recipe P. 188) is also good on the puffs.

NOTE: to keep frozen for later use, remove frozen squares from baking sheet and seal in freezer bags.

THE PEPPER LADY'S CHILE CON QUESO

This is about as Tex-Mex as it comes, but an informal gathering in these parts of Texas wouldn't be the same without it.

Makes 8 to 12 Servings. More as a Dip

1   2-pound package Velveeta® cheese, cut into 1-inch cubes

1   pound sharp cheddar cheese, shredded, light if available

1   10-ounce can Rotel® diced tomatoes and green chiles

2   fresh Poblanos peppers or Long Green/Red Chiles, roasted, skinned, deveined, and cut into fine, 2-inch long strips

Salt and freshly ground black pepper to taste

Ground cayenne or Aleppo pepper to taste

Canned, evaporated milk for thinning

Melt Velveeta® cheese in a microwave or in a large double boiler, or crock pot, being careful not to scorch. Add cheddar cheese gradually; stir until melted and completely mixed with Velveeta® cheese. Add can of tomatoes to melted cheeses; mix well. Add chopped fresh poblano or Long Green/Red Chile. Stir until well mixed. Add seasonings to taste. Thin to desired consistency with canned evaporated milk; stir well. Serve immediately with freshly made corn tortillas or tostados. In the southwest, chile con queso is served warm from a chafing dish or fondue pot as a dip with toasted tortilla chips.

SUN-DRIED TOMATO CHEESE BALLS

A secret to using sun-dried tomatoes is to soften them in warm red wine for an hour or more before draining and using them. Keep the wine-softened tomatoes covered and on hand in the refrigerator.

Makes 6 (3-inch) or 1 Large Cheese Ball

3   8-ounce packages cream cheese, softened; or dripped plain yogurt (see P. 44)

1   cup sun-dried tomatoes, softened in warm red wine and drained

1   7-ounce jar or can roasted and peeled red peppers

2   teaspoons fresh or dried basil, chopped

1   tablespoon Aleppo pepper or ½ teaspoon cayenne pepper

1   garlic clove, peeled and mashed

½   cup pine nuts or sunflower seed, toasted

Place all ingredients, except nuts, in bowl of a food processor; process until smooth. Cover and chill. Divide cheese mixture into 6 equal portions: shape each portion into a ball. Dip each ball in nuts; lightly press nuts into cheese. Wrap each cheese ball in plastic wrap, refrigerate up to 5 days or freeze. Serve with favorite crackers.

SEVICHE (CEVICHE)

Seafood seviche (say-bee-chay) originated in pre-Columbian Peru. This uncooked dish makes a refreshing appetizer or a main course for a light summer meal. It is best made the day before it is to be served.

Makes 10 to 12 Servings

1½ pounds redfish, snapper, trout, or a mixture (use any good fresh fish your favorite fisherman brings home), filleted and cut into very narrow strips.

2 cups mixed clams, oysters, shrimp, and/or snails, chopped (if not available, use fish)

3 cups fresh lime juice (Key limes or Mexican limes preferred but NO bottled lime juice)

2 fresh green chilies (serranos, jalapeños, or Fresnos), seeded and chopped

1 large, ripe tomato, chopped

1 large red onion, finely chopped

3–4 cilantro (fresh coriander) sprigs, chopped

1–2 tablespoons olive oil

Salt and freshly ground black pepper to taste.

Place all chopped seafood in a non-reactive bowl. Cover with half the lime juice; marinate in refrigerator at least 4 hours, preferably overnight. Drain; wash in cold water (important). Drain again. Return to bowl. Pour in remainder of lime juice and remaining ingredients. Some like to add sliced stuffed olives. Adjust seasonings. Serve in cocktail dishes before dinner; from a bowl sitting in ice as an appetizer; or on a bed of lettuce as a luncheon entrée. Serve with crackers.

ECUADORIAN SEVICHE DE CAMARONES (SHRIMP SEVICHE)

Seviche (say-bee-chay), a marinated seafood classic, can be enjoyed at any meal. It was created in Peru and became an Andean favorite. Popcorn, the authentic accompaniment, probably also originated in the same region before Columbus because it is used there in so many different ways. The popped corn is not buttered and salted as we have come to expect at our movie theaters and is frequently used as we do croutons.

Makes 4 to 6 Servings

1 pound headless shrimp, cooked 1 minute in 2 cups of boiling water; drained, shelled and cleaned. Set aside 1 cup of the cooking water (shrimp broth)

6 tablespoons fresh lime juice

1 teaspoon salt

1 red onion, thinly sliced and separated into rings; cured (see P. 38)

1 tablespoon fresh lime juice for curing onion

1 serrano, seeded and chopped

1 Roma tomato, seeded and chopped

½ cup fresh orange juice

3 tablespoons catsup

2 tablespoons olive oil

1 tablespoon cilantro (fresh coriander), minced

Salt and freshly ground black pepper to taste

1 quart of popped popcorn

Lime wedges for garnish

In a large, flat, non-reactive container mix lime juice and salt. Marinate shrimp with lime juice in refrigerator for 1 hour or more; stir occasionally. Add onions, serranos, and tomatoes to marinated shrimp. Drain; mix in reserved cooking water, orange juice, catsup, olive oil, and cilantro. Chill thoroughly; serve in small bowls with a teaspoon provided. Garnish with lime wedges. Pass the popcorn.

NOTE: For seviche, shrimp of 40 to 50 count per pound are a nice size. If larger, you might need to cut them in half and increase marinating time slightly.

BLACK BEAN QUESADILLAS

Inspired by a favorite appetizer served at the Old Granite Café in Austin, Texas. It is an ethnic style but with southwestern overtones.

Makes 8 Servings

- 3 cups black beans; canned refried beans can be substituted
- 1 chipotle *adobado* (canned), puréed, (use more if desired)
- 16 flour tortillas
- 1 pound smoked chicken, diced; substitute grilled chicken or rotisserie from the market, or omit if desired
- 1 pound Monterey Jack cheese, grated
- 3 poblanos, roasted, peeled, and cut into strips

Mix puréed black beans (see preparation below) and chipotle adobo; spread on eight tortillas; top with smoked chicken, Jack cheese, and poblano strips. Place the other tortillas face down on top of first eight. Place each *quesadilla* on a preheated grill or oiled skillet for a minute or so. If using a grill, turn each at a 45-degree angle until there is a good crisscross grill pattern. Repeat same procedure for other side. Be careful not to burn. Once they are done, take them off grill or skillet, and cut each into 6 to 8

wedges. Serve hot with a tomatillo sauce (see Recipe P. 154) and guacamole (see Recipe P. 66) or sour cream and salsa picante.

Black Bean Preparation:

- 1 pound black beans, picked over
- 4 tablespoons oil
- 2 large onions, diced
- 1 garlic clove, peeled and minced
- 2 tablespoons ground cumin (comino)
  Salt to taste
- 4 tablespoons fresh epazote (see P. 35), chopped; optional

Soak beans in water for several hours or overnight. Heat oil in a large saucepan (2¾ quart) over low heat; cook onions and garlic; stir for 5 minutes. Add drained beans, enough fresh water to cover, cumin, and *epazote*; bring to a boil. Reduce heat to medium-low; simmer until tender, about 2 hours, stirring occasionally; make certain there is enough water to cover beans. If additional water is needed, add only boiling water. Purée beans in a food processor—you may have to do this in batches.

NOTE:
1. You can cheat a little by using canned bean dip and seasoning it to your taste.
2. When epazote, an easily grown Mexican herb, is cooked with beans they no longer cause flatulence.

TEX-MEX NACHOS

A nacho is a crisp tortilla chip topped with tasty tidbits and a crosswise slice of jalapeño. This botaña (appetizer) was created some time ago, at least before 1980, by Ignacio "Nacho" Anaya at the Victory Club in Piedras Negras, Mexico across the Rio Grande River from Del Rio, Texas. Today pickled jalapeño slices are called "nacho slices." In 1985, after my first pepper book, Ignacio's banker son in Del Rio called to tell me that his father first made the appetizers for a group of women from Midland who drove down often to eat at the club where his father worked—soon they were calling them nachos. In 2004, I found them on a menu down in Guanajuato, Mexico.

Serves 6 or More

> 5 ounce tostados (tortilla chips), large size, flat or round
>
> 1–2 cups frijoles, pinto, or black beans, cooked Vegetable oil for frying beans
>
> 2 cups cheddar cheese, shredded
>
> 2–3 jalapeños, pickled and sliced cross ways. Canned ones are easiest

A day or two ahead boil beans in water to cover until tender. If desired, season with onion, ham, bacon, cilantro when cooking. Drain beans, reserving liquid. Place beans and 1 cup reserved juice in a bowl and mash with a potato masher until all beans are mashed and mixed well, adding more liquid if too dry. In a heavy skillet over low heat, melt 1 or 2 tablespoons shortening or butter. Add mashed beans to skillet and stir until thickened to desired consistency.

Preheat oven to 475°F. Smear each chip with a ¼ to ½-inch dab of refried beans; arrange in a single layer on a 12 x 18-inch baking sheet or oven-proof platter. Sprinkle cheese evenly over beans. Place a jalapeño slice in center of each chip. Bake for 4 to 6 minutes until cheese is melted. Place on a plate; serve immediately.

NOTE:

1. You can cheat a little by using canned bean dip and seasoning it to your taste.

Variations:

1. Instead of beans use chopped cooked chicken (breast or mixed) and shredded Monterey Jack cheese instead of cheddar. Top with jalapeño slice.
2. Make same as originals but after cooking add a dollop of guacamole (recipe Page 66) with the jalapeño slice on top.
3. Top with salsa cruda (recipe P. 144) instead of jalapeño slice.

JICAMA WITH CHILI-PEPPER SALT

The jicama, (hick-a-ma) is a Mexican legume; however, only the tuberous root is eaten. It is now grown in some western states of the United States. It adds a crunchy texture along with a very mildly sweet flavor to salads and vegetable appetizer trays.

Makes 8 to 10 Servings

> 1 tablespoon salt
>
> ¼–½ teaspoon chili powder, or to taste; Gebhardt® suggested; or Aleppo Pepper
>
> 1 jicama, peeled
>
> 1–2 limes, cut into wedges

Mix salt and chili powder to taste. Add a little cayenne if not pungent enough. Place mixture in a small bowl. Rinse and cut peeled jicama into ¼-inch thick sticks, 3 to 4 inches long. Arrange lime wedges, jicama sticks, and bowl of chili salt on a platter. To eat, rub jicama with lime, then dip in chili salt.

THE PEPPER LADY'S VERSION OF JEFFREY'S OF AUSTIN OYSTER NACHOS

These to-die-for oysters originated with Chef David Garrido of Jeffrey's, the favorite restaurant of President George W. and Laura Bush when they lived in Austin. The main problem may be finding the firm yuca chips, which are made from yuca, the root of cassava or manioc, a South American native plant. Look in Latin American or ethnic food stores.

Makes 4 Servings

      Canola oil for frying
      Buttermilk for dredging
      All-purpose flour, or masa for dredging
16 oysters, shucked
16 yuca chips or nacho chips if yuca not available
½ cup *pico de gallo,* recipe following
½ cup chipotle mayonnaise, recipe following

In a small skillet, pour in canola oil to a depth of 1 inch; heat to 375°F. Put buttermilk and flour or masa into 2 separate, shallow bowls. Coat oysters with buttermilk, then dip them in the flour or masa. When oil is hot, slide the oysters in, a few at a time; fry for 45 seconds to 1 minute, or until lightly browned. Transfer oysters to paper towels to drain. Keep warm until all are cooked.

To serve, put a heaping teaspoonful of *pico de gallo* on each chip, then a fried oyster. Top each with a heaping teaspoonful of chipotle mayonnaise. Serve immediately.

NOTE: Often the chips are small or broken making it necessary to use more by overlapping them so that they will hold an oyster.

PICO DE GALLO

Makes 1 ½ cups

1 cup ripe tomato, diced
½ cup onion, diced
1 serrano chili pepper, stemmed, seeded and minced
¼ cup fresh cilantro, chopped
1 tablespoon fresh lemon juice
    Salt to taste

Combine all ingredients in a bowl, including salt. Mix well; refrigerate for 30 minutes to allow flavors to blend before serving.

CHIPOTLE MAYONNAISE

Makes 1½ cups

2 tablespoons Dijon mustard
2 tablespoons honey
½ cup fresh cilantro, chopped
1 teaspoon chipotle adobado purée, or to taste
2 egg yolks
1 tablespoon fresh lemon juice
½ teaspoon sea salt
¾ cup olive oil

In a blender combine mustard, honey, cilantro, chipotle, egg yolks, lemon, and salt. Pulse blender on and off briefly to mix. Remove center section of blender lid, if possible, if not, remove lid. With blender running, gradually pour in oil in a thin, steady stream, processing until mixture thickens to a mayonnaise. Transfer to a bowl; cover and refrigerate for up to two days.

NOTE: You can cheat a little by using 1 cup of Hellmann's® Lite Mayonnaise and adding mustard, honey, cilantro, and chipotle adobado purée to it.

BOURSIN CHEESE

This delicious cheese is expensive to purchase, but now you can beat that price and make it with fewer calories to boot. If the soy cream cheese or dripped yogurt is used, even more guilt is removed.

Makes 2 ½ cups

   2 packages light cream cheese, at room temperature; or Soya Kaas (cream cheese style tofu), or dripped, nonfat yogurt

   ¼ cup or ½ stick butter, room temperature

   2 garlic cloves, peeled and mashed

1½ tablespoons marjoram, chopped

1½ tablespoons fresh chives or green onion, fresh chopped

   2 tablespoons fresh basil, chopped

   1 teaspoon thyme, fresh if available, chopped

   1 tablespoon fresh parsley, chopped

   2 teaspoons Aleppo pepper or ½ teaspoon cayenne

      Salt and freshly ground black pepper to taste

Place cheese and butter in bowl of a food processor; pulse until smooth. Add garlic; mix well. Add chopped herbs and salt and peppers; mix well. Chill slightly. Form into logs. Wrap tightly in plastic wrap; refrigerate or freeze. Serve at room temperature with toasted French bread, melba toast, or a favorite snack cracker. Corn chips are not recommended.

Salads

INDIA RAITA

The actual mouth cooling effect of casein (here, from the yogurt) has been proven. Traditional Indian dishes like this one are delightful complements to burning curries or any other peppery foods.

Makes 6 to 8 Servings

- 2 cucumbers, onions, or ripe tomatoes, or a combination, diced
- 2 cups plain low fat yogurt
- ½ teaspoon ground coriander
- ½ teaspoon cumin (comino) seeds, sautéd in 1 tablespoon vegetable oil until golden brown (reserve oil)
- ½–1 teaspoon ground cayenne pepper
  - Pinch of turmeric
  - Pinch of garam masala (see P. 198)
- ¼ teaspoon freshly ground black pepper
  - Salt to taste
  - Cilantro (fresh coriander) sprigs for garnish

Mix together vegetables and yogurt. Add salt, cumin seed and oil seed was sautéd in; mix well. Sprinkle all spices on top; toss lightly. The spices can be mixed with yogurt; reserve a bit to use with the cilantro sprigs, for garnish.

NOTE: Although not typically Indian, chopped fresh dill weed goes well when using cucumbers.

RUBY RED GRAPEFRUIT AND AVOCADO SALAD

Texas is the home of the 'Ruby Red' grapefruit. Texans are so proud of it that it was declared the state fruit and given a special automobile license plate. It is not only delicious, but also beautiful.

Makes 3 Servings

- Leaf lettuce
- 1 grapefruit, peeled and sectioned (Ruby or pink preferred)
- 1 avocado, peeled and sliced
- 1 small, red Bell Pepper, seeded and sliced in thin rings
  - Zesty Poppy Seed Dressing (see Recipe P. 159) or Creamy Serrano Dressing (see Recipe: P. 160)

On each chilled salad plate prepare a bed of lettuce. Alternate overlapping slices of grapefruit, Bell Pepper, and avocado. Drizzle generously with dressing and serve.

TABBOULEH

A popular appetizer in the Middle East where it is made of cracked wheat, one of the staples of the region. Both couscous and quinoa serve wonderfully in this recipe. Over there I have noted that much more fresh parsley is used in the recipe than most American cooks would have used—and always fresh mint— I recommend both.

Makes 6 Servings

1 cup cracked wheat, couscous, or quinoa, prepared according to directions on package

1 small onion, grated

3 scallions, finely chopped

2 small, ripe tomatoes, peeled, seeded, and chopped

1 small, red Bell Pepper or ethnic type, seeded and chopped

2 tablespoons chopped fresh mint leaves

1 cup fresh parsley, chopped—can use up to 2 cups

½ cup olive oil

½ cup lemon juice, freshly squeezed

2 teaspoons Aleppo pepper or ½ teaspoon cayenne
Salt and freshly ground black pepper, to taste

12 calamata olives for garnish, or black olives
Fresh, small romaine lettuce leaves

Prepare cracked wheat or starch of choice; drain very thoroughly. It must feel dry. Put it into a large mixing bowl; add onion, scallions, tomatoes, mint, parsley, salt, and pepper to taste. Thoroughly blend mixture using your clean hands. In a cup, mix lemon juice and oil; pour over mixture in bowl and toss, using a fork. Correct seasoning. Let stand 2 to 3 hours in a cool place or over night in a refrigerator before serving. To serve: line each salad plate with 2 or 3 lettuce leaves. Shape tabbouleh into 6 small cones; place on lettuce leaves; garnish with olives. For a buffet, it may be served from a bowl lined with lettuce leaves.

NOTE: ½ cup of toasted pine nuts is a nice addition before mixing.

QUINOA-TOMATILLO SALAD

This unique salad combines two ingredients rather new to North American kitchens—quinoa (keen wah) and tomatillos. Both are not only tasty but healthful. It can be made the day before and garnished just before serving.

Makes 6 to 8 Servings

2 cups quinoa, toasted in 350°F oven or microwave oven

3 cups water

½ pound (about 8) tomatillos, husked and blanched

1 medium yellow onion, chopped

¼ cup fresh cilantro, chopped

7 tablespoons fresh lime juice

⅓ cup fresh parsley, chopped

⅓ cup extra-virgin olive oil

2 tablespoons rice vinegar

1 serrano pepper, seeded and minced

1 clove garlic, peeled and minced
Salt and freshly ground black pepper to taste

Garnish:

1 medium, red onion, sliced into thin rings

1 red Bell Pepper, seeded and sliced into thin rings

1 8½-ounce can yellow whole kernel corn

¼ cup Feta cheese, crumbled

1 tablespoon fresh lime zest; grate whole limes before juicing

In a 2 quart sauce pan over high heat, bring water to a boil. Reduce heat to medium; add toasted quinoa; cover; simmer until tender and water is absorbed, about 15 minutes. Cool and set aside. In a blender jar, place blanched tomatillos, yellow onion, cilantro, lime juice, parsley, oil, vinegar, serrano, and garlic; pulse until puréed. Place purée in a large bowl; stir in quinoa. Season with salt and pepper. Just before serving, garnish with red onion, Bell Pepper, corn, feta cheese, and lime zest. Serve at room temperature.

JÍCAMA AND PEPPER SALAD

Crunchy, tasty, and beautiful, the ingredients for this salad can be prepared earlier for last minute assembly.

Makes 8 to 10 Servings

- 1 head bibb or leaf lettuce, washed and crisped
- 1 each orange, red, yellow, green, and purple Bell Peppers, seeded and carefully cut into 8 thin rings
- ¾ pound jícama, peeled, thinly sliced and cut into ½-inch by 2 to 3-inch strips
- 1 medium size red onion, thinly sliced and separated into rings
  Creamy Serrano Dressing (see Recipe P. 160)

Tear lettuce into bite sized pieces; prepare a bed on each salad plate. Overlap rings of each color pepper on lettuce bed. Leave space for 4 to 5 jícama slices laced through several onion rings. In the center place a generous spoonful of dressing. Serve very cold.

BERRY BLEU SPINACH SALAD

This beautiful salad can be turned into a luncheon entrée with the addition of cooked chicken, shrimps, clams, or scallops. One of my favorites.

Makes 4 to 6 Servings

- 2 bunches fresh spinach, preferably baby sized leaves; stemmed, washed and well-dried (about 2 quarts or 2 packages of prepared salad spinach)
- 1 pint fresh blueberries or raspberries, do not mix
- ⅔ cup bleu cheese, crumbled (fatty but tasty)
- ½ cup pecans or walnuts, toasted and coarsely chopped

Toss all together and set aside.

Berry Vinagrette

- ½ cup fresh blueberries or raspberries
- 1 shallot, minced
- ½ teaspoon salt
- ¼ teaspoon cayenne pepper
- 1½ teaspoon granulated sugar
- 3 tablespoons raspberry vinegar
- ½ cup vegetable oil

Combine berries, shallots, salt, cayenne, sugar, vinegar, and oil in a blender; pulse until smooth. Toss with salad before serving.

NOTE: Add cooked meats if desired just before adding salad dressing.

GARDEN POTATO SALAD

When entertaining guests, it is always a blessing to be able to make some dishes well before the event. This is one that must be made ahead of time so that the flavors will meld and be absorbed into the potatoes.

Makes 6 to 8 Servings

For the Salad:

2 pounds red, new potatoes, un-peeled
1 tablespoons canola oil
1 medium-size red or purple onion, thinly sliced
5 garlic cloves, peeled and minced
3 medium Bell Peppers, 1 each red, yellow, orange; seeded and julienned
1–5 jalapeños, seeded and chopped (depends on desired pungency)
½ cup green celery, coarsely chopped

For the Dressing:

1 tablespoon dry mustard
1 teaspoon freshly ground black pepper
½ teaspoon ground cayenne pepper or Aleppo pepper, or to taste
2 teaspoons salt
¼ cup olive oil
2 tablespoons cider or herbed vinegar

Boil potatoes with skins on in water to cover until quite tender (can be cooked in a microwave). Drain; cool until easy to handle; cut each potato into large chunks. Heat oil in a heavy skillet over medium heat; cook onion, garlic, peppers, and celery, stirring until tender. Combine with warm potatoes. In a small bowl, blend dressing ingredients with a wire whisk until smooth. Pour over warm vegetables; toss gently. Refrigerate for several hours or overnight to let flavors blend. Allow salad to stand at room temperature 1 hour before serving.

GUACAMOLE (AVOCADO SALAD)

It's a long, long road to guacamole and there are many variations of the dish on the way—most of them loaded with fat. Following the traditional recipe I have shown here, I have added some suggestions for reducing the fat.

Makes 2 Cups

4 ripe avocados, peeled, and mashed with a fork
1 small tomato, chopped
1 tablespoon minced onion
1 clove garlic, juice only
1–2 serranos, seeded and minced
2 teaspoons cilantro leaves, finely chopped
Lime or lemon juice, to taste
Salt and pepper to taste

Mix all ingredients in a bowl. This mixture should have some texture. If a processor is used, care must be taken to keep mixture from becoming too smooth. Never use a blender. The addition of 1 teaspoon of FRUIT FRESH® (ascorbic acid) will allow you to make this several hours ahead of serving time without fear of it turning black on top; cover closely (no air space) with Saran® wrap; otherwise, make it at the last minute. Serve with toasted tortilla chips.

Alternates:

1. For each avocado blend in ½ cup low-fat cottage cheese; follow directions as given above. This is less

fat than the same size serving as straight avocado guacamole recipe. Serve with baked low-fat tortilla chips or raw vegetables.

2. Substitute thawed and puréed frozen green peas for avocado; proceed with guacamole recipe. A little extra serrano may be needed, or try half peas and half avocado the first time. Serve with baked low-fat tortilla chips or raw vegetables.

NOTE: To peel an avocado; cut in half and remove seed. Using a table-spoon, insert spoon between peel and meat. Work spoon to other side; scoop out entire half; dip avocado quickly into a solution of water and ascorbic acid (a commercial preparation such as Fruit Fresh®) or wipe it with lemon juice to prevent darkening.

If avocado is not ripe; wrap in newspaper or place in a paper sack; place in micro-wave. Using a half-minute to start with, and more or less as needed as you progress, heat avocado until it is desired softness. Take care to not "cook" it.

Soups

CREAMY CRIMINI MUSHROOM SOUP

This is a wonderful soup to serve when you only want soup and salad. Crimini look like miniature portabella mushrooms. If you can't find crimini mushrooms substitute a nice brown or white button mushroom.

Makes 6 to 8 Cups

2 cups yellow onion, chopped
2 teaspoons butter, melted
2 pounds crimini mushrooms, sliced
3 tablespoons fresh dill, chopped
4 teaspoons paprika
¼ teaspoon cayenne pepper
4 teaspoons tamari sauce or soy sauce
3 cups vegetable or chicken stock
2 tablespoons sauce or gravy flour
1 tablespoon butter
2 cups low-fat milk
1 cup nonfat yogurt
1 tablespoon fresh lemon juice

Over medium heat, in a large skillet or Dutch oven, sauté onions; add mushrooms, dill, paprika, cayenne, tamari, and stock; stir. In a separate pan, make a roux with flour and butter (see P. 46); add milk gradually, stirring constantly. When roux has thickened, gradually add one cup of the vegetable/stock mixture; whisk until there are no lumps.

Gradually pour roux mixture into vegetable and stock mixture (the soup); stir constantly; simmer for 15 minutes. Remove from heat. When soup has cooled for about 10 minutes, add yogurt and lemon juice; stir to mix. Reheat and serve immediately.

EASY—AND HEALTHY—SOUP

This soup is full of vitamins, minerals, protein, flavor, and is so easy. I make the recipe for myself and have it for lunch with a fresh green salad. I change the main vegetable depending on the season and what is on special at the market.

Makes 4 Cups

6 medium scallions, with tops or ½ large onion peeled, and quartered
6 sprigs fresh parsley
6 sprigs of fresh herb to compliment the vegetable; basil, thyme, oregano
4 cups broccoli, or one of the following: zucchini with green skin, spinach (packed), butternut squash, yellow squash, or asparagus, (or any highly-pigmented vegetable) cut into 1-inch cubes
1 serrano or jalapeño, seeded and chopped
2 cups water
2 teaspoons chicken base, Better Than Bouillon® or similar product

1 cup nonfat, plain yogurt

Salt and freshly ground black pepper to taste.

Place all ingredients except chicken base, yogurt, salt, and pepper in a medium sauce pan. Bring to a boil; reduce to a simmer; cook until primary vegetable is very tender, 15 to 20 minutes. This can also be done in a microwave using a microwave safe covered dish. For safety sake, allow to come to room temperature before putting cooked ingredients and liquid in a blender; purée. When very smooth, add chicken base and yogurt; pulse to blend thoroughly. Season with salt and pepper. Serve hot, cold, or at room temperature with whole grain crackers or toast.

NOTE: For better nutrition, use vegetables rich in chlorophyll (green color) and/or carotene (orange, yellow, red) which are both soluble in fat. Chlorophyll will leak into water but carotene is not affected by cooking. To retain nutrients, it is important to use ALL of the water the vegetable is cooked in; however more liquid can be added until desired consistency is reached.

ANDALUCIAN-STYLE GAZPACHO

This recipe is the result of my visits to kitchens in Andalucia, Spain, and eating gazpacho every day for a month. That area became renowned for gazpacho after its introduction by the Moors long before Columbus discovered America, the home of the tomato and pepper. The ancient soup brought to the Iberian peninsula with the Moorish conquest was originally made of oil, vinegar, onion, garlic, water, bread and perhaps cucumbers. Today it comes in many forms.

Makes 6 to 8 Servings

6 cups peeled and chopped ripe tomatoes or canned plum tomatoes

1 small onion, coarsely chopped

½ cup seeded green Bell Pepper chunks

1 serrano, seeded

½ cup cucumber chunks

4–5 fresh basil leaves

½ cup stale French bread crumbs, or similar type of bread

2 cups tomato juice

1 garlic clove, peeled and minced

freshly ground black pepper

¼ cup olive oil, 'Extra Virgin'

¼ cup white wine vinegar

For the Garnish

½ cup finely chopped onion

½ cup finely chopped ripe tomato

½ cup finely chopped cucumber

½ cup finely chopped and seeded green Bell Pepper

Garlic croutons

In a blender, purée tomatoes, onion, peppers, cucumbers, basil, and bread crumbs. Add tomato juice, garlic, and pepper. Stir in oil and vinegar. Cover and chill. Serve this smooth, creamy soup in chilled bowls. Pass side dishes of chopped onion, Bell Pepper, cucumber, and tomato separately. Garnish with croutons.

NOTE: In Andalucia the soup is served icy cold in bowls that have been chilled until frosty as we do beer mugs. The crisp vegetable bits are passed and each diner selects those to add to his bowl.

LOCRO DE PAPA— ANDEAN POTATO SOUP

This very hearty soup can be a meal in itself when served with a hot cornbread or French bread (whole grain if available) and a light green salad. Pass a bowl of Salsa Ají with it. I learned to make it in Ecuador, but it is traditional throughout the Andes where potatoes were first domesticated. Although VERY delicious, it is high in carbohydrates—include some beans or berries in the meal to balance the effect.

Makes About 5 Cups

Step 1:

2	tablespoons vegetable oil
1	pound potatoes, peeled and finely chopped
1	leek or small red onion, finely chopped
2	serranos, seeded and minced
1	potato, peeled and cut into 1-inch cubes

Step 2:

4–8	bibb lettuce leaves, washed
⅓	pound white farmer's cheese or Monterey Jack, cut into 1-inch cubes
1	teaspoon annato paste or turmeric
1	teaspoon salt
¾	cup milk
1	ripe avocado, peeled and cut into ½-inch thick slices

Step 1: In a large saucepan (2¾ quart) heat oil over medium heat. Add finely chopped potatoes, onion, and chilies; cook until onion is golden. Add warm water until potatoes are just covered; add 1 cup more water; bring to a boil. Reduce heat and simmer; stir, until potatoes are very tender. Stir briskly in one direction to almost pureé cooked vegetables. Add cubed potato; cook until tender and potatoes are dissolved, about 30 minutes.

Meanwhile, line deep soup bowls with lettuce leaves; place a cube or two of cheese in bowl.

Step 2: Dissolve annato and salt in milk; add to cooked potatoes; stir in one direction until soup almost boils. Remove from heat; spoon immediately into bowls so that cheese melts. Top each bowl of soup with a slice of avocado.

NOTE: The second step can be done in a blender but the texture of the potatoes become too slick. It has been served to me made that way, and if I had not had it the "old fashioned" way I might have thought that it was good, however, it is NOT recommended. Stick to the traditional method.

EASY TORTILLA SOUP

Tortilla soup is so good, but it need not be a searing experience. I have been served tortilla soup with a whole chipotle swimming on the surface, but I don't recommend it for the novice.

Makes 8 Cups

1	small onion, finely chopped
2–4	cloves of garlic, peeled and minced
1	tablespoon vegetable oil
6	cups chicken broth (homemade from chicken cooked with herbs, onions, celery, and carrots is best, but canned will do)
2	10 ¾-ounce cans chopped tomatoes and green chiles (for example Rotel®)
3	tablespoons fresh coriander (cilantro), chopped
1	teaspoon ground cumin (comino)
	Salt and freshly ground black pepper to taste
1	teaspoon sugar
	Juice of 2 limes
½–1	cup shredded cooked chicken (optional)

½–1 cup shredded Monterey Jack cheese

Lightly salted, corn tortilla chips, broken

Sprigs of fresh coriander (cilantro)

In a small skillet, wilt onion and garlic in oil over a low heat; or omit oil and wilt them in a microwave. Place onion mixture in a large stock pot; add all ingredients except cheese, tortillas, and cilantro sprigs. Stir mixture well; cover; simmer soup over low heat for about 1 hour. If it cooks down too much, add hot water to bring it back to 8 cups.

To Serve: Warm bowls; bring soup to a boil, but don't boil. Add a heaping tablespoon of cheese and a few tortilla chips in each bowl. Fill bowls with very hot soup; top each with several sprigs of cilantro. Serve immediately. This soup, served with corn tortillas or Jalapeño Cornbread (see Recipe P. 83), can make a meal. Serve smaller amounts if it is to be eaten before a meal.

ROASTED POBLANO BISQUE

A very tasty soup that can be served with or without shredded chicken.

Makes 8 Cups

2 cups rotisseried chicken, boned and shredded (optional)

3 cups chicken broth, fat skimmed (see below)

1½ pounds poblanos, cut in half lengthwise, stemmed and seeded

1 pound leeks, or onions, cut crosswise into ½-inch thick slices

2 cups half-and-half or non-dairy creamer

Salt and freshly ground black pepper to taste

1 ripe avocado, sliced

2 ripe Roma tomatoes, cored and chopped

¼ cup fresh cilantro, minced

Purchase a rotisseried chicken. Remove all meat and skin from bones. Shred meat; set aside. Crush leg, thigh, and wing bones to reveal bone marrow. Place all bones and skin in a large stew pan over medium heat; add 5 cups of water; boil for 1 hour. Remove from heat; strain into a large bowl; discard bones. Allow strained broth to sit until fat rises to top; remove fat and discard. Set broth aside.

On a broiler pan, arrange poblanos, with cut side down, and onions in a single layer. Broil 4 to 6 inches from heat until vegetables are soft and slightly charred, 20 to 25 minutes; turn onions as needed to brown evenly. When poblanos are cool enough to handle, remove and discard skin.

In a blender or food processor, pulse half of the poblanos and onions with ¾ cup chicken broth until smooth; scrape container sides as necessary. Rub mixture through a fine strainer into a bowl; discard residue. Repeat with remaining poblanos and onions and ¾ cup broth; strain into a bowl. Stir in 1½ cups chicken broth, cream, and chicken (if using). Add salt and pepper to taste. Cover; chill up to 1 day.

When ready to serve, heat bisque in a 3 to 4-quart pan over medium-high heat; stir often until steaming, about 15 minutes. Place avocado, tomato, and cilantro in individual soup bowls. Ladle bisque into bowls. Serve immediately. Tostados are good with this bisque.

CREAMY PEPPER AND TOMATO SOUP

A recent and very delicious addition to our grocer's shelves, flavorful roasted red peppers from the Balkan lands are now readily available to harried American cooks. They are at their best in this easy soup that may be a little on the "too rich" side.

Makes 8 Servings

- 2 tablespoons butter
- 2 tablespoons all-purpose flour
- 1 11½-ounce can tomato juice
- 1 cup whipping cream
- 42 ounces diced tomatoes (one 28-ounce can, plus one 14-ounce can), do not drain
- 1 cup canned roasted red peppers, drained and chopped
- 1 garlic clove, peeled and mashed
- 1 teaspoon granulated sugar
- 1 teaspoon dried tarragon
- ¼ teaspoon cayenne
  Salt and freshly ground black pepper to taste
- ½ cup low fat sour cream
- 1 ripe tomato, rinsed, cored, and chopped finely
- 2 tablespoons fresh parsley, chopped

In a 3 to 4-quart pan over medium heat, melt butter. Add flour; stir until mixed. Gradually whisk in tomato juice and cream until smooth. Add canned tomatoes, red peppers, garlic, sugar, tarragon, and cayenne; stir often until soup begins to simmer, about 10 minutes. Add salt and pepper to taste. Pour into bowls. Garnish each with a spoonful of sour cream, fresh tomato, and parsley.

TOM KAI, THAI CHICKEN COCONUT MILK SOUP

I attended a wonderful Thai cooking school at the Oriental Hotel in Bangkok. That week-long event inspired this soup—my absolute favorite Thai dish! You may need an oriental grocery for the ingredients.

Version 1:
Makes 6 to 8 Servings

- 4 cups coconut milk. Canned light, if possible
- 1½ cups chicken stock
- 3 pieces dried galangal (Kha, or a type of ginger root) or 2 teaspoons ground galangal, or 2 tsp. peeled, minced fresh ginger
- 3 stalks fresh lemon grass, cut in half lengthwise, then into 2-inch lengths and crushed
- 3 fresh serranos, halved and seeded
- 1 large whole chicken breast, skinned, boned and cut into ½-inch chunks
- 5 fresh or dried citrus or lime leaves, if available
- ½ cup canned straw mushrooms, (optional)
- 4 tablespoons fish sauce (Nam Pla), (see P. 29)
  juice of 2 limes
- 1 fresh red serrano or jalapeño, cut into rounds for garnish
- 2 tablespoons fresh cilantro leaves, (fresh coriander) for garnish

Bring coconut milk, chicken stock, galangal, lemon grass, and serranos to a boil in a large saucepan (2¾ quart). Reduce heat to medium; simmer, uncovered for 15 minutes. Strain; discard galangal and lemon grass. Add chicken and citrus leaves; simmer until chicken is tender (about 3 minutes).

Stir in straw mushrooms and fish sauce; simmer 1 minute longer. Pour into soup tureen, stir in lime juice; adjust seasoning. Garnish with red chili peppers and cilantro leaves. Serve hot.

NOTE: May be served over cooked rice (see P. 40). Pass rice separately.

Version 2:
Serves 4

2 13-ounce cans coconut milk, light if available

6 pieces galangal (Kha, or a type of ginger root) sliced thin

2 stalks lemon grass, lower portion cut into 1-inch pieces and crushed

5 fresh makrut lime leaves, torn in half

8 ounce chicken breast, skinned, boned, and sliced

5 tablespoons fish sauce (Nam Pla)

2 tablespoons sugar or Splenda®

¼ cup fresh lime juice

1 teaspoon black chilli paste (Nam Phrik Pao)

5–6 sprigs fresh cilantro, leaves only

5 green Thai chili peppers or 2 green serranos, seeded and crushed

In a 2 quart sauce pan, combine half the coconut milk with the galangal, lemon grass, and lime leaves; heat to boiling. Add the chicken, fish sauce, and sugar; simmer for about 4 minutes until chicken is cooked. Add remaining coconut milk; heat just to boiling. Remove from heat and add lime juice and chilli paste; stir to mix. Serve in a tureen or individual bowls garnished with cilantro and chili pepper slices.

NOTE: May be served over cooked rice (see P. 40). Pass rice separately.

TOMATO AND ORANGE GAZPACHO

A refreshing, yet satisfying summertime soup that is best made the day before so that flavors are enhanced and it becomes well-chilled.

Makes 5 Cups

1 14-ounce can diced tomatoes (petite if available)

½ cup fresh orange juice

1 garlic clove, peeled and minced

2 tablespoons white wine vinegar

¼ cup croutons or dried French type bread

2 teaspoons salt

2 tablespoons olive oil

1½ teaspoons orange rind, grated

2 navel oranges, peel and pith cut away, fruit segmented and chopped coarsely

½ cup cucumber, peeled, seeded, and finely chopped

½ cup red Bell Peppers, stemmed, seeded and finely chopped

⅓ cup red onion, peeled, finely chopped and soaked in cold water for 15 minutes, drained

Cayenne pepper to taste

Freshly ground black pepper to taste

In a blender or processor put one half of the tomatoes, reserve other half. Add orange juice, garlic, vinegar, croutons, salt, oil, orange rind, and oranges; purée. Transfer purée to a bowl; add remaining tomato, cucumber, Bell Pepper, onion, cayenne, and black pepper; stir to mix. Cover and chill until very cold. (I like to put it in the freezer until it just begins to form ice but does not freeze.) Serve in chilled bowls.

MIDDLE EASTERN LENTIL SOUP

Lentils are not as appreciated by Americans as they deserve to be. They are tasty, cook quickly compared to other legumes, and are also highly nutritious. This soup is very basic and invites you to give it your own twist.

Makes 10 or More Cups

    4   tablespoons butter or vegetable oil
    1   large red or yellow onion, chopped
    1   celery stalk with leaves, chopped
    1   carrot, chopped
    1   small red Bell Pepper, seeded and chopped
    1   serrano or jalapeño, seeded and chopped
    2   tablespoons all-purpose flour
    1½ cups lentils
    7½ cups meat or chicken stock
    1   marrow bone, cracked
        Salt and freshly ground black pepper to taste
    1   lemon, juiced
    1   teaspoon cumin, ground
        Aleppo pepper or crushed red pepper to taste
        Croutons, if desired

Melt butter in a large soup pot; add onion, celery, carrot, Bell Pepper, and serrano; cook until soft. Add flour gradually; stir constantly until smooth. Add lentils, stock, and marrow bone; bring to a boil. Reduce heat; simmer gently, covered, until lentils are very soft. This may take up to 1½ hours. Red or yellow lentils will disintegrate; brown ones will not.

When lentils are cooked, season soup with salt, pepper, lemon juice, and cumin. Simmer a little longer; remove marrow bone. Put soup in a food processor in batches to make a smooth purée. Return soup to soup pot; add water if you want a thinner soup, or cook it down if you want it thicker. Add Aleppo pepper, to taste. Croutons are a good accompaniment.

2

BREADS

SAVORY TARTS

PASTAS

Introduction to Breads, Savory Tarts, and Pastas

Choosing the Right Flour

Flour is the finely powdered particles of any substance; in this case it is finely ground particles of cereal grains used for making breads. The word "flour" comes from the "flower" or the best part of the grain left after milling. Here we refer specifically to flour made from wheat (*Triticum*) although there are many others. Wheat flours may look alike, but there are important differences that make some better than others for certain cooking jobs. Should you use unbleached all-purpose flour, cake flour, or bread flour for pie crusts, crisp cookies, or crusty light breads? A few facts will clarify the difference between flours.

Cereal grains are the seed-like fruits from the grass family of plants. Several were among the first cultivated crops. It is generally believed that domestication of cereal grains was a prerequisite to civilization. Today about a dozen of the thirty-five cultivated grains are significant, of which barley, wheat, rye, oats, rice, corn, and sorghum are probably the most important. First barley, then wheat, both popular in biblical times, were domesticated in the Middle East. Indian corn (maize) is the only major grain domesticated in the New World. The grains of barley and the earliest wheat, *T. momococcum,* a diploid, were parched (parching removed the husks) on hot stones or boiled into a paste or gruel to make them palatable. It was discovered that the paste made of wheat, barley, or other grains could also be parched, making flat bread, the only bread of Stone Age people.

Later other wheats arose that were easily husked without being heated, and their endosperm was very high in protein. These proteins, gliaden and glutenin, are collectively known as gluten. When wheat is ground up and mixed with water its proteins stored in the seed form an elastic and plastic structure that can stretch under pressure. Heat denatures the protein making the glutens retain their shape around the carbon dioxide gas bubbles formed by yeast in the dough, causing the paste or dough to rise and become light. Only rye has similar proteins, but rye gluten is very inferior to wheat gluten. Gluten is necessary for raised bread, which originated in Egypt around 4,000 B.C. following the domestication of hexaploid wheat that has a large amount of gluten. It was not until 1857 that Louis Pasteur discovered the nature of yeast as a living organism and with it, the leavening process.

Several kinds of wheat are grown today, each with a typical kernel composition or protein-to-starch ratio resulting in particular culinary applications. Kernel "hardness" is determined by protein content. More protein and less starch makes harder grains, which contain more gluten. Durum semolina, *Triticum turgidum* var. *durum,* is used for pastas. *T. aestivum* is the source of hard flours for bread, and soft flours for biscuits, cakes, pastries, and cookies. High processing removes the protein-rich endosperm of wheat resulting in a white flour that produces tender, crumbly products, such as cakes and biscuits. A blend of hard and soft wheat flours produces "All-purpose" white flour that is used in a wide range of foods, but it seldom produces the same results as commercially baked breads or cakes that are made with specialized flours. The modern technique for grinding and milling to make white flour by removing the nutritious bran and germ is one of the unhealthiest products of food technology.

Finely ground grain, used by most commercial bakers, is more rapidly digested than more coarsely ground grain and thus breaks down more quickly into glucose (sugar) that causes blood sugar to rise quickly. Millers produce "all-purpose" flour by blending several hard and soft white flours that have different amounts of two gluten-forming proteins. With the addition of water to flour, and the kneading process, the proteins are aligned. This forms strong, elastic sheets of gluten, that trap gases from the yeast, which make the dough rise. This is a blessing to the bread maker but a disaster when a flaky pie crust is the goal. That is the reason for using high-protein flour for yeast breads and low-protein flours for tender cakes, muffins, and pie crust. The pigments that cause the light yellow color of wheat flour have no practical nutritional value. That color is oxidized by bleaching, a process that destroys flour's small amount of vitamin E but enhances its elasticity. Semolina is never bleached.

Keep in mind that the processing of energy-producing whole-grain carbohydrates removes the fiber-rich outer bran and vitamin-and mineral-rich germ of those cereal grains. This processing greatly influences how quickly the carbohydrates raise blood sugar. Whenever possible, replace highly processed grains and cereals with minimally processed whole-grain products.

Storage: In humid climates flour absorbs moisture from the air. Storing in the freezer will eliminate this but space is often a problem. Freezing will also eliminate the insect larvae that may be in flour. Freeze flour and other dry starches such as corn meal, which harbor larvae, then put them in tightly sealed containers before placing in the pantry.

Guide to Flour

Read package label carefully!

A mixture of flour and water is either dough or batter, depending on the ratio of flour to water. Batter contains more water than dough and is thin enough to pour while the stiff dough is manipulated by hand. Regardless of the proportion of flour to water, the ingredients commonly added—sugar, eggs, milk, shortening, salt, leavening—alter the balance in significant ways. Your choice of flour will depend on the type of product you plan to make.

WHOLEMEAL OR WHOLE GRAIN FLOUR contains all the bran and germ.

WHOLE WHITE-WHEAT FLOUR looks like refined wheat flour but is made from hard white wheat varieties developed in America, but not new in Australia and China. It has all the fiber and nutrients of regular, brown, whole wheat flour, but tastes a bit sweeter. When buying flour or items made of flour, make certain it is one-hundred percent whole wheat flour, whether or not it is regular whole wheat flour, or whole white wheat, or it is combined with other whole grains.

WHEATMEAL or brown flour is intermediate.

WHITE FLOUR is nutritionally inert because it has had all the bran and wheat germ removed but may be "enriched" with synthetic vitamins. It is differentiated by hardness. The types are:

1. Bread flour: High-protein flour. Use for yeast breads, pasta, and pizza. 14 grams protein per cup.
2. Nationally available all-purpose flour: Bleached and unbleached. Use for cookies but it has too much protein for best pie crusts, quick breads, muffins, or pancakes and too little for the best yeast bread. It

will work if it is all you have but it will not produce the best products. 12 grams protein per cup.

3. Southern all-purpose flour: Superior for pie crusts, muffins, biscuits, and quick breads. (Brands: Martha White®, White Lily®; or use 2 parts all purpose flour and 1 part cake flour). 9 grams protein per cup.

4. Cake flour. Use for best cakes. 8 grams protein per cup.

UNBLEACHED FLOUR. Because the miller assumes that a bread is the goal of most cooks, this flour is milled with a higher protein content than bleached flour. 13 grams protein per cup.

SEMOLINA. (Durum wheat) Use for pasta and bread. 10 or more grams protein per cup.

SELF-RISING FLOUR: A white flour to which a leavening agent has been added before packaging. Use for quick breads, muffins, and pancakes. Always bleached. Low in protein. 9 to 11 grams protein per cup.

WHITE WHOLE WHEAT FLOUR: A new high protein and high fiber flour, lighter in taste and body than regular whole wheat. Use as all-purpose flour. 13 grams protein per cup.

SAUCE AND GRAVY FLOUR: Use for gravies and sauces because it has been pregelatinized so that it will not clump when mixed with liquid. 2 grams protein per cup.

Nutritional Value of Grains (Per 100 Grams)

U.S. Department of Agriculture Handbook, 8–20, 1989

(Grams of Protein, Fat, Carbohydrates, Fiber; Milligrams of Vitamins, Iron & Calcium)

PROTEIN		IRON		DIET FIBER		CALCIUM	
RYE	.12	QUINOA	.7.9	BARLEY	.15.6	MASA HARINA	.81
WILD RICE	.11.8	MASA HARINA	.4.1	RYE	.11.5	QUINOA	.51
QUINOA	.11.2	WHITE RICE	.4	WHOLE WHEAT FLOUR	..7.3	BARLEY	.29
SEMOLINA	.11	SEMOLINA	.3.7	MASA HARINA	.5.5	RYE	.26
BARLEY	.10	WHOLE WHEAT	.3.4	WHITE CORN MEAL	..4.4	WHITE RICE	.26
BULGAR	.8.6	BLEACHED FLOUR	.2.9	YELLOW CORN MEAL	..4.4	BULGAR	.25
WHOLE WHEAT FLOUR	..8	UNBLEACHED FLOUR	..2.9	OATS	..4.4	BROWN RICE	.22
BROWN RICE	.8	BARLEY	.2.5	BROWN RICE	.3.5	WHOLE WHEAT FLOUR	..21
UNBLEACHED FLOUR	..6.5	RYE	.2.1	SEMOLINA	.3.3	OATS	.20
BLEACHED FLOUR	.6.5	YELLOW CORN	.2.1	UNBLEACHED FLOUR	..1.7	WILD RICE	.17
WHITE RICE	.6	WHITE CORN	.2.1	BLEACHED FLOUR	.1.7	SEMOLINA	.14
OATS	.6	OATS	.1.8	BULGAR	.1.3	BLEACHED FLOUR	.9.9
MASA HARINA	.5.5	BULGAR	.1.7	WILD RICE	.1.2	UNBLEACHED FLOUR	..9.9
WHITE CORN MEAL	.5	WILD RICE	.1.6	WHITE RICE	.1.2	YELLOW CORN MEAL	..4
YELLOW CORN MEAL	.5	BROWN RICE	.1.4	QUINOA	.unknown at this time	WHITE CORN MEAL	..3.5

CARBOHYDRATES		SATURATED FATS		TOTAL FAT		VITAMIN A	
BARLEY	.78	BROWN RICE	.0.6	QUINOA	.4.9	YELLOW CORN MEAL	..29
WHITE RICE	.74	QUINOA	.0.5	OATS	.2	OATS	.4
BROWN RICE	.72	OATS	.0.4	RYE	.2	BARLEY	.2
SEMOLINA	.61	YELLOW CORN MEAL	..0.3	WHITE CORN MEAL	.2	WILD RICE	.2
WILD RICE	.60	WHITE CORN MEAL	..0.3	YELLOW CORN MEAL	.2	OTHERS ON LIST	.0
QUINOA	.59	MASA HARINA	.0.3	MASA HARINA	.2		
RYE	.55	WHOLE WHEAT FLOUR	..0.2	BROWN RICE	.2		
BULGAR	.53	SEMOLINA	.0.2	WHOLE WHEAT FLOUR	..1	**VITAMIN C**	
WHITE CORNMEAL	.47	BULGAR	.0.2	BARLEY	.1	NONE CONTAIN ANY	.0
YELLOW CORNMEAL	.47	WHITE RICE	.0.2	SEMOLINA	.1		
UNBLEACHED FLOUR	.47	BARLEY	.0.2	WILD RICE	.0.9		
BLEACHED FLOUR	.47	RYE	.0.2	BULGAR	.0.9		
MASA HARINA	.44	BLEACHED FLOUR	.0.1	BLEACHED FLOUR	.0.5		
WHOLE WHEAT FLOUR	..44	UNBLEACHED FLOUR	..0.1	UNBLEACHED FLOUR	..0.5		
OATS	.28	WILD RICE	.0.1	WILD RICE	.0.2		

Breads

AZTEC PANCAKES

These can also be served as bread. They may be made ahead of time and warmed up just before serving. They are good with a pepper jelly.

Makes 24 (3½-inch diameter) cakes

  1⅓ cups masa harina (see P. 37) or white cornmeal (use quinoa flour for Inca Pancakes)

  1¼ teaspoons salt

   ½ teaspoon baking soda

   ½ teaspoon cayenne pepper or 1 teaspoon Aleppo pepper

   ¼ cup all-purpose flower, sifted

   ¼ cup cold butter

   2 cups nonfat yogurt

   1 egg, beaten

Mix dry ingredients together in a bowl. Cut in butter with a pastry blender. In another bowl, combine yogurt and egg. Stir liquid into dry ingredients quickly. Barely moisten, leaving lumps. Do not over beat. Rest covered for 3 to 6 hours. Heat a large skillet and spray with butter spray. Make 3½-inch pancakes in skillet so that they do not touch. Turn only once. Do not stack until ready to serve. If to be used later, cover with a clean dish towel; re-heat in oven or toaster oven just before serving.

AZTEC SCONES

The key ingredients—masa (corn,) sunflowers, chili pepper, and tomatoes—in this tasty, healthful, easy bread are pre-Columbian Mexican Indian in origin, hence the name. What makes the recipe so handy is that it can be prepared ahead of time and served at room temperature.

Makes 16

  1½ cups Bisquick®

   1 cup masa, (see P. 37) or use quinoa flour and call them Inca Scones

   1 teaspoon granulated sugar

   2 teaspoons Aleppo pepper or red pepper flakes

   ½ teaspoon baking soda

   ½ teaspoon salt

  12 tablespoons butter (1½ sticks), unsalted, chilled, cut in small chunks

   1 cup plain yogurt, low-fat or light

   ½ cup sun-dried tomatoes, soaked in red wine (see note below)

   ½ cup sunflower seed or pepitas (squash seed), toasted

Preheat oven to 400°F. Butter or butter spray a cookie sheet. In a food processor place the Bisquick, masa, sugar, chili pepper flakes, salt, baking soda; whir together. Scatter butter over dry ingredients; pulse mixture just until it re-sembles coarse meal. Pour in yogurt; pulse mixture until combined. Turn dough out onto a floured work surface;

scatter tomato pieces and sunflower seed over it. Gently pat out dough; fold it back over itself about six times, until smooth, but do not over mix. Divide dough in half; pat it out again into two ¾-inch circles. Cut each circle into 8 wedges. Transfer wedges to prepared cookie sheet. Bake for 12 to 15 minutes until golden. Serve at room temperature. Pepper jelly and/or sour cream or both are good with these scones.

NOTE: To moisten those tough, sun-dried tomatoes: In a small, microwave proof container place a cup or two of whole sun-dried tomatoes, cover with red wine (a good way to use left over wine). Place container in a microwave for 2 or 3 minutes, depending on amount; heat through. Set aside. When cool, remove tomatoes from wine and place in container; cover uncut tomatoes tightly; store in refrigerator for future use.

DRIED CHERRY OR CRANBERRY SCONES

These scones are a tasty addition to a Sunday brunch.

Makes 14 Scones

   ½ cup dried cherries or cranberries
   2 tablespoons cherry brandy
1½ cups White Lily® flour or all purpose flour
   ¼ teaspoon salt
3½ tablespoons sugar
   1 tablespoon baking powder
   6 tablespoons butter, chilled
   1 egg, beaten
   ⅓ cup half and half cream, plus 1 tablespoon plain, nonfat yogurt

Preheat oven to 400°F. Soak fruit in brandy 15 minutes; set aside. Do not drain.

In a mixing bowl, combine flour, salt, sugar, baking powder; stir. Add butter; cut butter into flour mixture using pastry blender or two forks. In a small bowl, combine undrained fruit, egg, ⅓ cup of the half and half with yogurt (reserve 1 tablespoon) and blend gently. Add to flour mixture; stir only until moistened. Turn dough onto a lightly floured surface. Knead 12 to 15 strokes, until nearly smooth. Lightly roll dough to ¾-inch thick. Cut into desired shape. Place on ungreased baking sheet. Brush tops lightly with reserved half and half. Sprinkle with remaining sugar. Bake 12 to 15 minutes until lightly browned. Serve with butter and/or jalapeño jelly.

RICE POPOVERS

These puffy bits of bread with steamy centers and crisp crusts are nice for a change but especially good for those allergic to wheat.

Makes 8

1½ teaspoons butter, soft
   1 egg, large
   ½ cup milk, non-fat or low-fat
   ½ cup rice flour
   ¼ teaspoonful cayenne pepper
   ¼ teaspoon salt

Preheat oven to 375°F. Butter eight 2½-inch muffin cups. Put all ingredients into a small bowl; beat together with a spoon. Immediately, fill greased muffin cups equally with batter. Bake until well browned, about 35 minutes. Ease out of cups with a knife. Serve hot.

NOTE: Do not allow batter to stand. Popovers will not be crisp or puffy (because rice flour, which has no gluten, soaks up the liquid rapidly) and they may sink as they cool.

TOUCH OF SPICE BISCUITS

This is my variation on a southern biscuit recipe that will make a biscuit lover out of a Yankee.

Makes 10 to 12 biscuits

Vegetable cooking spray
1½ cups southern self-rising flour such as White Lily® or Martha White®
1 teaspoon granulated sugar
½ teaspoon salt
1 teaspoon Aleppo pepper or ½ teaspoon crushed red pepper or cayenne
3 tablespoons shortening or unsalted margarine
1 cup plain yogurt or heavy cream (if you dare)
½ cup toasted, unsalted pecans, coarsely chopped
½ cup coarsely grated Parmesan cheese
½ cup all-purpose flour

Preheat oven to 475° F. Spray an 8-inch round cake pan with cooking spray. In a medium bowl, mix 1½ cups of flour, sugar, chili, salt until blended. Cut in shortening with a pastry blender or work in with fingertips until lumps are pea-sized. Stir in yogurt or cream; let stand 2 to 3 minutes. The dough should be very moist.

Pour all-purpose flour onto a plate. Flour hands well. Scoop about 2 tablespoons of dough into flour. Sprinkle more flour over dough. Gently lift the clump of dough and form it into a ball. Shake off excess flour and place biscuit in the middle of prepared pan. Shape other biscuits in same manner; place in pan. Bake 15 to 18 minutes or until golden brown. Serve with butter.

NOTE: If the southern self-rising flour cannot be found substitute 1 cup Bisquick® and ½ cup cake flour plus ¼ teaspoon baking powder.

ZESTY SPOON CORNBREAD

The 500°F cooking temperature in this recipe is NO mistake! A meal by itself!

Makes 8 Servings

1 cup sharp American or Cheddar cheese, grated
2 tablespoons pickled jalapeño peppers (nacho slices), drained and chopped. Use long green chiles if jalapeño peppers are too pungent
1½ cups yellow cornmeal, or half cornmeal and half dry masa, or cornmeal and Quinoa flour
½ teaspoon salt
2 teaspoons baking powder
2 large eggs, beaten
1 cup buttermilk or nonfat, plain yogurt
3 tablespoons vegetable oil
1 4-ounce can chopped long green/red chiles, hot or mild
1 17-ounce can cream-style corn
shortening to grease pan

Preheat oven to 500°F. Combine cheese and jalapeños and set aside. In a large bowl, combine dry ingredients with baking powder and salt. In a small bowl, combine eggs, yogurt, and oil; mix thoroughly; add to dry ingredients and stir until just blended. Add corn and green chiles; stir. Liberally grease a 10-inch iron skillet with shortening; place in oven for 5 minutes; remove and pour batter into hot skillet. Sprinkle cheese and jalapeños mixture over batter. Bake for 15 minutes. Remove and let stand for 5 minutes before spooning. It should have a very soft center.

EASY JALAPEÑO CORNBREAD

This should never be a sweet cornbread. It is great topped with stewed tomatoes and lots of butter—real country style. Another country favorite is cold left-over cornbread crumbled into a glass of sweet milk and eaten with a spoon—called "crumble-in" or "crumblin."

Makes 4 to 8 Servings

   3 canned or pickled jalapeños, drained and chopped

1½ cups yellow stone-ground cornmeal

  ½ cup all-purpose flour

  1 teaspoon granulated sugar, or up to 1 tablespoon depending on taste

  ½ teaspoon baking soda

  1 teaspoon salt

  2 teaspoons baking powder

  2 large eggs, at room temperature

  1 cup buttermilk

  1 tablespoon vegetable oil, plus enough to grease pan

Preheat oven to 400°F. In a mixing bowl, combine cornmeal, baking soda, sugar, flour, salt, and baking powder; set aside. In a separate bowl, mix eggs, buttermilk, and oil; stir until smooth and creamy. Add jalapeños; mix. Stir liquid into cornmeal-flour mixture. Blend with spoon to form smooth batter; do not over stir. Grease 9-inch pan (preferably cast iron) with oil and preheat in oven. Remove; pour batter into hot pan. Return to oven; bake for 20 to 30 minutes or until a toothpick inserted in the bread comes out clean. Cut and serve immediately.

Savory Tarts

Most of us think of tarts as sweet, single crust, dessert dishes made of butter pastry filled with fruits and they usually are. These, however, are savory tarts that evolved from them but with some inspiration from the pizza. They are made in traditional round tart pans with a removable rim. The base is either an unsweetened tart pastry or a flaky phyllo (filo) pastry.

TART PASTRY

Makes one 12-inch tart crust

- 2 cups Southern all-purpose flour (see P. 77)
- ½ teaspoon salt
- 10 tablespoons unsalted butter, cold and cut in pieces (1 stick plus 2 tablespoons)
- 1 egg
- 4 tablespoons ice water

In a food processor, combine flour, salt, butter. Process mixture until it resembles very coarse meal. In a small bowl mix egg and water together. Add 2 tablespoons of egg and water mixture to processor; process until just incorporated. Add additional water, a little at a time, processing briefly after each addition, until dough just holds together without being wet and sticky. Turn dough out onto plastic wrap; knead it lightly into a ball. Wrap dough and chill at least 1 hour; can be kept chilled up to one week.

Preheat oven to 375°F. On a lightly floured surface roll out dough into a 12-inch circle about ¼-inch thick and fit it into a 12-inch tart pan with removable bottom. Chill dough for at least 30 minutes. Lightly prick dough with a fork; weigh down by covering dough with wax paper or foil and then adding dried beans or rice. Bake in center of oven for 15 to 20 minutes, until golden. Set aside and let cool until ready to fill.

NOTE: The pastry is suitable for large tarts or small tartlets. Up to a day ahead, bake crust, leave in pan and cool, wrap airtight; keep at room temperature. This can also be sealed and frozen unbaked for use later. Remove tart pan rim; leave pastry on tart pan bottom. When ready to use, replace rim on tart pan and bake as directed. Fill with one of the recipes that follow.

PHYLLO TART PASTRY

Sometimes called puff pastry. This is a very difficult pastry to make from scratch but it can now be found in the frozen food section of most grocery stores. Most are somewhat tedious to prepare, but using the butter flavored cooking spray used to grease pastry sheets and baking pans instead of brushing on melted butter makes preparation easier. However, frozen Pepperidge Farm® puff pastry sheets are ready to bake after thawing. Follow directions on package. Bake in traditional 9-inch tart pan with removable rim which has been sprayed with butter flavored cooking spray.

NOTE: Remember to put a couple of inches of dry beans or rice for weight on top of foil-covered tart pastries before baking. This will keep them flat. After baking, the beans are removed before the filling is added.

PHYLLO (FILLO) TARTLET CUPS

Preheat oven to 350°F. Prepare 4 mini-muffin pans (1¾ by 1-inch cups) by spraying with butter flavored cooking spray or make repeat batches with one or two pans. Prepare phyllo pastry using three sheets phyllo according to directions on package. Cut stacked phyllo lengthwise into 4 strips and crosswise into 6 strips to make twenty-four 3-inch squares. Trim off corners of each square and cover with plastic wrap. Turn muffin pan over; spray with butter flavored cooking spray. Cover outside of each muffin cup with 1 trimmed phyllo square, allow edges to curl naturally; set a metal cookie sheet on top of covered muffin cups as a weight; bake in middle of oven until nicely browned, about 10 minutes. Carefully transfer phyllo cups to racks to cool. Fill with your favorite tart filling and bake. Serve tartlets warm or at room temperature.

NOTE: Cups may be made 1 week ahead and kept wrapped in plastic wrap, at room temperature, or 1 month ahead and frozen.

MASA TART SHELLS

Try using these shells filled with huevos rancheros, lightly scrambled eggs, or pepper cream—great for breakfast or brunch.

Makes 24 Tarts

½ cups all-purpose flour

1½ cups dry masa (Quaker brand) and ½ cup water, or ¾ pound prepared masa from a market that sells Mexican or Latino foods

⅓ cup Crisco® or similar shortening

1 teaspoon salt

2 teaspoons Ancho or Guajillo chili peppers, powdered (not chili powder)

¼ cup chicken stock made from Better than Bouillon® base; directions on jar

¼ cup cotija cheese (a Mexican cheese) or other semi-dry white cheese

Preheat oven to 300°F. Spray or oil 1½ inch diameter muffin tins. In bowl of electric mixer or food processor, combine prepared masa, and shortening or dry masa, water, and shortening. Run machine until well mixed. Add salt and powdered chili pepper; mix again. Add chicken stock in 3 batches, mixing well with a spoon after each addition. Dough should be a thick paste; add more masa if too thin. Using finger or a small spoon, press dough ⅓ inch thick into each muffin cup. Bake until golden. Cool and remove from tin. Reheat or serve at room temperature with hot eggs.

CHIPOTLE-PORTABELLA TARTLETS

This impressive first coarse or appetizer will make your guest think you slaved for hours instead of opening a package of prepared pastry. A very tasty time saver.

Makes 24

24 Phyllo tartlet shells, uncooked (see P. 84)

2 cups Portabella mushrooms, caps and stems, diced finely (2–3 mushrooms)

3 tablespoons prepared oyster sauce

1–2 tablespoons chipotle adobado, puréed, or to taste (see note below)

Non-fat sour cream

Paprika

Preheat oven to 450°F. In a food processor, put mushrooms, oyster sauce and chipotle purée. Whirl until mixed. Divide mushroom mixture equally among tartlet shells. Bake until phyllo pastry is golden, about 15 minutes. Serve hot or at room temperature. A dab of sour cream with a dash of paprika is very good on these.

NOTE: Open a 7-ounce can of chipotle adobado (see P. 28) and empty the contents into a blender jar; pulse until smooth. Put the purée in a tightly covered jar and store in the refrigerator for future use. Keeps a month or more.

ROASTED RED PEPPER, TOMATO, AND CHEESE TART

This tart is an ideal way to use those fully ripe, home or locally grown tomatoes.

Makes 6 to 8 Servings

- 1 tart shell, well-baked
- 5 slices lean bacon
- ½ cup fresh basil leaves, firmly packed
- ¾ cup ricotta
- 2 large eggs, beaten lightly
- 1 teaspoon salt
- ¼ pound mozzarella, grated coarsely
- ½ cup Parmesan, freshly grated
- ½ teaspoon cayenne pepper
    Salt and freshly ground black pepper to taste
- 3 roasted red peppers, well-drained and cut into 3 lengthwise pieces
- 4 large (about 2 pounds) fully-ripe tomatoes, sliced crosswise ⅓ inch thick, drained on paper towels
- 1 teaspoon salt for sprinkling tomatoes
    Olive oil for brushing tomatoes
    Basil sprigs for garnish

Preheat oven to 350°F. Cook bacon in a skillet over a hot fire or in microwave until crisp; drain, cool, and crumble; set aside. In a food processor or blender, purée basil and ricotta; add eggs, pulse until smooth; add mozzarella, Parmesan, cayenne, and salt and pepper to taste; blend until just combined; set aside. Place tomato slices on paper towel, sprinkle with salt; allow to drain along with red pepper slices. Sprinkle baked tart shell evenly with bacon crumbles; cover with the red pepper slices and spoon cheese mixture over this. Pat tomato slices dry with paper towels; arrange them in one layer, overlapping slightly, over cheese mixture; brush them with oil. Bake tart for 40 to 50 minutes, or until cheese mixture is set. Transfer tart to a rack to stand for 20 minutes; remove rim and garnish with basil sprigs. Serve warm or at room temperature.

FRENCH TOMATO TART

Still another flavorful savory tart.

Makes 6 to 7 Servings

- 1 tart or phyllo crust, pre-baked
- 3 tablespoons olive oil
- 3 tablespoons tomato paste
- 1 garlic clove, peeled and minced
- 2 teaspoons fresh thyme leaves
- 2 teaspoons fresh marjoram leaves, chopped or 1 teaspoon dried marjoram
- 1 teaspoon fresh oregano leaves, chopped or ½ teaspoon dried oregano
- ½ teaspoon cayenne pepper
- 6 canned anchovy fillets, drained
- 8 calamata or niçoise olives, pitted
    Salt and freshly ground black pepper to taste
- 2 tablespoons Dijon mustard
- 2 cups (½ pound) Swiss cheese, shredded
- 5 ripe Roma tomatoes, rinsed, cored and sliced into 1-inch thick slices
    Aleppo pepper or crushed pizza pepper, to taste
    Salt and freshly ground black pepper, to taste

Preheat oven to 400°F. In a small bowl, add oil, tomato paste, garlic, thyme, marjoram, oregano, and cayenne; mix well. On a baked tart or phyllo crust, spread mustard to cover. Over mustard, sprinkle 1½ cups cheese evenly. Fit tomato slices snugly in a single layer on cheese. Cut remaining tomato slices into pieces to fill gaps; reserve extra tomato for other uses. Spread tomato paste mixture over tomatoes. Sprinkle with Aleppo pepper, salt and pepper. Sprinkle with remaining cheese. Arrange anchovies and olives on top of tomato mixture. Bake until cheese is lightly browned, about 25 minutes. Remove rim from pan. Cut tart into wedges and serve hot or warm.

SWISS TARTS

You don't have to be able to yodel to eat these delicious tarts.

Makes 4 to 6 Servings

- 1   tart or phyllo crust, pre-baked
- 9   slices lean bacon
- 1   medium onion, chopped finely
- 2   tablespoons red Bell Pepper, chopped finely or the canned roasted red peppers
- 1   pound Swiss cheese, shredded
- ¾   cup low-fat sour cream
- 2   eggs, lightly beaten
- ½   teaspoon cayenne pepper
       Salt and freshly ground black pepper to taste

Preheat oven to 375°F. In a skillet, fry bacon until crisp; drain, reserving 2 tablespoons fat. Crumble bacon; set aside. To the fat in skillet add onion and Bell pepper; cook until tender; remove and drain. In a bowl combine bacon, onion, Bell Pepper, cheese, sour cream, eggs, cayenne, salt and pepper; mix well. Spoon bacon mixture evenly over tart pastry in tart pan. Bake for 12 to 15 minutes or until cheese melts. Run under broiler until light brown. Cool for 10 minutes; remove rim, cut into wedges and serve hot or warm.

ROQUEFORT AND CARAMELIZED ONION TART

Find how to prepare the almost sinfully good caramelized onions on page 127.

Makes 6 to 7 Servings

- 1   tart or phyllo pastry, pre-baked and in pan
- 2   tablespoons butter
- 1   pound onions, peeled and finely chopped
- 2   tablespoons canned Long Green Chiles, chopped
- 1   egg
- ½   cup heavy cream
- ½   teaspoon cayenne pepper
       Salt and freshly ground black pepper, to taste
       Ground nutmeg, to taste
- 2   tablespoons Roquefort cheese, crumbled

Preheat oven to 325°F. In a skillet over medium heat, place butter; cook until melted. Add onions and chiles; cook until light brown and tender; stir occasionally. Remove from heat; allow to cool. In a bowl, combine egg and cream; whisk to blend. Add onions; season with salt, pepper, cayenne, and nutmeg. Blend in cheese, lightly. Pour mixture into tart shell in tart pan. Bake about 25 minutes until lightly browned. Cool for 10 minutes; remove rim; cut into wedges. Serve warm.

FETA CHEESE AND OLIVE TART

Goat cheese is often labeled Chèvre, the name for goats in French. Although Feta cheese is made from goats milk it is not Chèvre; however, either can be used in this tasty tart.

Makes 6 to 7 Servings

> 1 tart or phyllo crust, baked
> 4 eggs, lightly beaten
> 2 cups heavy whipping cream
> 4 ounces Feta cheese, crumbled
> 2 teaspoons fresh thyme, minced.
> 10 Calamata olives or a Greek olive, pitted and halved
> ½ teaspoon Aleppo or cayenne pepper
>   Salt and freshly ground black pepper to taste
>   Paprika for garnish

Preheat oven to 350°F. In a bowl, combine eggs, cream, cheese, thyme, and olives. Add red pepper, salt, and black pepper to taste; stir to mix. Pour mixture into tart mold over pastry; bake for about 30 minutes, until set and golden. Garnish with paprika. Cut into wedges; serve warm or at room temperature. Pass some Red Pepper Ajvar as a table sauce.

BLEU CHEESE AND SPINACH TART

Tarts are a nice change from quiche or chicken salad served in pastry shells; great for a luncheon or as a savory first course at dinner.

Makes 6 to 7 Servings

> 1 tart or phyllo pastry, baked
> 1 cup, (5-ounces) gorgonzola or Stilton cheese, shredded
> 1 tablespoon vegetable oil
> 1¼ pounds fresh spinach, washed, drained, and stemmed
> 1 small, red Bell Pepper, stemmed, seeded, and finely chopped
> ½ teaspoon cayenne pepper
>   Salt and freshly ground black pepper

Preheat oven to 300°F. On top of baked pastry in rimmed pan sprinkle cheese evenly. Place in oven and bake until cheese is melted, about 5 minutes or longer. While cheese is melting, in a skillet over medium heat, warm oil; add spinach and Bell Pepper; cook until tender. Season with cayenne, salt and pepper; stir to mix. Remove from heat; drain hot cooked vegetables in a colander, pressing with a spoon to extract liquid. Spoon evenly over cheese on pastry. Remove rim from tart pan, cut into wedges; serve immediately.

ROASTED RED PEPPER AND RED ONION ON RICCOTA TART

Another way to use those tasty roasted red peppers now available bottled at the market.

Makes 6 to 7 Servings

> 1 tart or phyllo pastry, baked
> 2 tablespoons unsalted butter
> 2 red onions, peeled and thinly sliced. Reserve several uncooked rings for garnish

½ cup Ricotta Salta cheese, grated

½ cup roasted red pepper, chopped

2 teaspoons cilantro, chopped

Salt and freshly ground black pepper to taste

1 tablespoon olive oil, heated

Red onion, chopped for garnish

Preheat oven to 400°F. In a heavy saucepan place butter; melt over low heat. Add sliced onions; cook until very soft and caramelized; stir frequently; this is a slow process. Remove pan from heat. Mix in cheese, roasted red pepper, cilantro, cayenne, salt and pepper to taste; stir until mixed. Spoon mixture over tart pastry in tart pan. Bake for 10 minutes. Remove from oven and lightly brush top of filling with oil. Garnish with chopped onion. Cut into wedges; serve warm.

CHÈVRE AND PISTACHIO TART

Chèvre is the way the French say goat. Sounds more uptown than goat cheese, doesn't it?

Makes 6 to 7 Servings

1 tart or phyllo pastry, baked

1 pound fresh goat cheese, if not available use packaged

1 cup pistachio nuts, toasted and coarsely chopped

½ pound prosciutto, torn into bite-size pieces

1 tablespoon Dijon mustard

2 tablespoons fresh tarragon, chopped

4 eggs, whisked

1½ cups heavy cream or non-fat yogurt

½ teaspoon Aleppo or cayenne pepper

½ teaspoon freshly ground black pepper

Preheat oven to 375°F. In a bowl, with a rubber spatula, mash together cheese, mustard, and herbs until soft and smooth. Add nuts and prosciutto; stir to mix. In another bowl, whisk eggs; add cream and black and red pepper; whisk to mix. Add egg mixture to cheese mixture. Pour onto pastry in tart pan. Bake 20 to 25 minutes, until center of filling is set. Cool on a rack; cut into wedges, serve warm or at room temperature. Can be prepared a day ahead, covered, refrigerated, then warmed in a 250°F oven for 10 to 15 minutes.

Pastas

Introduction to Pasta

Carbohydrates from semolina pasta do not raise blood sugar as high as white and whole wheat breads made of finely ground wheat flour. If the pasta is cooked *al dente* (with a little tooth) in the Italian manner it is even better for you. Check the package label to make certain that the pasta is made with semolina, a flour made of hard durum wheat (see P. 78).

Pasta comes in many shapes and some have several names. The most common are the long types, all of which are long, straight, and straw-like but descend in thickness from: (1) spaghetti, (2) thin spaghetti, (3) vermicelli, (4) capellini. Other long types are flattened with widths that narrow: (1) egg noodles, widest, (2) fettuccini, (3) macaroni ribbons, (4) linguine.

The short types are: (1) large and small elbow macaroni, (2) small and large shells (like sea shells), (3) Rigatoni, a large, cut, striated tube, (4) Mostaccioli/Penne/Trenne, a medium tube cut on the bias, (5) Ziti, a medium sized straight cut tube, (6) Rotelle/Rotelli/Rotoni, a short spiral shape, (7) Acini di Pepe or Orzo, small, rice shaped, (8) Bow ties/Fargalle/Far Fallini, bow shaped.

To cook pasta you will need:

A kettle or large sauce pan, a colander, a measuring cup, a long-handled spoon or fork, and a timer.

How Much to Cook:

Short Types (for example, elbow macaroni):
    1 cup 6-ounces uncooked = 2 cups cooked
    (except noodles)

Noodles:
    1 cup 6-ounces uncooked = 1¼ cup cooked

Long Types: Bunch the lengths together to form a cylindrical shape, measure the diameter of the circle.
    ¾-inch diameter, or 6 ounces uncooked = 2 generous cups cooked
    1-inch diameter, or 12 ounces uncooked = 4 cups cooked
    1½-inch diameter, or 16 ounces uncooked = 9 cups cooked

Note: According to label a 1 pound package of spaghetti serves 8.

Size Pot to Use: Pot must be able to hold the amount of water called for in package directions. Pasta must be able to move freely.
    1 cup uncooked pasta—1 quart water in 2 quart pot = 2 cups cooked
    2 cups uncooked pasta—2 quarts water in 4 quart pot = 4 cups cooked
    1 pound uncooked pasta—4 quarts water in 6 quart pot = 9 cups cooked
    2 pounds uncooked pasta—8 quarts water in 12 quart pot = 18 cups cooked

Note: The volume of cooked noodles does not increase as much as other types of pasta.

How to Cook Pasta:

1. Bring water to a rapid boil. Water in a covered pot boils faster.
2. Add pasta. Add short pasta gradually, stirring with a long-handled spoon. Long pasta should be fanned out and stirred with a long handled fork to keep strands separate.
3. Do not cover while pasta is cooking. Follow package directions because cooking time varies according to shape and size.
4. Place pasta in a colander to drain. Rinse with cold water for casseroles and salads; rinse with hot water for pour-over sauces.
5. To keep pasta pieces separate, add a small amount of vegetable oil to the drained pasta and toss lightly. (This also works with rice.)
6. If too much pasta has been cooked, toss in oil as in #5. Store in a covered container in the refrigerator up to 3–4 days. To reheat: drop pasta in boiling water, stirring to separate until hot or reheat in a microwave oven. Freeze by placing cooled, oiled pasta in plastic freezer container and seal; freeze up to a month; use microwave safe containers. To reheat on a conventional stove, remove pasta from container and add to boiling water, stirring to separate. Bring water to a boil again and heat until hot.

COOKING PASTA IN THE MICROWAVE IS NOT RECOMMENDED. The containers required are too large, it takes more time to boil the water and because the water does not boil rapidly enough, the pasta will be sticky. However, initial heating and reheating of prepared dishes containing pasta can be done satisfactorily. Stirring recipes that can be stirred permits you to distribute the heat evenly throughout the dish being reheated.

RED CHILE PASTA

This is home-made pasta, or pasta from scratch. You'll need a pasta machine for this.

Makes 4 Servings

1 teaspoon olive oil
1½ cups all-purpose flour, or more as needed
½ teaspoon salt
2 large eggs
1 tablespoon water, or more as needed
½ cup Gebhardt's Chili Powder® or an available red chili powder

Combine all ingredients in a large mixing bowl; mix until it has consistency of fine meal. Adjust water or flour as needed to make the mixture stick together when kneaded. Knead dough by hand for 5 minutes; cover; let rest 30 minutes. Set pasta machine to thickest setting. Work a quarter of dough through pasta machine at one time; take care to cover remainder with a damp cloth. Repeat 8 times; gradually reduce thickness. Hang processed pasta to let it rest and air dry for 20 minutes before cooking. Place dried pasta in a large pot of rapidly boiling water. Cover; boil until *al dente* (tender but still firm); this cooks very quickly. Serve with your favorite sauce in a contrasting shade of red. Experiment with colors and flavors for desired effect.

GREEN CHILE PASTA

Do it yourself pasta. This needs a pasta machine.

Makes 4 Servings

- 1 7-ounce can Herdez Salsa Verde or Salsa Verde with Tomatillos (see Recipe P. 154)
- ¼ cup fresh spinach, finely chopped; tightly packed
- 2 large eggs
- 1½ teaspoons olive oil
- 2½ cups all-purpose flour
- 1 teaspoon salt

Strain salsa through cheese-cloth to remove all seeds. Place it in a small saucepan over medium-high heat; reduce it to 2 tablespoons. Place spinach and eggs in a blender and purée. Add salsa to blender; purée. Add purée to all the other ingredients in a large mixing bowl. Mix until consistency of fine meal. Adjust water or flour as necessary to make mixture stick together when kneaded. Knead dough by hand for 5 minutes; cover; let rest. Air dry 30 minutes. Set pasta machine to thickest setting. Work a quarter of the dough through pasta machine at one time, taking care to cover remainder with a damp cloth. Repeat 8 times; gradually reduce thickness. Hang processed pasta; let rest for 20 minutes. Place pasta in a large pot of rapidly boiling water. Cover; boil until tender but still firm (this cooks very quickly). Serve with your favorite sauce or a green pesto. Experiment with colors and flavors for desired effect. See Sauce Section P. 142.

PEPPER AND SPAGHETTI FRITTATA

Vegetarians, this is for you! A mouth-warming experience.

Makes 6 to 8 Servings

- 6 tablespoons olive oil
- 2 medium-size onions, chopped
- 5 medium-size garlic cloves, minced
- 6–8 red, orange, and green Bell Peppers, chopped and minced (about 4 cups)
- ¼ cup sun-dried tomatoes, chopped
- 1 jalapeño, seeded and minced
- ½ teaspoon dried oregano
- 1 teaspoon salt
- ¼ teaspoon freshly ground black pepper
- 6 ounces thin spaghetti, cooked according to package instructions and drained
- 8 large eggs
- ½ cup freshly grated Parmesan cheese
- ¼ cup fresh parsley, minced
- 1 tablespoon fresh basil leaves, minced

Preheat oven to 350°F. In a large oven proof skillet, heat olive oil over medium-high heat. Add onions, garlic, peppers and tomatoes; cook over moderately high heat; stir frequently until vegetables begin to brown, taking care not to burn. Season with oregano, half of the salt and black pepper. Add the cooked spaghetti to the skillet and toss well. Cook, stirring occasionally, until the pasta is lightly browned, about 10 minutes. In a medium bowl, beat the eggs with ¼ cup of water and the remaining salt and black pepper. Stir in ¼ cup of the cheese and 2 tablespoons of the fresh parsley and the fresh basil. Pour egg mixture over pasta; stir with a fork to distribute evenly. Cook without stirring until eggs are set around edges. Place in the oven; bake until eggs are set; about 10 minutes. Slide frittata onto a platter; cut into wedges. Toss together remaining ¼ cup cheese and 2 tablespoons parsley; pass separately. Serve with a tasty sauce such as Salsa Cruda (Recipe: P. 144), Pepita Salsa Verde (Recipe: P. 154), Chipotle Sauce (Recipe: P. 156) or your choice.

POBLANO PASTA

The simplicity of this rich pasta dish will surprise the diner. It freezes well.

Makes 8 to 10 Servings

- 16 ounces pasta, fettuccini, vermicelli or a light type
- 10 cups water
- 1 teaspoon chicken or vegetable base
- 3 fresh poblano peppers, roasted, skinned, deveined and seeded
- 16 ounces sour cream or low fat plain yogurt or 8 ounces of each
- 8 ounces Monterey Jack or mozzarella cheese, grated
  Salt and freshly ground black pepper, to taste
  Cayenne pepper, to taste

In a large saucepan add 10 cups water; bring to a boil. Add pasta and base; bring to a boil and cook until pasta is just tender. Drain thoroughly. While pasta cooks, prepare poblanos. Place peeled poblanos in blender; add sour cream or yogurt; pulse until well mixed. Salt and black and red pepper to taste. Add poblano cream to pasta with half the grated cheese. Mix well. Place pasta in a rectangular 9 by 12 inch baking dish. Sprinkle with remaining cheese. When ready to serve, bake in the oven at 375°F until

cheese melts. Garnish with red and green Bell Pepper rings or paprika. Can be prepared ahead, wrapped and stored in refrigerator or frozen.

NOTE: Some poblanos are more pungent than others. Make a taste test. If too pungent, use only one or two poblanos.

CHIPOTLE SHRIMP PASTA

Tasty and simple. Shrimp fans will love it.

Makes 6 Servings

- 1¼ pounds penne pasta
- 1½ teaspoons olive oil
- 1 medium onion, peeled and diced
- 3 large tomatoes, diced
- ¾ cup chicken broth (chicken base can be used)
- 1½ teaspoons chipotle adobado, puréed
- ½ pound large shrimp, boiled and peeled
- 3 tablespoons heavy cream
  Salt and freshly ground black pepper to taste
  Fresh cilantro, chopped, for garnish

In large pot, cook pasta al dente; drain. In a large nonstick skillet, over medium heat, place olive oil; add onion and sauté for 3 minutes. Stir in tomatoes, broth and chipotle adobado. Lower heat slightly; simmer 5 minutes. Add shrimp; cook for four minutes. Reduce heat to low; stir in cream, salt and pepper; simmer until thickened, about 2 minutes. Divide pasta among 6 pasta bowls; spoon sauce over it. Garnish with cilantro. Serve hot.

PASTA PUTTANESCA

This is a rather aggressive Italian tomato sauce that is quick and easy. It was supposedly created by Italian "ladies of the night." A puta means a "lady of the night" in Italian and Spanish. Perhaps the sauce is called that because it has her aggressive attributes and is so salty. If you use the anchovies do not add any salt to the sauce or the pasta water. Originally spaghetti was suggested but I find it especially tasty on ravioli of any type. This one is my spin.

Makes 4 Servings

1 pound pasta (boiled according to directions on package while making sauce, then drained)

2 tablespoons olive oil

5 garlic cloves, peeled and mashed

1 tablespoon water

1 teaspoon Aleppo or red pepper flakes, more to taste

8 anchovy filets, 1–2 ounce can, rinsed and mashed.; OPTIONAL, (see Note)

1 28-ounce can diced petite tomatoes, drained, ½ cup juice reserved

3 tablespoons capers, rinsed

½ cup black calamata olives, pitted and chopped coarse (Alfonso, Gaeta, Greek or calamata pitted black olives lack attitude)

¼ cup fresh basil leaves, minced
Parmesan cheese, shredded

Heat oil in a 2 quart sauce pan; add garlic and water; cook until soft but not browned over medium heat; stir frequently. Add pepper flakes and anchovy; cook 2 to 3 minutes; stir frequently. Stir in tomatoes; simmer until slightly thickened, about 8 minutes. Add capers, olives and parsley; cook and stir for 2 minutes. Return drained pasta to its pot; add reserved ½ cup tomato juice; toss to combine. Pour sauce over pasta; toss to combine. Serve with shredded Parmesan cheese.

NOTE: The addition of anchovy to the sauce may make it too salty and fishy for some. Try using anchovy strips on top of a serving as done on pizza.

FABULOUS FETTUCCINE

This pasta dish, a real crowd pleaser, is so quick and easy your guests won't believe it if you tell them.

Makes 6 to 8 Servings

½ cup red wine

½ cup sun-dried tomatoes, packed firmly

4 tablespoons olive oil

4 garlic cloves, peeled and minced

1 tablespoon fresh basil, finely chopped

1 pound Portabella mushrooms, wiped and sliced

1 red Bell Pepper, stemmed, seeded and coarsely diced

1 14-ounce can artichoke hearts (not marinated), quartered

½ cup non-fat sour cream

1 teaspoon chicken base in ½ cup water (Better Than Bouillon®)

½ cup Parmesan cheese, grated

1 teaspoon Aleppo pepper or ½ teaspoon cayenne
Salt and freshly ground black pepper to taste

12 ounces Fettuccini noodles

In a small microwave safe container place wine and sun-dried tomatoes; microwave for 3 minutes; set aside to soften, then coarsely chop; set aside again. In a large sauce pan heat oil over medium heat; add mushrooms, garlic, and basil; cook until just tender, about 6 minutes. Add Bell Pepper; cook for 3 minutes more. Add artichoke, tomatoes, cream, chicken base, cheese, and cayenne pepper; stir to mix. Season with salt and black pepper. Remove from heat and cover; set aside to mellow while cooking pasta. Cook pasta for 8 minutes. Drain. Toss pasta with sauce. Pass additional cheese. The sauce can be made earlier or the day before.

NOTE 1: Shredded cooked chicken is a nice addition for a heartier meal.

NOTE 2: A larger quantity of sun-dried tomatoes may be softened in this manner and stored in a tightly covered container in the refrigerator for future use.

NOTE 3: Pass sour cream or plain, nonfat yogurt as a nice addition to individual servings.

PORTABELLA AND FUSSELI/ROTINI

A simple but very flavorful vegetarian dish that can be whipped up at the last minute.

Makes 4 Servings

 12 ounces dried fusseli pasta; or any short pasta such as penne or small shells
  1 tablespoon olive oil
 ½ cup onion, chopped
  2 garlic cloves, peeled and chopped
 ½ cup red Bell Pepper, veined and chopped
  2 tablespoons fresh basil, minced
  1 tablespoon chipotle adobado, puréed
 12 ounces Portabella mushroom caps, rinsed and cut into ½-inch pieces
 ⅓ cup dry red wine
  1 28-ounce can diced tomatoes
    Salt and freshly ground black pepper to taste
 ½ cup Parmesan cheese, shredded

In a 5 to 6-quart pan over high heat, bring 4 quarts water to a boil. Add pasta; stir occasionally until tender, 7 to 9 minutes. Drain, return to pan; set aside. Pour oil into a 10 to 12-inch frying pan over medium-high heat; when hot, add onion, garlic, Bell Pepper, chipotle, basil, and mushrooms. Stir frequently until onion and mushrooms are soft, about 8 minutes. Add wine and cook until most liquid has evaporated, 1 to 2 minutes. Add tomatoes; bring to a boil; reduce heat: simmer to blend flavors, about 10 minutes. Add salt and pepper to taste. Pour over hot pasta and mix to coat with sauce. Spoon into four wide, shallow bows and top evenly with cheese.

3

MEAT

FOWL

SEAFOOD

Meats

Four Old Time Texas Favorites

FRITO PIE

The incomparable, favorite chip, Frito, was originated about 1932 by Elmer Doolin in San Antonio, Texas, in a little old house on South Flores Street. His wife, Daisy, made the first Frito pie when she dumped her bowl of chili directly into a bag of Fritos. Her handy innovation caught on with kids of all ages and is still going strong—but has graduated to a bowl. You can use chili made from one of the recipes in this book or just open and heat a can of Wolf Brand® Chili without beans. Wolf Brand® Chili is also a native of Texas but now owned by Quaker Oats. If not in your store, order from Wolf Brand Products, P.O. Box 617, Corsicana, TX, 75151.

Makes—depends on amount of chili on hand.

> Fritos
> Chili con carne
> Onions, chopped
> Longhorn cheddar cheese, shredded
> Salsa picante

In each individual bowl spread about ¾ cup Fritos and sprinkle onion equally on top. Put equal amounts of hot chili on top of the Fritos and top with cheese. Pass the salsa at the table.

NOTE: Originally a small, individual bag of Fritos was split down one side and spread open to allow entry of chili. The other side was flattened so that the package of Frito pie would sit on a table.

PEDERNALES RIVER CHILI (PRONOUNCED: "PURR-DIN-ALICE")

The late Frank Tolbert reported in his A Bowl of Red, that President Lyndon B. Johnson said: "One of the first things I do when I get home to Texas is to have a bowl of red. There is simply nothing better." This recipe got its inspiration from the chili made at the LBJ Ranch which is located on the Pedernales River near Johnson City in Blanco County, Texas. In the late 1950s, Frank and I were Dallas neighbors. Our pre-teen sons played together for years.

A word about chili con carne. Most evidence points to its beginnings in Texas, probably San Antonio, in the early nineteenth century and becoming known in the 1880's when chili queens sold cooked chili con carne from caldrons at dusk in downtown plazas. This practice continued until about 1943. O. Henry was the first to write about the chili queens.

Makes—a lot!

> 4   pounds of chili meat; coarsely cut beef or venison (deer)
> 4   tablespoons vegetable oil
> 1   large onion, chopped
> 4   garlic cloves, peeled and minced
> 1   teaspoon oregano
> 1   teaspoon cumin seeds, ground
> 7   teaspoons chili powder, more if desired. Gebhardt's® preferred

2   16-ounce cans of tomatoes, diced
2   cups of boiling water
    Cayenne pepper, to taste
    Salt and freshly ground black pepper to taste

In a large skillet or Dutch oven heat oil. Add ground meat, onion, garlic; sear until a grayish color. Add rest of the ingredients; bring to a boil and lower heat. Simmer for an hour, covered. Skim off grease. Cooked pinto beans (Recipe: P. 59) or black beans may be added, but never kidney beans!

NOTE: Leftovers freeze well when tightly wrapped and sealed.

KING RANCH CHICKEN

Because I was born and grew up within a mile or two of the headquarters of the King Ranch, named Santa Gertrudis after the original Spanish land grant, I will include this recipe—although it didn't get popular until sometime after World War II. Campbell's introduced their cream of mushroom soup in 1934 and cream of chicken soup in 1947. Rotel first produced their famous tomatoes and green chiles in the 1940s. My mother would never have prepared anything with canned soups.

Who first made this dish? It was not in a local area cook book, "What's Cooking in South Texas," compiled by the Chemcel Women's Club of Kingsville and Bishop in 1950, which included ads by the King Ranch and eight recipes from the ranch. I don't know where it came from, but I doubt that it came from the kitchen at the Santa Gertrudis headquarters and I'm certain that the Kineños (King Ranch vaquero's families) never made or ate it back then. However, today many Texans seem to have their own version of this "classic." This one is adapted from a recipe sent to me from the King Ranch Saddle Shop in Kingsville, Texas.

As a post script: In 1915 my father bought the original Santa Gertrudis land grant from the Kleberg family whose ancestors founded the King Ranch with that grant. That is where I grew up. Sadly, in January 1972 the U. S. Navy forced him to sell the land. It is still a part of the Kingsville Naval Air Station.

Makes 8 to 10 Servings

1   rotisserie chicken, purchased; skin, debone and tear into bite sized pieces
2   packages corn tortillas, 10-ounce; tear into quarters
1   large onion, chopped
1   green Bell Pepper, seeded, veined, and chopped
1   red Bell Pepper, seeded, veined, and chopped
2   cups or 8-ounces Cheddar cheese, shredded; or Monterey Jack cheese
1½ teaspoons chili powder, Gebhardt's® preferred
2   garlic cloves, peeled and minced
1   can, 10½-ounce condensed cream of chicken soup, mixed to directions on can
1   can, 10½-ounce condensed cream of mushroom soup, mixed to directions on can
1   can, 10-ounce can Rotel® tomatoes and green chiles, diced. Do not drain

Preheat oven to 350°F. Lightly grease a 13 x 9 x 2-inch baking dish. Into this dish, place half of the chicken, onion, garlic and green pepper; layer half the tortilla pieces over chicken pieces. In a bowl, combine mixed soups and tomatoes; pour half of the soup-tomato mixture over tortillas and chicken. Top with half the cheese. Repeat layers—chicken, tortillas, soup-tomato mixture, ending with cheese. Bake for 45 minutes or until thoroughly heated. Serve immediately.

NOTE 1: The tightly wrapped dish may be frozen to cook later or the baked dish may be cooled, then wrapped and frozen. Allow several hours to thaw before reheating or baking.

NOTE 2: Early versions did not contain Rotel® tomatoes because they were not yet on the market.

TAMALE PIE

An old fashioned Texas dish but still a winner and easy to pre-pare. It can be made a day early and cooked before serving or sometime ahead and kept in the freezer to be thawed and cooked when needed.

Makes 6 Servings

- 1 tablespoon vegetable or canola oil
- 1 medium onion, chopped
- 2 garlic cloves, peeled and chopped
- 1 small poblano pepper, roasted, peeled and chopped
- ¼ cup lean pork, ground
- 2 cups tomato sauce, canned
- 12 ounce can whole kernel corn
- ½ cup black olives, pitted and chopped
- 1 teaspoon granulated sugar
- 1 tablespoon chili powder
- 1½ cups processed American cheese, shredded
  Salt and freshly ground black pepper to taste

Topping

- ¾ cup masa harina or yellow cornmeal (masa is more nutritious)
- 2 cups water
- 1 tablespoon butter or margarine

Preheat oven to 375°F. In a large skillet over medium heat, place oil and add onions, poblano, garlic; cook until soft. Add meat and brown slightly; drain off excess fat. Add tomato sauce, corn, olives, sugar, chili powder; stir. Add salt and pepper to taste, then simmer over medium heat until thick, 20 to 25 minutes. Add cheese, stir until melted. Pour into a 10 x 6 x 1½-inch baking dish; set aside. Put masa or cornmeal, salt, and water in a medium-size sauce pan over medium heat; cook until thick. Add butter; mix well. Spoon over the meat mixture. Bake for 50 minutes or until topping is browned. Serve immediately. Salsa Cruda (see Recipe P. 144) is good with this dish.

BREAKFAST ENCHILADAS

This can be made up the day before for company on Sunday morning. With Tequila Bloody Mary's (see Recipe P. 52) and guacamole (see Recipe P. 66) this is a real winner.

Makes 12 Servings

- 1 pound chorizo, Mexican sausage
- 1 large onion, finely chopped
- 1 poblano pepper, roasted, seeded and finely chopped
- 2 eggs, beaten
- 1 pound Monterrey Jack cheese, grated
- 2 cups medium white sauce, recipe below
- 24 flour tortillas, medium size

In a heavy skillet, sear sausage; add chopped onions and green pepper; cook until browned. Pour off grease. Add beaten eggs to sausage mixture; stir to scramble. Soften tortillas in a sealed bag in a microwave oven for 1½ minutes.

For Rolled Enchiladas:

Put about a tablespoon of sausage mixture and a little cheese in a tortilla and roll. Place seam side down in a greased 3-quart casserole. Continue to fill casserole. This can be prepared to this point, covered well and refrigerated several days ahead. To serve, make a white sauce and pour over rolled tortillas. When ready to serve, sprinkle with cheese and heat in a 350°F oven until cheese is melted.

For Casserole Dish:

Preheat oven to 350°F. Oil the bottom of a 9 x 13-inch casserole dish; cover bottom of dish with tortillas then layer with the sausage mixture. Place another layer of tortillas; cover with white sauce. Top with grated cheese. Bake until cheese is melted.

WHITE SAUCE

1 cup milk
1 tablespoon flour
1 tablespoon butter
  Salt and freshly ground black pepper to taste

Melt butter in a saucepan over low heat. Add flour; stir until smooth. Over low heat, slowly add milk, stirring constantly. Cook until thick. Season with salt and pepper to taste.

ANCHO-PECAN AND TWICE COOKED PORK TACOS

A zippy, nutty flavored way to use leftover pork roast or chops. "Twice-cooked" meat, especially pork, is favored in Chinese cooking. The raw meat is first simmered, then stir-fried; leftovers need only be stir fried. We should use it more often.

Makes 8 tacos

3 cups water
¼ cup canola or vegetable oil

1½ pounds boneless pork loin
1 green onion with stalk, cut in 1-inch sections
1 garlic clove, peeled and crushed
½ cup red Bell Pepper, diced
½ teaspoon cayenne pepper
  Salt and freshly ground black pepper to taste
1 tablespoon butter
1 cup pecans, chopped
2 ancho chili peppers, stemmed, seeded, finely chopped
8 flour tortillas, warmed
2 cups guacamole at room temperature (see Recipe P. 66)

Place water and pork in a heavy pan; bring to a boil; simmer, covered until well done; about 1 hour. Drain, reserving stock for other use. Cool. Cut pork across the grain in ¼-inch slices, then in strips 1 by 2 inches. In a wok or a large skillet, heat oil; add pork and stir-fry to brown, 2 to 3 minutes. Add onion, garlic, Bell Pepper, cayenne, salt and black pepper and stir-fry to blend well; 2 to 3 minutes more; set aside. In a small skillet over low heat melt butter. Add pecans and anchos; cook for 3 to 5 minutes or until butter begins to turn reddish brown. Season with salt and transfer to a small bowl.

To prepare tacos: lay each warm tortilla flat; divide the warm pork, ancho-pecans and guacamole equally among them. Roll, or fold in half, and serve.

NOTE: Meat can be done before-hand and kept refrigerated in closed container.

GREEN CORN TAMALE PIE

This succulent casserole can be prepared and refrigerated several days before it is baked and served. If possible use white "field" corn but in this day and time that is almost impossible to find. It has a much higher starch content than sweet corn, consequently extra corn starch must be added to make up for the difference.

Makes a 3 Quart Casserole

8–10 ears of corn, (7 cups) cut off the cob; reserve un-torn shucks, keeping them moist; discard cobs
¾ cup masa harina; dry, not moist (see P. 37)
⅓ cup corn or vegetable oil
2 cups Monterrey Jack cheese, shredded
1 7-ounce can green chiles, diced
6 ounces chorizo, Mexican sausage, casings re-moved; (all are made of pork)
   Fresh cilantro, chopped
   Salt and freshly ground black pepper, to taste
   Green salsa, recipe follows

Preheat oven to 350°F. Working in batches in a blender or food processor (fill blender only half full), add corn, masa, and oil; pulse until finely ground. Scrape mixture into a bowl; add cheese, chiles, salt and pepper; mix well. Line a 3 to 3½-quart casserole with the green corn shucks, over-lapping them and letting ends stick up 3 or 4 inches over the rim. Discard any extra shucks. Drop spoonfuls of the corn mixture onto shucks, being careful that they remain in place. Spoon remaining corn mixture into casserole; spread level. Fold ends of shucks over corn mixture. Cover casserole tightly with foil. Bake in oven until corn mixture is steaming and slightly firm to touch in the center (un-cover to check), about 1 hour. Let casserole stand, covered, for 10 minutes.

Meanwhile, cut chorizo into ¼ inch slices. In a 10 to 12-inch skillet, over medium-high heat, brown chorizo, stirring often, about 5 minutes. Remove; drain on paper towels. Uncover casserole and unfold husks. Spoon sausage over tamale pie and sprinkle cilantro on top. Serve with green salsa.

GREEN SALSA

Makes 1½ cups

½ pound fresh tomatillos, cooked; or one 12-ounce can tomatillos, drained
1 7-ounce can green chiles, diced
¾ cup fresh cilantro, lightly packed
¼ cup scallions, chopped
1 tablespoon fresh lime juice

Place all ingredients in a food processor; pulse until mixture is finely chopped. Put into a small bowl and serve.

PEPPERED PORK CHOPS WITH BALSAMIC-PEACH GLAZE

Tasty but simple and quick.

Makes 2 Servings

2 boneless pork chops, ¾ inch-thick
1 teaspoon seasoned pepper (garlic pepper, lemon pepper or a pepper blend)
½ teaspoon cayenne pepper
½ jalapeño chilli-pepper, or to taste; seeded and minced
½ tablespoon onion, chopped

½ cup chicken broth, chicken base can be used

¼ cup peach jam

1 tablespoon balsamic vinegar

Fresh cilantro, chopped, as garnish

Rub chops on both sides with seasoned pepper. Heat olive oil in nonstick skillet over medium-high heat; cook chops to brown on one side; turn chops; add onion and jalapeño to pan. Continue to cook, stirring occasionally, until onion is tender, about one minute. Add broth, jam and vinegar to pan; cover, lower heat and simmer 8 to 10 minutes. Serve chops with pan sauce, garnished with chopped cilantro.

LAMB TAGINE

This Moroccan stew is enhanced when served with harissa, a deep-red, North African relish made from a paste of dried red peppers.

Makes 6 Servings

4 pounds lamb shoulder or cut suitable for stewing, boned, fat-trimmed, rinsed, cut into 1½-inch pieces.

1 pound onions, peeled and thinly sliced

5 garlic cloves, peeled and minced

1 tablespoon *each* ground cinnamon, tumeric, and fresh ginger, minced

½ teaspoon cayenne pepper

1 tablespoon Aleppo pepper

⅛ teaspoon cardamom, ground

1 14½-ounce can diced tomatoes

2 tablespoons tomato paste

2½ cups chicken broth, fat skimmed or use Better Than Bullion® paste as directed for that amount

Salt and freshly ground black pepper

Couscous prepared by directions on package

for 6 Servings

⅓ cup calamata olives, pitted

⅓ cup fresh cilantro, chopped

Place meat in a heavy 5 to 6-quart pan. Add ½ cup water; cover; bring to a boil over high heat. Reduce heat; simmer briskly over medium heat for 15 to 20 minutes. Uncover pan; increase heat to high; stir often until most of the liquid has evaporated, another 15 to 20 minutes. Reduce heat to medium-high; stir often until meat juices have caramelized and meat has browned, about more 5 minutes. Be careful to not scorch. Discard all but 2 tablespoons fat from pan.

Add onions and garlic to pan; stir often over medium heat until onions become limp. Add dry spices; stir until very fragrant; about 30 seconds. Add broth, tomatoes with juice, and tomato paste. Bring to a boil over high heat. Reduce heat, cover, and simmer, stirring occasionally, until lamb is tender when pierced, about 1 hour. Skim off and discard any fat. Season with salt and pepper.

On a large rimmed platter or on individual dinner plates, mound couscous and form a well in the center. Using a slotted spoon, transfer lamb and vegetables to the well. Measure pan juices; if less than 3 cups, add water to make that amount; return to pan; bring to a boil over high heat. Add salt to taste. Pour juices into a bowl and pass. Scatter olives and cilantro over lamb.

STUFFED PEPPERS NOGADA

If stuffed peppers could be thought of as decadent, these from Mexico would be the ones referred to. Use turkey to cut down on fat and calories a little.

Makes 8 Servings

       2   tablespoons vegetable oil
       1   medium-size onion, chopped
       1   16-ounce can tomatoes, drained and chopped
       2   tablespoons fresh parsley leaves, chopped
       ½   teaspoon ground cinnamon
       ½   teaspoon ground cayenne pepper
       2   pounds ground meat, beef, pork, or fowl
       ¼   cup raisins, soaked in hot water to cover and drained
       ½   cup pecans, roughly chopped, or blanched almonds, slivered; or a mixture
       2   large eggs, lightly beaten
           Salt and freshly ground black pepper to taste
       4   large red or green Bell Peppers, cleaned, halved and par boiled 3 minutes and patted dry
           Nogada Sauce (recipe follows)
           Parsley sprigs for garnish

Preheat oven to 325°F. Heat oil in a large sauce pan over medium high heat. Add onion; cook until soft. Add tomatoes, parsley, cinnamon and cayenne; cook slightly. Add meat, raisins, and nuts; cook, stirring for 20 minutes or until browned and done. Allow to cool; stir in eggs. Season with salt and pepper. Stuff Bell Pepper halves with meat mixture. Bake 30 minutes until thoroughly heated, or microwave until heated. Pour nogada sauce on top of stuffed peppers; garnish with parsley. This may be served hot or at room temperature as it is done traditionally.

NOGADA SAUCE

       3   slices whole grain bread, no crust
       ½   cup cold milk
       2   cups milk
       1   cup pecans or almonds
           salt to taste

Soak bread in ½ cup cold milk. Purée milk-soaked bread in a blender with 2 cups of milk, nuts, and salt. The sauce should be fairly thick; adjust with milk. You may warm it slightly before serving on hot stuffed peppers but do not cook it.

Variations: Instead of rich nogada sauce, try tomato sauce or the following:

WHIPPED NOGADA SAUCE

Makes 3 Cups

       2   cups whipping cream
       ½   cup walnuts or pecans, ground in a blender
       ½   cup blanched almonds. ground in a blender
       2   tablespoons fresh parsley, finely chopped
       ½   teaspoon ground cinnamon
           Salt to taste

Whip cream with a whisk or electric beater until it forms soft peaks. Fold in ground nuts, parsley, cinnamon, and salt. Serve at room temperature on top of stuffed pepper halves.

TABASCO STEAK

I was shown how to prepare this by George O. Jackson, better known as Georg-O, who was born in Houston of a Texan father and Mexican mother. As a result of his maternal family background he has spent much of his life in Mexico. He was the originator of several restaurants in Houston, Texas, but is best known for his photography, hospitality, and love of peppers. This recipe sounds crazy, but it isn't. The pepper sauce acts as a tenderizer and when heated over coals, it seals the juices in the meat. Advance planning necessary.

Makes 10 to 15 Servings

- 5 pounds of 3½-inch thick sirloin butt beef steak, the best you can buy
- 2 small bottles of Tabasco Pepper Sauce®, depending on amount of meat
- 1 zip-lock bag, large
- 1 stick of soft butter
- 2–4 garlic cloves, peeled and crushed

Place the beef in a plastic zip-lock bag with contents of 2 bottles of sauce. Soak beef in sauce in refrigerator for 3 days; turn often. Remove beef from sauce; cook over mesquite wood coals. When coals are at hottest point, put steak on a grill 2 inches above fire. Care must be taken to prevent flame-ups during cooking. Cook for 10 minutes; turn; cook on other side for 10 minutes; repeat for 2 more 10 minute periods. While meat is cooking, blend garlic into softened butter; melt slightly. After meat has cooked for 40 minutes, remove from fire; place on a cutting board; allow to rest for 10 minutes before carving. After carving, brush slices with garlic butter. The meat will have a tangy crust but is not pungent in spite of the sauce.

NOTE: If meat is room temperature at time of cooking, the final product will be medium rare; if it has just come from refrigerator, it will be rare. After cutting, if a serving is too rare for some tastes, return meat slices to the grill for a bit more cooking.

BEEF TENDERLOIN MARINATED IN MOLASSES AND PEPPERS

This tasty main course can be started the day before and cooked just before serving.

Makes 4 Servings

- 1 cup molasses
- 2 tablespoons balsamic vinegar
- 2 tablespoons freshly ground black pepper
- 1 tablespoon Aleppo pepper or ½ tablespoon cayenne pepper
- 2 garlic cloves, peeled and finely chopped
- 1 large shallot, peeled and finely chopped
- 2 teaspoons fresh ginger, finely grated
- 1 teaspoon fresh thyme, finely chopped. Dry can be used
- 2 pounds center-cut beef tenderloin, trimmed of fat and silver skin
- 2 tablespoons vegetable oil
  Salt to taste

In a small bowl, combine molasses, vinegar, peppers, garlic, shallot, ginger, thyme; mix; pour over beef in a glass dish. Cover; marinate in refrigerator 24 hours; turn meat occasionally. Remove meat; reserve marinade to glaze meat. Cut meat into 8 medallions; season with salt. Heat oil in large cast-iron skillet over medium heat; brown medallions 3 minutes on one side, 2 minutes on other side, until desired doneness. Just before removing beef, add 4 tablespoons marinade to skillet; glaze both sides of meat quickly.

ROCOTO RELLENO (PERUVIAN STUFFED PEPPERS)

Arequipa, Peru, is the world capital of the rocoto pepper and its most famous culinary achievement, the Rocoto Relleno. I never dreamed that I would be able to eat anything made from the fiery rocoto. The way this dish is done in Arequipa made my trip worth while in order to experience it at its finest. Rocotos will probably not be available in your area. Actually, red Bell Peppers or poblanos work almost as well.

Makes 8 to 12 servings

- 12 rocotos or small red Bell Peppers or poblanos. Roast and skin poblanos
- 3 tablespoons vegetable oil
- 12 baking potatoes, washed, boiled until almost tender and peeled
- 2½ pounds lean pork, beef, or turkey cut into fine cubes or ground as for chilli (ask butcher for "chili grind")
- 2 tablespoons vegetable oil
- 1 small red onion, chopped finely
- 4 red jalapeños or serranos, seeded and finely chopped
- 1 tablespoon ground cumin
- 2 large eggs, hard boiled, and chopped
- ½ cup raisins, soaked in hot water and drained
- 3 tablespoons butter, melted
  Salt to taste
  Paprika
  Fresh cilantro sprigs

For the Peppers

Preheat oven to 350°F. If using rocotos, wear gloves. Cut tops off peppers carefully; set aside to use as lids. Remove seeds and veins. Place peppers and their tops in water to cover with 1 teaspoon of salt in a large covered saucepan over high heat; bring to a boil. Reduce heat to low; simmer for 3 minutes; with rocotos, repeat with fresh water as often as necessary if still too pungent. Remove from pan; drain; pat dry with paper toweling. Set aside.

In a skillet; heat oil over medium heat; add onion; cook until translucent. Add meat and spices, then increase heat; cook until done but not browned and most juice is cooked down. Remove from heat; add egg and raisins; season with salt; mix well. Fill each pepper with meat mixture; cover with its pepper lid and set aside.

Peel the almost tender potatoes; cut lengthwise into quarters. Using as many flat greased baking dishes as are necessary, arrange potatoes and peppers in equal groups (for example, 2 slices of potato with each pepper). Brush potatoes with butter. Bake in oven until the potatoes are tender and slightly browned.

For the Sauce

- 1 large egg, beaten
- 1 tablespoon vegetable oil
- 1 cup milk
- ¾ pound white cheese, Farmer's or Monterey Jack, grated
  Salt and freshly ground black pepper to taste

In a small sauce pan, beat egg and oil together until well blended. Place over low heat; gradually add milk while stirring continuously; cook until thickened, do not allow to boil. Gradually add one-half of the cheese, saving remainder. If sauce separates or curdles, pour it into a blender; process until smooth.

To assemble, pour some sauce over each pepper and potato group, then sprinkle with remaining cheese; continue baking until cheese is melted. Place portions on a plate; cover with any sauce remaining. Garnish with paprika and cilantro sprigs. Serve immediately.

NOTE: If you have individual ovenproof dishes, place a serving of pepper and potatoes in each dish, add sauce; sprinkle with cheese; heat until cheese is melted. Garnish with paprika and cilantro sprigs.

Alternate: Add 1 cup of dry roasted peanuts, finely chopped, to meat mixture along with raisins and eggs.

PORTUGUESE PORK CHOPS OR CHICKEN BREASTS

This recipe is in honor of the Portuguese explorers who did so much to introduce peppers to the Old World. Start this the day before you plan to serve it so that the pepper paste can really flavor the meat, that is, if you don't eat all of the paste before you put it on the meat.

Makes 6 Servings

- 6 1-inch pork chops or boneless chicken breasts
- 6 tablespoons Portuguese Style Red Pepper Paste (see Recipe P. 155)
- ½ teaspoon freshly ground black pepper
- 2 cups dry white wine
- 2 olive oil
  parsley, chopped for garnish

Rub meat on both sides with pepper paste; place in a shallow bowl, pour wine on meat, cover; refrigerate overnight, turning meat once or twice. Make a basting sauce by placing marinade and olive oil in a sauce pan; simmer until consistency of gravy; adjust seasoning with salt and pepper. Cook meat on a charcoal grill, baste with sauce. To cook in a skillet, heat a little olive oil until almost smoking; add meat and brown both sides; add basting sauce to meat; reduce heat to low; cover, and cook until well done. Sprinkle with chopped parsley; serve with brown or wild rice, quinoa, or pasta.

EASY TACO PIE

A quick microwave recipe that your kids will love.

Serves 6

- 1 pound lean beef, pork, chicken or turkey, ground
- ½ cup onion, chopped
- 1½ cups Monterey jack cheese, shredded
- 1½ ounce taco seasoning mix
- 14 ounce can green chiles, drained and chopped
- ½ cup salsa cruda or chopped tomatoes
- 1 cup cornbread mix
- 3 eggs
- 1 cup milk
- 1 teaspoonful Aleppo pepper or hot pepper sauce

Garnish

Pickled jalapeño slices, black olive slices, and shredded cheese

Preheat oven to 400° F. In microwave safe dish, combine meat and onions; heat on high for 3 minutes. Stir to break up meat; microwave another 3 minutes; drain well. Stir in cheese, taco seasoning, green chiles and salsa; spread mixture evenly into a round microwave safe dish; cover. Let stand 5 to 10 minutes until cheese melts. In a bowl, combine cornbread mix, eggs, milk and Aleppo pepper or pepper sauce; beat until smooth. Pour thin mixture over meat mixture; bake 35–40 minutes until top is browned and a knife inserted into center comes out clean. Garnish with cheese, olives, and jalapeños. Let stand 10 minutes before serving.

RACK OF LAMB WITH RASPBERRY CHIPOTLE SAUCE

This elegant dish requires an oven-proof serving plate or individual oven-proof dinner plates. The sauce and garlic puree can be prepared well in advance.

Makes 4 Servings

- 1 lamb rack, with at least 8 chops
- 2 tablespoons olive oil
  Salt and freshly ground black pepper
- 8 tablespoons goat cheese mix, recipe follows
  Raspberry chipotle sauce, recipe follows

Trim rack of lamb of all fat. Cut into 8 equal chops each with bone left on. Rub all chops with olive oil. Salt and pepper both sides. Grill over charcoal, live wood, or gas grill to desired doneness. Remove from fire; place 1 tablespoon of the goat cheese mix (recipe follows) on the top of each chop. Set aside until serving time.

To Serve: Preheat oven to 450°F. Place 2 chops, with the bones crossed and goat cheese on top on each oven-proof serving plate or place all of them on an oven-proof serving platter. Place plates in the oven for 2–3 minutes to lightly brown the cheese and heat the meat and the plate. Ladle 2 tablespoons of raspberry chipotle sauce over each chop. Garnish with a sprig of a favorite fresh herb.

GOAT CHEESE MIX

Makes 1 Cup

- ¼ pound cream cheese or dripped yogurt
- ¼ pound fresh goat cheese

- 3 tablespoons oven-roasted garlic, recipe follows
- 2 teaspoons Hidden Valley Ranch® dressing mix, dry

Mix all ingredients in food processor until well blended. Refrigerate until 1 hour before serving.

ROASTED GARLIC PURÉE

Makes ¼ Cup

- ½ cup garlic cloves, peeled
- 1 tablespoon olive oil
- ¼ teaspoon salt

Preheat oven to 375°F. Coat garlic with oil and season with salt. Wrap in foil and bake until garlic is golden brown. In food processor with knife blade, process garlic to a smooth paste.

RASPBERRY CHIPOTLE SAUCE

- 1 cup granulated sugar
- 1 cup raspberries, fresh or frozen
- 1 cup red wine vinegar
- 1 quart veal or beef stock; use canned or Better Than Bouillon®
- 6 chipotle chilies, adobado, pureéd, or finely chopped
- 1 tablespoon freshly ground black pepper
  Salt to taste

In a heavy saucepan, caramelize sugar until golden brown. Add raspberries, chipotles, and pepper. Continue cooking until sugar is brown, but not burned. Add vinegar, stirring constantly, until mixture is smooth. Add veal stock and cook slowly until reduced by half. Strain through a fine strainer into a clean double boiler; add butter and salt and pepper to taste. Cook over boiling water until desired thickness. Reserve until serving time.

To Serve: Place the plates into oven for 2–3 minutes to lightly brown the goat cheese and to heat the food. Ladle raspberry sauce over meat before serving or put sauce in a bowl and pass.

Fowl

CHICKEN TERIYAKI INDONESIAN STYLE

An exotic but easily made main course with oriental overtones.

Makes 6 Servings

- ⅓ cup ginger tamari sauce or lite soy sauce
- ⅓ cup honey
- ¼ teaspoon sesame oil
- 1 tablespoon fresh ginger, finely chopped
- 3 cloves garlic, peeled and minced
- 3 chiltepín peppers or 1 teaspoon cayenne pepper
- 4 chicken breasts, skinless and partly frozen
- 4 green onions, finely sliced
- 2 tablespoons sesame seeds
  Fresh cilantro leaves
  Cooked brown or wild rice

In a medium bowl, stir together soy sauce, honey, sesame oil, ginger, garlic, and chili peppers. Set aside ⅓ of the mixture. Slice chicken into ½-inch thick strips. Add to marinade and stir. Refrigerate, covered, for 1 to 2 hours, stirring occasionally to coat chicken thoroughly. Drain chicken; reserve extra marinade in refrigerator. Place on foil; grill or broil about 4 minutes per side, until lightly browned and cooked through. Just before serving, heat reserved marinade; brush chicken with marinade. Serve over brown or converted rice with onions, sesame seeds, and cilantro sprinkled on top.

CHICKEN-PISTACHIO TAGINE

Tagine, a spicy stew, named for the container it is cooked in, is from the Maghreb—Tunisia, Algeria and Morocco. It is an easily prepared, tasty dish that has traveled to Mediterranean lands and France and now here!

Makes 4 Servings

- 4 chicken breast halves, boneless and skinless
- 1 tablespoon olive oil
- 2 red onions, (about 1 pound), peeled and slivered
- 4 garlic cloves, peeled and minced
- 1 serrano pepper, seeded and chopped
- 2 teaspoons ground cumin
- 2 teaspoons ground ginger
- ½ teaspoon ground cinnamon
- ½ teaspoon ground dried turmeric
- ½ teaspoon cayenne pepper
- ½ teaspoon paprika
- ¼ cup dark raisins
- ¼ cup golden raisins
- ½ cup pistachios, shelled and toasted
- 1 cup chicken broth, fat-skimmed (or use Better Than Bouillon®, or chicken base)
- 1½ cup semolina couscous
- ¼ cup fresh mint leaves, finely chopped
- ¼ cup fresh cilantro leaves, finely chopped
  Salt and freshly ground black pepper to taste

Rinse chicken; wipe dry; cut into 1 to 2 inch pieces. Pour olive oil into a 10- to 12-inch frying pan over medium-high heat; when hot, add chicken; cook until brown, turning often for 5 to 8 minutes. With slotted spoon, transfer chicken to bowl. Add butter to pan; when melted add onions, garlic, and serrano; stir often until onions are soft and begin to brown, 5 to 7 minutes. Return chicken to pan; spread evenly. Sprinkle cumin, ginger, cinnamon, turmeric, cayenne, paprika, raisins, and pistachios over chicken. Pour chicken broth over all. Cover and bring to a boil, then reduce heat and simmer, stirring occasionally, until chicken is no longer pink in the center, 5 to 6 minutes. Add salt and pepper to taste.

Meanwhile, in a 3 to 4-quart sauce pan over high heat, bring 1½ cups water to a boil; stir in couscous; return to a boil. Cover pan; remove from heat; let stand until water is absorbed, about 5 minutes. Fluff couscous with a fork; stir in mint. Scoop couscous equally onto dinner plates or into wide bowls. If chicken tagine is drier than desired, thin with additional broth. Spoon over couscous; sprinkle with cilantro.

LEMON AND CHILLI ROAST CHICKEN

The late Tim Coltman-Rogers was an engaging young Englishman with a contagious joy for living and love of peppers. He collected them on his worldwide travels and grew them in special green-houses at his estate in Northumberland where he showed me how to prepare this dish. Peppers brought Tim into my life for ten years. I never see a Chiltepín without remembering him.

Makes 6 or More Servings

 1 large roasting chicken; figure ½ pound
   per serving
 ½ pound (2 sticks) butter or margarine, clarified

 2 large lemons
6–8 chiltepínes, to taste (fresh or dry); substitute
   Thai, de árbol or serrano
2–6 garlic cloves, peeled and minced
 2 tablespoons honey
   Freshly ground black pepper; to taste
 1 cup chicken broth, fresh, canned, or chicken base;
   reserve for roasting

Preheat oven to 375°F. Wash chicken; dry thoroughly. Peel lemons, being careful not to include any bitter white pith. Chop rind finely; put in boiling water for 1 minute; drain. Squeeze lemons; reserve juice. Mash chiltepínes; add with butter, lemon rind, garlic, and black pepper in a sauce pan. Heat for 2 to 3 minutes over medium heat.

Gently lift skin from chicken's breast meat; fill the space between skin and breast meat with lemon-pepper mixture. Use any surplus sauce to cover chicken inside and out. Thread a long wooden skewer; sew thread though the flaps of skin on each side of cavity. Take thread through the skin flaps to close the cavity. Place uncovered bird breast side down on a v-rack (if you have one) in a roasting pan. Bake in oven for 40 minutes. Remove pan from oven; raise temperature to 450°F; using paper towels, turn chicken breast side up; return pan to oven; add ½ cup of chicken broth. Cook another 35 to 40 minutes, basting from time-to-time. Allow 15 minutes per pound, plus another 15 minutes. Chicken is done when juices run clear at a joint or thick part of thigh and temperature registers 170° on meat thermometer. Transfer chicken to platter; let rest uncovered for 30 minutes. Déglace (see P. 45) the roasting pan with remaining broth, lemon juice, and honey (totaling about 1½ to 2 cups). Serve chicken and its gravy separately.

CHICKEN AND GREEN CHILE CASSEROLE

This is an adaptation of a prize-winning recipe that is not only flavorful but also very easy to prepare. It can be made the day before, refrigerated, and baked an hour before serving.

Makes 6 to 8 Servings

- 1 pound boneless chicken breasts, cooked and cut in 1-inch pieces or use the meat from a skinned rotisseried chicken
- 1 16-ounce bottle salsa picante, such as Pace® brand
- 2 4-ounce cans green chiles, diced
- 1 cup frozen corn kernels, thawed
- ¾ cup instant rice
- ½ cup water
- 1 2¼-ounce can ripe olives, drained and sliced
- 12 crisp taco shells, crumbled
- 2 cups (8-oz) cheddar cheese, shredded
  Green onions, chopped
  Sour cream

Preheat oven to 375°F. In a large bowl, combine chicken, salsa, green chiles, corn, rice, water, and olives; stir to mix. Spoon into ungreased 13-by-9-inch baking dish. When ready to bake, combine taco shells and cheese in a medium bowl. Sprinkle over chicken mixture just before baking. Bake for 40 to 45 minutes until top is golden brown. Garnish with onions and sour cream. Serve hot. This can be prepared the day before but do not add taco shells and cheese until ready to put into the oven.

BUTTER CHICKEN FROM NORTHERN INDIA

The spicy gravy of this dish is what the British called curry. Serve a good flat bread—chapatis, naan, paratha, or flour tortillas—to "sop" up the buttery sauce as we do gravy in Texas.

Makes 6 to 8 Servings

- 2 pounds boneless chicken breast, skinned and cut into 1-inch pieces

Marinade

- 5 garlic cloves, peeled and chopped
- 1 teaspoon fresh ginger, chopped
- 1 teaspoon turmeric powder
- ½ teaspoon cayenne pepper
- 2 serrano or jalapeño peppers, seeded and chopped
- 1 cup plain yogurt
  Salt and freshly ground black pepper to taste

Put all ingredients into a blender; process into a smooth paste. Rub paste into chicken pieces; place in an airtight container. Marinate in refrigerator for at least two hours or overnight.

Gravy

- 3 tablespoons butter
- ¼ teaspoon cinnamon, ground
- ¼ teaspoon nutmeg, ground
- 3 cloves
- 3 cardamom pods, use the seeds
- 2 red onions, finely sliced
- 1 teaspoon cumin, ground
- ½ teaspoon cayenne pepper

1 teaspoon coriander, ground

Salt and freshly ground black pepper, to taste

¼ cup fresh cilantro, chopped, for garnish

In a heavy pan or Dutch oven, melt butter; add cinnamon, nutmeg, cloves, cardamom. Sauté for one minute until spices release their aroma. Add onions; fry until golden. Add cumin, cayenne, and coriander. Sauté for 2 more minutes. Add marinated chicken along with excess marinade, water, salt, and pepper. Bring to a boil; turn down heat; simmer partially covered, until chicken is tender; at least 15 minutes. Garnish with chopped cilantro.

JALAPEÑO-PEACH CHICKEN

Simple but elegant for family or guests. The chicken (murgh in India) will cook while you do other things.

Makes 4 to 6 Servings

1 roasting chicken, washed and blotted dry

1 16-ounce jar peach preserves

¼ cup pickled jalapeños (nacho slices)

2 teaspoons juice from pickled jalapeños

1 tablespoon fresh lemon juice

2 fresh peaches, whole, studded with whole cloves

Preheat oven to 350°F. Stuff inside of chicken with clove-studded peaches. In a small saucepan combine peach preserves, lemon juice, jalapeños with their juice. Heat over moderate heat until hot and bubbly; stir constantly. Place chicken in a 9 x 13-inch baking dish. Glaze with sauce, reserving some for later. Bake until done (1½ to 2 hours); glaze 2 more times during baking. Add a little water (¼ cup) to dish if sauce is sticking. Discard peaches. Carve and serve.

ROTISSERIE CHICKEN CHEESE POCKETS

An imaginative way to put together already prepared foods from the market, which makes life much easier without taking away taste appeal.

Makes 4 Servings

2 cups cooked chicken from the rotisserie, skinned, chopped, and drained

1 8-ounce package refrigerated crescent rolls

¾ cup Monterrey Jack cheese, grated

¼ cup red onion, finely chopped

¼ cup green chiles, canned, chopped

¼ cup sour cream or non-fat yogurt

¼ cup Monterrey Jack cheese, shredded for topping

Aleppo pepper or paprika for garnish

Preheat oven to 375°F. Unroll crescent dough onto ungreased baking sheet. Separate into 4 rectangles; press diagonal seams to seal. Pull sides of rectangles slightly to enlarge. In a bowl, combine chicken, ¾ cup of cheese, onion, and chile; mix well. Divide chicken mixture into 4 portions; press into compact rectangles. Place the chicken in the center of dough rectangles. Fold long sides of each rectangle over filling, pressing at top to seal. Press ends to seal. Sprinkle pockets evenly with remaining cheese. Bake until golden brown, 13 to 16 minutes. Dust with paprika and serve with sour cream.

NOTE: Cooked turkey or roast beef can be substituted for the chicken.

ANATOLIAN STEW

I named this hearty stew Anatolian because the flavors remind me of the superb foods of Turkey. With a salad it is really a one-dish meal. Best prepared several days before eating so the flavors can meld.

Makes 8 Servings

            2   tablespoons olive oil
            1   medium-size red Bell Pepper, seeded and
                chopped
          1–2   jalapeños or serranos, seeded and chopped
            1   pound ground turkey or beef
            1   medium-size red onion, chopped
            1   28-ounce can Italian-style tomatoes, chopped,
                with liquid
            1   medium-size eggplant, peeled and cut into
                large dice
            ½   cup diced carrots
            ½   cup chopped celery
          3½   cups beef, chicken, or turkey broth
            1   tablespoon chopped fresh basil
            1   teaspoon salt
            1   teaspoon sugar
            ½   teaspoon ground nutmeg
            ½   cup uncooked pasta (small shells)
            2   tablespoons fresh parsley, chopped
          1–2   garlic clove, peeled and minced
                Grated Parmesan cheese for garnish

Heat oil in a large stockpot over medium high heat. Add Bell Peppers, and jalapeño, and onion; cook, stirring, until soft. Add meat and brown; drain off any fat. Add tomatoes, eggplant, carrots, celery, broth, basil, salt, sugar, and nut-meg. Bring to a boil and cover. Reduce heat to medium-low; simmer 1 to 1½ hours. Add pasta, parsley, and garlic; cover, and simmer until pasta is tender. This is a thick stew. Add hot water for desired thickness. Ladle into bowls and sprinkle with Parmesan. Serve with hot garlic toast and a green salad.

NOTE: Standing improves flavor.

TURKEY ENCHILADAS

Here is a tasty way to use left over turkey, chicken, or those "store bought" rotisserie chickens and your favorite salsa. Pace® is a flavorful one.

Makes 6 Servings

            3   cups turkey or chicken, cooked, skinned and
                shredded
            2   cups sour cream, low fat; try a Central America
                style sour cream (not low fat, available at some
                ethnic food stores)
            2   cups sharp cheddar, shredded
            ¼   cup onion, chopped
            1   teaspoon salt
            ⅓   cup canola or vegetable oil
           12   corn tortillas
            1   8-ounce jar salsa

Preheat oven to 350° F. In a bowl, mix fowl, sour cream, cheese, onion, and salt. Heat oil in a 10-inch frying pan over low heat. Dip tortillas, one at a time, in hot oil until just limp. (To avoid oil's fat, the tortillas can be softened in a microwave oven.) Fill each tortilla with an equal amount of meat mixture; roll up and arrange side by side, seam down, in a 9 x 13-inch baking dish. Pour salsa evenly over top. Bake in oven until thoroughly heated, about 20 minutes. If desired, sprinkle more shredded cheese over enchiladas and return to oven for a minute or two. Pass extra sour cream and sliced pickled jalapeños at the table.

CHICKEN PATTIES WITH TOMATO-BASIL RELISH

A tasty way to use one of those nice rotisserie chickens that can be had so handily in most food stores. When you get home with the chicken, remove skin and take the meat off the bone. What you don't use, package well and freeze for future chicken salad, a pasta dish, or more patties. Save bones and skin in freezer to make chicken broth.

Makes 8 Patties

- 3 cups chicken, cooked on rotisserie, both light and dark meat; skinned and chopped
- 1 cup Italian bread crumbs,
- ¼ cup mayonnaise, low fat
- ¼ cup pesto, prepared
- 1 egg, lightly beaten
- 2 teaspoons honey mustard
- ⅓ cup roasted red peppers, canned; drain and chop
- 1 teaspoon Aleppo pepper or ⅓ teaspoon cayenne pepper
- ⅓ cup red onion, finely chopped
- 2 tablespoons olive oil
- 1 package (5-ounce) mixed salad greens
- ⅓ cup balsamic vinegar and oil salad dressing, prepared
  Golden Aioli (recipe follows)
  Tomato Basil Relish (recipe follows)
- ⅓ cup basil pesto, prepared

In a large bowl place chicken, half of the bread crumbs, mayonnaise, egg, pesto, honey mustard, roasted peppers, Aleppo pepper, and onion; mix well. Using a ⅓ cup measure, shape chicken mixture into 8 patties; lightly coat each with remaining bread crumbs. In a large nonstick skillet, place oil and heat over medium high heat until a small test piece of bread turns golden. Add chicken; cook until golden brown, about 3 minutes per side; drain on paper towels. Toss salad greens with dressing; spread on a platter. Top greens with the chicken patties; drizzle each with Golden Aioli. Top each patty with dollop of Tomato-Basil Relish. Serve immediately.

GOLDEN AIOLI

- 1 tablespoon chipotle adobado purée
- ½ cup mayonnaise, low fat
- 2 tablespoons honey mustard

Place the chipotle, mayonnaise, and mustard in a small bowl; mix well.

TOMATO-BASIL RELISH:

- 1 cup Roma tomatoes, seeded and chopped
- ⅓ cup red onion, chopped
- 3 tablespoons sun-dried tomatoes, soaked in warm red wine, drained and chopped
- 2 tablespoons fresh basil leaves, slivered
- 2 tablespoons balsamic vinegar and oil dressing, prepared
- 1 teaspoon basil pesto, prepared

Place all of ingredients in a small bowl and mix well.

SOUTH TEXAS TURKEY WITH TAMALE DRESSING

Once upon a time a national magazine asked me to write a story on a Southwestern Christmas dinner. I told them I could write about a South Texas Christmas dinner, being a South Texan, but I knew little about what folks who lived in the Southwest did at Christmas. This turkey was the centerpiece of my story—it is really an easy way to make an outstanding dressing.

Makes—allow ½ pound per person

- 1 10 to 12 pound un-basted or butter-basted turkey, with neck and giblets
- 6–8 fresh red chiltepínes (use dry, if you must)
- 2½ dozen tamales with shucks removed (allow at least 3 for each guest)
- 3–4 tablespoons vegetable oil (more if necessary)

For the Gravy

- Giblets and neck from turkey
- 1 large onion, peeled and quartered
- 8–10 fresh basil leaves or 1 tablespoon dried basil
- 1 serrano or jalapeño, chopped
- 2 celery stems with leaves, chopped
- Salt and freshly ground black pepper to taste
- Water to cover
- ½ cup all-purpose flour (add more for a thicker gravy)

Preheat oven to 300°F. Thaw turkey thoroughly if frozen; remove giblets and neck; set aside. Wash turkey well, making certain cavity is clean; dry it with a clean cloth or paper towels. Place turkey breast-up on a cooking rack in a pan. Do not put any water in pan. With a larding needle or ice pick, make 6 to 8 evenly distributed deep holes in breast. Push 1 whole chiltepín into each hole as far as possible, as if you were larding meat.

Remove tamale shucks; break each tamale into about 3 pieces, being careful not to crumble them. Lightly fill both stomach and neck cavities with tamale pieces. Close cavities securely by sewing with cord and large needle (for example, a tapestry needle). Rub entire bird with some oil. Cut 4 pieces of aluminum foil large enough to wrap around each wing and drumstick to prevent them from overcooking and drying out. Mold a sheet or two of paper towels over turkey breast; saturate paper towel with remaining oil; use more if necessary. Next, mold a 12 inch square of foil over oil-saturated towel. This keeps skin from becoming hard and too brown.

Roast turkey in oven for 20 minutes per pound unstuffed, or 25 minutes stuffed. Remove toweling and foil during last hour of cooking so turkey will brown. A meat thermometer should register 180°F. When done, place it on a serving platter. Remove any stitching. Cover it with turkey baker lid or clean dish towels. The bird will slice better if it is allowed to sit covered while you prepare gravy and get the meal on the table.

NOTE: If you have the flavorful tropical herb *hoja santa* (*Piper auritun*) available, use large fresh leaves from the plant instead of tasteless paper toweling to cover the breast.

For Additional Dressing

If the number of tamales required for guests exceeds space in bird's cavity or if extra dressing is desired, layer those extra broken tamales in a square Pyrex dish and place dish on cooking rack directly under uncooked turkey (bird will be sitting on the extra tamales). In this position some turkey drippings will go into the tamales, infusing them with turkey flavor. Check tamales from time to time—you may need to remove them before bird is done so dressing doesn't become dry or overcooked.

Gravy

Place giblets, neck, onion, basil, chili peppers, celery, salt, and black pepper in a 1 quart saucepan; cover with water. Bring to a boil. Reduce heat; allow to simmer until you have a rich stock. Add more water as necessary to maintain a quart of liquid. (This may take an hour.) Remove meat when done; set it aside. Next, strain stock; put 1 cup in a blender with flour; process until smooth. Mix this with stock in saucepan. When turkey is done, remove as much melted fat from pan as possible; save all browned and caramelized drippings. Add a cup of hot water to pan; use a spoon to loosen browned juices; stir until dissolved. Add brown juices to flour and stock mixture in saucepan; they will give gravy a rich color and flavor. Place mixture over high heat until it boils; reduce heat; stir constantly until gravy reaches desired thickness. Season with salt and freshly ground pepper.

Alternative: Cornish game hens can be stuffed with tamales in the same manner.

IMPOSSIBLE POULTRY PIE

I didn't invent this but some years ago an imaginative home-maker found that baking mix poured over a pie filling would sink to the bottom of the pan and form a crust all by itself. Believe it or not!

Makes one 10-inch pie

    2   cups turkey or chicken, cooked and cut into
        bite-sized pieces
   14   ounce jar sliced mushrooms, drained
    ½   cup roasted red Bell Pepper, canned; chopped
    ½   cup scallions, chopped
    ½   teaspoon cayenne pepper
    ½   teaspoon salt
    1   cup Monterrey Jack cheese, grated
   1½   cup milk or non-fat plain yogurt
    ¾   cup Bisquick® buttermilk baking mix
    3   eggs

Preheat oven to 400°F. Lightly grease a 10-inch pie plate. Sprinkle the meat, mushrooms, red peppers, onions, salt, and cheese in pie plate. Place the remaining ingredients in a blender and pulse until smooth. Pour over ingredients already in pie plate. Bake until golden brown and knife inserted halfway between center and edges comes out clean, 30 to 35 minutes. Let stand 5 minutes before cutting. Refrigerate any remaining pie.

NOTE: Vegetarian pie: substitute 2 cups chopped fresh vegetables of your choice for the poultry.

CHICKEN TIKKA

Tikka is a Persian word used in Iran, Pakistan, and India for meat threaded on a skewer. Start this dish the day before you plan to cook it. It is so good and you won't believe how easy it is.

Makes 4 to 6 Servings

1	boneless chicken filet per serving
2	tablespoons white wine vinegar
¼	cup fresh lime juice
½–1	teaspoon ground cayenne pepper
½	teaspoon ground cumin
1	teaspoon turmeric
¼	cup cilantro leaves (fresh coriander), chopped
1½	teaspoons paprika
¼	cup fresh parsley, chopped
1	tablespoon ginger root, peeled and minced
1	cup low-fat plain yogurt
	Indian Mint Chutney (see Recipe P. 189) or any chutney

Place all ingredients, except chicken, in a blender and purée. Put chicken in a non-reactive bowl, pour blended ingredients over it and mix well. Cover and let marinate in refrigerator over night. Scrape off excess marinade; cook chicken on a charcoal grill 4 inches to 6 inches above coals but not directly over them. It can be threaded on a skewer. Cover; cook until tender. Serve with Indian Mint Chutney or any chutney. Tikka Masala, available at some Indian markets, can be substituted for the dry spices.

Seafood

SHRIMP PIPIÁN

From Fray Bernadino de Sahagún, the ancient Spanish chroni-cler, we learn that "the Aztec lords ate many kinds of casserole—one made of fowl with red chile and tomatoes, and ground squash seeds," a dish that is now called "pipián." My Spanish dictionary calls "pipian" an Indian fricassee. My English dictionary says a fricassee is "meat cut small, stewed, and served with gravy." It is pre-Columbian Mesoamerican in origin, but whatever it is, it is good. This one is done with shrimp, pepitas, and tomatoes.

Makes 6 Servings

For the Shrimp

2 pounds raw shrimp in their shells (about 25 to 30 to a pound)

1½ cups cold water

Shell and devein raw shrimp; wash them under cold run-ning water, pat dry with paper towels; set aside. Place shrimp shells in a 2- to 3-quart saucepan, add water, and bring to a boil over high heat. Reduce heat to low; sim-mer, uncovered, for about 15 minutes, or until liquid is re-duced to 1 cup. Strain stock through a sieve into a bowl; set aside. Discard shells.

For the Sauce

½ cup pepitas, toasted

3 medium-size tomatoes, peeled, seeded and coarsely chopped or 1 cup canned Italian plum tomatoes, drained

½ cup red onions, coarsely chopped

½ cup red Bell Pepper, seeded and coarsely chopped

6 dried chiltepínes crushed or 3 serranos or jalapeños seeded and chopped, or to taste

2 tablespoons cilantro (fresh coriander), chopped

1½ teaspoons ground coriander seeds

1 garlic clove, peeled and minced

½ teaspoon sugar

Salt and freshly ground black pepper to taste

3 tablespoons olive oil

2 tablespoons fresh lime juice

1 cup long-grain Basmati or brown rice cooked (3 cups)

Pepitas, whole, and fresh cilantro sprigs for garnish

Place pepitas in a blender; process until completely ground. Add tomatoes, onions, all peppers, cilantro, co-riander seeds, garlic, sugar, salt, and pepper; blend at high speed until mixture becomes a smooth purée. Heat oil in a heavy 10 to 12-inch skillet over medium heat; add shrimp; stir them in oil until they are pink and firm, about 2 to 3 minutes. Transfer shrimp to a plate. Add remaining oil to skillet; add sauce; cook, uncovered, over moderate heat, stirring frequently, for 5 minutes. Add cup of shrimp stock and lime juice; cook stirring, over low heat until heated through. Serve over cooked rice; garnish with pepitas and cilantro sprigs.

NOTE: Also great on chicken. Cook boneless chicken breasts on a grill or by your favorite method. In the sauce substitute chicken broth or one cup of hot water to which a teaspoon of chicken base has been added in place of shrimp stock.

SESAME-CRUSTED TUNA OR SALMON STEAKS

For a flavorful, crispy crust try sesame seed instead of the usual cornmeal or crumb coating before cooking any pan-fried/seared fish.

Makes 4 Servings

- ¾ cup sesame seeds (use a mix of white and black seed when possible)
- 4 tuna steaks, about 1 inch thick
- 2 tablespoons vegetable oil
- 1 tablespoon Aleppo pepper or red pepper flakes
  Salt and freshly ground black pepper

Spread sesame seed and Aleppo pepper in a 12-inch non-stick-skillet. Dry tuna steaks with paper towel; use 1 tablespoon oil to rub each side of fish; sprinkle with salt and pepper. Add remaining oil to skillet and heat. Add tuna; cook for ½ minute without moving fish. Reduce heat to medium-high; continue cooking 1½ minutes or until seeds are golden brown. With tongs, carefully turn tuna over; continue cooking until golden brown on second side. 1½ minutes for rare or 3-minutes for medium-rare. Check for doneness by nicking center with a paring knife. If more cooking is desired, remove from heat and leave in pan to allow residual heat to finish the job. Serve with Oriental Sauce, if desired. Recipe below.

ORIENTAL SAUCE FOR FISH

Makes 1 cup

- ¼ cup soy sauce
- ¼ cup rice vinegar
- ¼ cup water
- 2½ teaspoons granulated sugar
- 1 medium scallion, sliced thinly
- 2 teaspoons fresh ginger, minced
- 1½ teaspoons sesame oil, toasted
- 1 teaspoon Aleppo pepper or red pepper flakes

Combine all ingredients in a small bowl, stirring to dissolve sugar.

WRAPPED SHRIMP

The bacon-wrapped shrimp can be cooked in a skillet or on a grill and eaten prepared that way, but it is the tomatillo sauce that makes the difference.

Makes 4 Servings

- 24 jumbo shrimp, raw, peeled and deveined
- 1 cup Monterey Jack cheese, grated
- 5 jalapeños, cut into 24 thin slices
- 12 slices of bacon, cut in half, crosswise
  Toothpicks
- 2 tablespoons Canola oil
- 3–4 cups tomatillo sauce; recipe follows

Slice open shrimp along vein. Stuff opening with a small amount of cheese and a slice of jalapeño. Set aside remaining cheese. Wrap each shrimp in bacon; secure with a toothpick. In a large skillet, pour canola oil; place over medium heat. Add wrapped shrimp; sauté until bacon is lightly browned. Remove from skillet; drain on paper towels; place on serving plate. Pour sauce over shrimp; sprinkle with remaining cheese and serve immediately.

Tomatillo Sauce
- 1½ pounds tomatillos with husks removed
- 1 small onion, chopped

⅓ cup fresh cilantro, chopped

2 serranos, seeded and minced

1 garlic clove, peeled and minced

½ teaspoon cumin

1 teaspoon chipotle adobado, or more to taste

¼ cup tomato paste

salt and freshly ground black pepper, to taste

In a large sauce pan over medium heat, place tomatillos, onions, cilantro, serranos, garlic, cumin; barely cover with water; bring to a boil. Cook until tomatillos are soft to the touch, about 5 minutes; remove from heat. Add chipotle and tomato paste; whisk until it reaches a sauce-like consistency. Return pan to heat; simmer 2 minutes. Add salt and pepper to taste. If sauce is too thick add a little water. Serve with shrimp.

SHRIMP CREOLE

Most cooks tend to overcook this dish. Shrimp Creole is really just tenderly cooked shrimp in lightly stewed tomatoes with Creole seasoning. It must not be like a marinara sauce for pasta.

Makes 8 Servings

For the Shrimp Boil

1 small bunch celery with tops, chopped

1 large onion, quartered

12 bay leaves

4 cloves garlic, peeled and crushed

4 lemons, quartered

1 teaspoon ground cayenne pepper

4 tablespoons salt

1½–2 pounds medium-size shrimp; shells left on

For the Sauce

1 tablespoon olive oil

1 large onion, chopped

1 16-ounce can tomatoes or 12 large, ripe tomatoes; finely chopped

4 celery stalks, chopped

1–2 garlic cloves, peeled and minced

1 sprig fresh thyme or a pinch of dried

2 bay leaves

6 fresh basil leaves, chopped

½–1 teaspoon ground cayenne pepper or to taste

Put first seven ingredients into a 5-quart stock pot; cover with water. Boil for 10 minutes. Add shrimp (shells on); boil 10 minutes more, until shrimp are pink. Drain; peel shrimp; leave them whole; set aside. In a deep skillet or Dutch oven heat oil over medium heat; cook onion in oil. Add rest of ingredients; cook 20 minutes, stirring frequently. Add peeled shrimp; cook 10 minutes more. *Caution:* never pour water into stewed shrimp as tomato juice makes gravy enough. Remove bay leaves. Serve over steamed Basmati or brown rice.

BAKED FISH WITH YOGURT, INDIAN STYLE

Yogurt is a great accompaniment to dishes prepared with chili peppers because the casein reduces the degree of "burn." This Indian style sauce for your favorite fish—tuna, salmon, halibut, drum, red snapper—can be prepared ahead of cooking and serving time.

Makes 4 Servings

1	cup low fat yogurt, drained overnight; (see P. 44)
½	teaspoon ground turmeric
1	teaspoon ground cumin
1	teaspoon fresh ginger, grated
1	serrano, seeded and minced
1	garlic clove, peeled and minced
¼	cup fresh mint or dill, chopped
2	tablespoons fresh cilantro, chopped
2	tablespoons fresh lime juice
1½	pounds fish fillet

Place drained yogurt into bowl, add turmeric, cumin, ginger, serrano, garlic, mint, cilantro and lime juice; mix well. Let flavors blend for 30 minutes. If making ahead, cover; store in refrigerator; allow to come to room temperature. When ready to serve, preheat oven to 450°F. Line a baking dish that fits the fish with aluminum foil. Put fish in dish; spread ⅓ cup of the yogurt sauce on top. Bake for 12 minutes per inch of thickness, or until the fish tests done. Serve and pass yogurt sauce.

SHRIMP AMAL

Amal Naj, from India, is a former Wall Street Journal *writer and author of* Peppers: A Story of Hot Pursuits. *He and I have had fun cooking together and these succulent shrimp are one of the results. Prepare more than you'd planned because your guests will want seconds.*

Makes 4 Servings

4	tablespoons mustard oil or a vegetable oil
6	dried red chili peppers, Thai, japonés, de árbol
4	cinnamon sticks, broken
6	cardamom pods, crushed
6	whole cloves
1	teaspoon fresh ginger, peeled and chopped
3	bay leaves
1	pound large shrimp, shells left on
2–4	fresh green chili peppers; Thai, serrano
2	teaspoons cumin, ground
1	teaspoon turmeric
1	teaspoon salt
½	cup white wine

Heat the oil in a large, heavy skillet over medium heat. When oil starts to give off pungent vapor, toss in dried chili peppers, cinnamon, cardamom, and cloves. Stir until peppers begin to darken, add ginger and bay leaves. Stir with wooden spoon for 2 minutes. Raise heat to high; add shrimp; stir for two minutes. Add chopped green chili peppers, cumin, turmeric, and salt; stir for two minutes. Add wine; cover; cook over medium heat for 3 to 4 minutes. Serve shrimp immediately with shells on. These go well as an appetizer or as an accompaniment to another entrée served with steamed basmati or brown rice.

HOT ACAPULCO SHRIMP

From 1944 until 1966 I spent a lot of time in Mexico—much of it on the beach in "old Acapulco" (it's hard to find that beach today) where local vendors sold all sorts of foods from little thatched huts on the beach. My favorite were these succulent shrimp—so easy to prepare!

Makes 4 to 6 Servings

- 2 pounds raw jumbo shrimp with tails, shells left on
- 2 garlic cloves, peeled and crushed
- 1 teaspoon ground cayenne pepper, or more to taste
- ¼ cup fresh lime juice, preferably from Mexican *limones,* or Key limes
- ½ cup (1 stick) butter or margarine, melted

Split un-peeled, raw shrimp down the belly; be careful not to cut through the back. Butterfly each shrimp by spreading it open; remove the vein. Mix remaining ingredients with melted butter in a small bowl; hold each shrimp by tail; dip in mixture until coated. Spread opened shrimp on a cooking rack shell-side down. Cook until just pink on a charcoal grill or under broiler. Make a dip of same ingredients used on shrimp before cooking; serve in individual ramekins. Jean's Own Chutney (see Recipe P. 187) is nice with these shrimp as is Creamy Serrano Dressing (see Recipe P. 160).

4 VEGETABLES

CASSEROLES

SOUFFLÉS

Vegetable Dishes

GUJARATI CREAMED CORN

This unusual corn and coconut dish comes from exotic Gujarat, a state in India adjacent to Pakistan on the Indian Ocean— famous for its textiles and one of my favorite areas in India.

Makes 4 Servings

- 3 cups fresh or frozen corn kernels (1 lb)
- 2 cups milk
  Salt and freshly ground black pepper to taste
- 2 tablespoon canola or vegetable oil
- ½ teaspoon cumin seeds
- 2 serrano or jalapeño peppers, seeded and minced
- ½ inch piece of fresh ginger, peeled and grated
- ½ teaspoon ground turmeric
- 1 teaspoon Aleppo pepper
- 1 tablespoon butter
- 4 tablespoons fresh or dried coconut, grated
- 6 cilantro sprigs, chopped

Put corn and milk in a saucepan; cook over medium heat until milk is reduced to three-quarter original amount, stir frequently—30 to 40 min. Add salt to taste. Heat oil in a medium skillet over medium heat; toast cumin seeds. Add serranos, ginger, turmeric, Aleppo pepper, and corn mixture; mix well. Add butter, coconut and cilantro; mix well; cook just until well heated. Adjust seasoning.

GREEN-CORN TAMALES

These mouth-watering tamales are made with fresh white field corn, not sweet corn, and wrapped in the fresh, green, undried shucks. You have to eat them to believe how good they are.

Makes About 28 three-inch tamales

- green shucks from a dozen large ears of corn
- 5 cups fresh corn kernels (7 to 8 ears); if possible use dent (corn whose kernels contain both hard and soft endosperm and become indented at maturity) or flint corn (corn having long kernels composed primarily of hard endosperm)
- ½ cup margarine
- ¾ cup Monterey Jack cheese, cubed
- ¾ cup mild Cheddar cheese, cubed
- 1¼ cup masa harina
- 1½ teaspoon salt
- 6 large Long Green chiles, roasted, seeded, peeled and chopped or 24-ounce can chopped green chiles
- ¾ cup chicken stock (this may not be needed)

In the field, when milk in corn sets it is called "green-corn," the first edible corn-on-the-cob stage of soft Indian corn, dent corn, or flint corn. It is never a sweet corn such as 'Golden Bantam.' Buy a few extra ears of corn in order to have enough good shucks. If you must use sweet corn, add 1 teaspoonful of corn starch for each ear of corn because field corn has much more starch than sweet corn.

With a cleaver, chop off stem end of corn; remove ugly outer shucks. Carefully remove the others to keep shucks whole. Using kitchen scissors, trim pointed ends of each shuck. To make shucks more pliable, some tamale makers bring a pot of water to a boil, drop shucks in and turn heat off, leaving them in the hot water until they are ready to be filled; this may not be needed with green shucks. Shucks are removed from water and drained. Shucks should not dry out before being filled. Unlike regular tamales that use dry shucks, the masa is not spread on fresh shucks. Leave the last several husks on the extra corn to keep it from drying out before you use it.

Hold each ear in a deep bowl; cut the kernels from 7 to 8 ears, enough to have 5 cups. Cream the margarine in a food processor, taking care to scrape sides of the bowl several times. Add 4 cups of corn, cheese, masa, salt, and a little stock if mixture is too thick (it must not be runny. Type of corn used will determine consistency). Blend until smooth. Coarse chop reserved cup of cut corn; mix it and chili peppers into the smooth mixture; do not process again.

To Fill Shucks: Spread a husk out so that it will curl over filling. Place about 2½ tablespoons of filling in center of shuck lengthwise. Fold sides in over filling; then fold ends up. Stand tamales in a steamer or colander, folded ends down. Place steamer or colander in a pot with enough water to come just below bottom of steamer. Tamales should not be standing in water. Cover and place over high heat. When the water comes to a boil; lower heat to a simmer; steam tamales for about 1 hour. Take care to not let steamer run out of water. Using tongs, transfer tamales from steamer to a serving platter; serve hot. Serve with a table sauce such as: salsa cruda (see Recipe P. 144), or salsa verde (see Recipe P. 154).

NOTE: Tamales freeze well if wrapped properly. Put cool tamales in a plastic bag, close tightly. Wrap in freezer paper and seal. Label and date package.

CARAMELIZED ONIONS

Caramelized onions are a very "in" thing! Use them in sandwiches, scrambled eggs, sauces, casseroles, tarts, pasta, on potatoes, in salads, in fact—they make almost any ordinary dish a very special creation.

Makes 1 Cup

 1 tablespoon vegetable oil
 1 tablespoon unsalted butter
 ½ teaspoon light brown sugar
 ½ teaspoon salt
 2 pounds onions, Spanish or yellow; peeled and sliced ¼-inch thick
 1 tablespoon water
 1 teaspoon Aleppo or ancho pepper, ground
   Freshly ground black pepper, to taste

In a 12-inch nonstick skillet place oil and butter; heat over high heat; when foam subsides, stir in sugar and salt. Add onions; stir until well coated; cook, stirring occasionally, until onions begin to soften and release steam, about 5 minutes. Reduce heat to medium; cook, stirring frequently, until onions are caramel color and slightly sticky, about 40 minutes longer. **Watch carefully** and raise or lower heat as needed so that they brown, not burn. Remove from heat; stir in water; season to taste with red chili peppers. They will keep for a week in the refrigerator in an airtight container.

NOTE: After the onions are well coated with the oils and sugar some of the cooking can be done in the microwave in 5 minute intervals. Cook 5 minutes; stir well; repeat 4 or 5 times. This will make the cooking time on the stove shorter and less likely to burn the onions.

BAKED SERRANO GRITS

This dish can be made the day before and baked while you are grilling the steaks, chicken, or fish to serve it with.

Makes 12 portions

   2   serranos, seeded and minced
   6   garlic cloves, peeled and minced
   3   tablespoons olive oil
1½   cups buttermilk
1½   cups heavy cream
   1   cup water
       Salt and freshly ground black pepper to taste
   1   cup dry grits or quinoa
   2   tablespoons butter
   ¾   cups Monterey Jack cheese, grated

Place serranos, garlic and oil in a two quart sauce pan until lightly browned. Add buttermilk, cream, water, and grits or quinoa; season with salt and pepper. Simmer over low heat, stirring occasionally to prevent sticking. When grits have thickened, add cheese and butter and stir to mix well. Spread the mixture evenly 1 inch thick on a sheet pan and chill in refrigerator to set. When ready to use, preheat oven to 400°F. Cut into 12 portions. Place cut grits on a greased sheet pan and bake until toasted, about 20 minutes.

ARTICHOKE-RED PEPPER BREAD PUDDING

This isn't bread pudding like my grandma used to make, but it is good!

Makes 8 Servings

   4   tablespoons butter
   2   9-ounce packages frozen artichoke hearts, thawed
   4   green onions, finely chopped
   ½   cup red Bell Pepper, diced
   ½   teaspoon thyme, dried
   ½   teaspoon salt
   ¾   pound crusty bread, cut into 1-inch cubes
   ¾   cup Gruyère or Monterrey Jack cheese
   5   cups milk, lactose free or soy milk can be used
   5   large eggs
   4   egg yolks
   ½   teaspoon freshly ground black pepper
   ⅓   cup Parmesan cheese, shredded
       Red Bell Pepper rings for garnish

Preheat oven to 350°F. In a large, non-reactive skillet over moderately high heat, melt butter; add artichoke hearts, onions, Bell Pepper, thyme and salt; cook until onions soften, stirring frequently; about 5 minutes. Set aside. In a 9 x 13-inch baking dish, spread bread cubes. Pour artichoke and cheese mixture over bread cubes; mix well. In a bowl, whisk milk with eggs, egg yolks, pepper and salt. Pour milk mixture over the bread in baking dish; sprinkle with Parmesan. Set baking dish in a large roasting pan; add enough hot water to roasting pan to reach halfway up the sides of baking dish. Bake for about 50 minutes, or until custard is set and top of pudding is browned. Garnish with pepper rings; let cool slightly before serving.

VINITA'S NEW POTATOES WITH POPPY SEED

When I studied Indian cookery with Vinita, who is from Madras, India, she was a graduate student at the University of Texas at Austin. You'll never settle for plain "hash browns" again!

Makes 6 Servings

- 1–2 tablespoons vegetable oil
- 6 medium new potatoes, un-peeled, cubed
- 2–3 dried red chili peppers, crumbled (de Árbol, japonés, Thai)
- 1½ tablespoons white poppy seed (available in Indian food market)
- ½ teaspoon turmeric powder
- ½ teaspoons ground cayenne pepper
- 1–2 serranos or jalapeños, minced
- 1 cup hot water

Heat oil in a large saucepan over medium heat. Add potatoes and cook, stirring, until golden. Remove potatoes from oil; set aside. To same oil, add dry chili peppers and poppy seed. When lightly browned, return potatoes to pan. Add turmeric, cayenne, salt, serranos, and water. Simmer over medium heat until potatoes are tender and most of the water is absorbed. This is quite hot, so use less chili peppers if desired.

COUSCOUS-STUFFED EGGPLANT

I can't recall the origin of this dish, but it is so good it does not matter. Just enjoy!

Makes 4 Servings

- 4 small Italian or Asian eggplants
- 3 cups semolina couscous, cooked
- 3 Roma tomatoes, diced
- 1 tablespoon roasted red pepper, canned, chopped
- 3 garlic cloves, peeled and minced
- ¼ cup pine nuts, toasted
- 2 tablespoons fresh cilantro, chopped
- ½ jalapeño, seeded and chopped
- 1 tablespoon fresh lemon juice
- 1 teaspoon cumin, ground
  Salt and freshly ground black pepper, to taste

Preheat oven to 425°F. Prick eggplant with a fork; place on a flat baking pan and bake until soft, 20–25 minutes. When cool enough to handle, cut in half lengthwise; scoop out flesh; place in a large bowl. Reserve eggplant shells. Place remaining ingredients in bowl; stir to combine. Season with salt and pepper. Mound mixture in eggplant shells; keep warm in oven until ready to serve. Sprinkle with paprika.

NOTE: Try substituting quinoa for the couscous.

QUINOA WITH ROASTED PEPPERS AND EGGPLANT

Here's another way to serve quinoa—that nutritious, tasty Andean grain.

Makes 4 Servings

　　5　cups eggplant, peeled, cut in 1-inch cubes
　　¾　teaspoon salt, divided
　1½　cups red Bell Pepper, seeded and chopped
　1½　cups yellow Bell Pepper, seeded and chopped
　　1　serrano pepper, seeded and chopped
　　2　cups red onion, chopped
　　2　tablespoons olive oil, divided
　　　　Cooking spray
　　¼　teaspoon freshly ground black pepper
　　1　whole head garlic, papery skin removed but un-peeled
　　1　teaspoon Aleppo or red pepper flakes
　　1　teaspoon ground cumin
　　½　teaspoon ground turmeric
　　½　teaspoon ground ginger
　　2　cups chicken broth, home made, canned or from chicken base
　　1　cup quinoa, uncooked
　　2　tablespoons fresh parsley, chopped
　　1　tablespoon fresh lemon juice

Preheat oven to 450°F. Place eggplant in a colander. Sprinkle with ½ teaspoon salt; let stand 20 minutes. Drain; pat dry with paper towels. In a large bowl, combine eggplant, all peppers, onion, and 1 tablespoon oil; toss well. Coat a jelly-roll pan with cooking spray; spread eggplant mixture over pan evenly. Sprinkle with remaining salt and black pepper. Cut off and discard top ¼-inch of garlic head. Rub bottom of garlic head with ¼ teaspoon olive oil. Place garlic head with cut side up in middle of eggplant mixture. Bake for 40 minutes or until vegetables are browned; stir occasionally.

In a large Dutch oven on medium-high heat, heat 1 tablespoon olive oil. Add cumin, turmeric, ginger, red pepper flakes, and chicken broth. Bring to a boil. Stir in quinoa; cover; reduce heat; simmer for 20 minutes or until grain is tender and liquid is absorbed. Remove garlic from eggplant mixture. Separate garlic cloves; squeeze to extract pulp. Discard skins. Stir pulp, eggplant mixture, parsley, and lemon juice into quinoa mixture. Serve hot or at room temperature. Garnish with lemon slices and/or fresh parsley.

ONIONS STUFFED WITH CHILI PEPPERS AND CRUMBS

In the vast farming region of the Texas Rio Grande Valley a delicious, sweet onion was developed recently. It is known as '10–15' because in the semi-tropical valley where it originated it must be planted by October 15. Try them, they are super.

Makes 4 Servings

　　4　large sweet yellow onions, 10 to 16 ounces each
　　¾　cup dry bread crumbs
　　½　cup celery, chopped
　　¼　cup yellow corn meal
　　¼　cup butter or margarine, melted
　　2　teaspoons chili powder, Gebhardt's® preferred
　　2　teaspoons oregano
　　½　cup water
　　　　Paprika for garnish

Preheat oven to 400°F. Cut a thin slice from root end of onion. Leaving skin on, cut off a slice about ¾-inch from stem end of onion. With small knife or apple corer, scoop out onion; reserve to use in stuffing. Use a spoon as needed to make a ½-inch thick shell. Do not cut through bottom of shell. Each large onion will hold about ¾ cup of stuffing. Finely chop enough reserved onion to measure 1½ cups. In a bowl, mix chopped onion with remaining ingredients except water. Place onions in baking dish. Spoon filling into shells, mounding it up. Add water to baking dish and cover. Bake until onions are tender, about 35 to 40 minutes. Garnish with paprika.

NOTE: The onion can be prepared ahead and kept refrigerated until ready to bake. Let come to room temperature before baking.

MY GARDEN RATATOUILLE

Gardeners will love this way to use their produce. It freezes beautifully. In a trip to Indonesia I was served a delicious ratatouille made with those cucumbers that get too big and turn yellow—try it.

Makes 4 to 6 Servings

- 1 large eggplant, peeled and cut into 1-inch cubes
- 1 6-inch-long zucchini, cut into 1-inch cubes
- ¼ cup olive oil
- 2 medium-size onions, finely chopped
- 6 ripe tomatoes, peeled and cut up
- 1 Bell Pepper, seeded and chopped
- 1 jalapeño or serrano, seeded and chopped
- 1 garlic clove, peeled and minced
- 1 tablespoon chopped fresh parsley
- 1 bay leaf
- 1 tablespoon Worcestershire sauce
- Salt and freshly ground black pepper to taste

In a large sauce pan over medium heat, boil eggplant and zucchini in water to cover; or microwave until just tender; drain. Heat oil in a large saucepan over medium heat. Add onions; cook, stirring, until browned. Stir in remaining ingredients; simmer until juices are cooked down and mixture is semi-dry. Allow to cool. Serve next day either hot or at room temperature.

NOTE: Usually squash does not freeze well but this does when sealed in freezer containers.

PEPPERONATA

Tired of plain old potatoes—try this for a change.

Makes 4 Servings

- ¼ cup olive oil
- 1 large onion, coarsely chopped
- 1 garlic clove, peeled and minced
- 2 large new potatoes, peeled and cubed (More nutritious un-peeled)
- 2 large, ripe tomatoes, peeled, seeded, and cut into large chunks
- 3 large Bell Peppers of several colors, seeded and julienned
- 1 jalapeño, seeded and chopped
- ¼ teaspoon dried thyme, crumbled
- ½ teaspoon dried basil
- ½ teaspoon ground cayenne pepper, or to taste

In a large skillet, heat oil over medium heat. Add onion and garlic; cook, stirring, until onion is limp. Stir in potatoes; cover, cook 10 minutes, stirring occasionally. Stir in remaining ingredients, cover, and cook 10 minutes longer, until the potatoes and peppers are crisp-tender.

CANARY ISLAND POTATO TORTILLA OR TORTA

This is not the kind of corn tortilla Americans associate with that word, it is more like an omelet and is one of the most popular dishes in Spain, of which the Canary Islands are a distant part. They are usually served at room temperature but can be served hot. Tortas are a favorite lunch or tapa. For a main course add chopped, cooked ham, chicken, or beef and top with cheese if desired. Return to oven to melt the cheese.

Makes 4 Servings

  1 pound new potatoes or ¼ pound per serving, peeled and diced
  ¼ cup olive oil
  1 cup onion, finely chopped or ¼ cup per serving
  ½ cup red Bell Pepper, chopped
  5 large eggs, separated; add 2 eggs for each additional serving
     Salt and freshly ground black pepper
     Dash of cayenne pepper

In a large sauce pan, boil potatoes until just tender; drain and set aside. In a large, heavy skillet, heat oil over medium heat; add onions and Bell Pepper; cook until onions and pepper are soft but not brown; stir occasionally. Drain onions and Bell Pepper in a strainer over a bowl, reserving the oil. Put onions and Bell Pepper in the container with drained potatoes; mix carefully. In a large bowl, whip egg whites with a wire whisk until slightly stiff. In another small bowl beat egg yolks with salt, black pepper and cayenne; fold them into egg whites. Pour blended eggs over vegetable mixture, mix gently; let stand 10–15 minutes. Wipe out skillet; add 2 tablespoons of reserved oil to coat pan; then heat oil over moderate heat. Pour egg mixture into skillet; spread it evenly over the bottom. Cook over moderate heat; shake pan occasionally to prevent sticking. When bottom of tortilla begins to brown, place a plate over it; invert pan; slide tortilla onto plate. Add a little more oil to pan; heat it. Return tortilla to heated pan with brown side up. Cook just long enough to brown underside. Transfer tortilla to a warmed plate; serve hot or at room temperature. Cut into 4 wedges for a main course or into smaller wedges for *tapas*. Serve with *mojo rojo* sauce (see Recipe P. 147).

CHEESE GRITS WITH LONG GREEN CHILES

Jean's version of an old Southern favorite.

Makes 12 Servings

  6 cups water or chicken stock
  1½ cups instant grits
  2 teaspoons salt
  1 teaspoon paprika
  1 teaspoon cayenne pepper
  3 large eggs
  1 pound sharp cheddar cheese, grated (try a mixture with Jack or chèvre)
  1 4-ounce can Long Green chiles chopped

Bring water to a boil in a large sauce pan; stir in grits gradually. Cover; cook until thickened. Stir occasionally to prevent sticking. Add salt, paprika, and pepper sauce. In a large mixing bowl, beat eggs lightly. Add a small amount of hot grits to eggs; stir constantly so eggs do not cook. Gradually stir in remaining grits. Add grated cheese and chiles. Pour into a buttered 2-quart casserole and bake for 45 minutes. Serve immediately.

CHEF GREWAL'S KHATTA ALOO (POTATOES)

Chef Grewal was my cookery teacher in Aurangabad, India where I learned about these potatoes. Indians have a special way with potatoes.

Makes 4 Servings

 2 tablespoons vegetable oil
⅛ teaspoon cumin seeds
⅛ teaspoon caraway seed
½ teaspoon ground cumin/comino seed
⅛ teaspoon ground coriander
 1 small purple/red onion, chopped finely
 1 garlic clove, minced
 1 serrano or jalapeño, chopped finely
 1 teaspoon ginger root, peeled and minced
 1 teaspoon turmeric
½–1 teaspoon ground cayenne pepper
 1½ cups diced new potatoes, boiled until tender, un-peeled
 2 tablespoon cilantro (fresh coriander) leaves, chopped
 2 tablespoons mint leaves, chopped
 Juice of 1 lime
 Salt and freshly ground black pepper to taste

Heat oil in a heavy skillet over medium-high heat. Add cumin seeds, caraway, ground cumin, and coriander; stir until fragrant. Add onion, garlic, serrano, and ginger; sauté until soft. Add turmeric, and cayenne; mix well. Add potatoes, cilantro, and mint and lime juice; stir to mix. Season with salt and black pepper. Heat thoroughly. Serve with grilled meats or as you would hash browned potatoes.

Alternate: Cauliflower, cooked *al dente,* is exciting prepared this way.

WRINKLED POTATOES WITH MOJO ROJO-PAPAS ARRUGADAS

These rather dry, small potatoes are served with almost every meal in the Canary Islands. They use a small, white potato with a slight brown skin, but unless you have access to a specialty market, use golf ball size red or new potatoes. Sea salt with large crystals is the secret. The potatoes are prepared ahead and served at room temperature. Use the traditional Canary island sauces: green or red mojo (see Recipe P. 147) or the ever present garlic sauce (see Recipe P. 146.

Makes 4 servings

3–4 golf ball size new potatoes per person, washed well
 ½ cup sea salt crystals

Place potatoes in a large saucepan; fill with water that does not completely cover potatoes; add salt. Boil over high heat until tender, about 20 or 30 minutes. Drain water from saucepan; return drained potatoes to heat. Dry them, tossing occasionally, until salt forms a light crust on skin. Remove from pan; cut if large; place on serving dish. These are traditionally served at room temperature as an accompaniment to meat dishes with *Mojo Rojo, Mojo Verde,* or To Die For Garlic Sauce. Try them with caramelized onions (see Recipe P. 127).

Casseroles

CHIPOTLE HOMINY CASEROLE

In the Deep South hominy has been looked upon as 'po' folks' food but don't let that put you off. It kept southerners of all classes alive during and after the American Civil War. Hominy is mature, hard, whole corn grains soaked in a lye solution to soften them, then the outer hulls removed, a process which improves the nutritional value (see Masa P. 37). When dried and ground, hominy becomes grits. Today it is principally a canned vegetable; few make it the traditional way.

Makes 6 to 8 Servings

    2 tablespoons corn or canola oil
    ½ medium red onion, chopped
    ½ red Bell Pepper, chopped
    ½ yellow Bell Pepper, chopped
    3 garlic cloves, minced
    1 teaspoon dried oregano
    1 teaspoon cumin seeds
    ½ chipotle chili pepper in adobo, puréed or chopped (more to taste)
    1 15½-ounce can diced tomatoes in juice
    2 15½-ounce cans white hominy, rinsed and drained
    1 cup chicken or vegetable broth
    1 lime, juiced
    2 tablespoons fresh cilantro, minced

Salt and freshly ground black pepper to taste
    ½ cup Monterey jack cheese, shredded
    Low fat sour cream or plain yogurt at room temperature, 1 tablespoon per serving
    Avocado slices for garnish

Preheat oven to 350°F. In a large non-reactive saucepan over medium heat place oil, peppers, garlic, oregano, and cumin seeds; cook until slightly softened; about 3 minutes. Add chipotle, tomatoes with juice, hominy, and broth; bring to a boil; reduce heat and simmer uncovered for 35 minutes. Add lime juice, cilantro; season with salt and pepper. Pour into an oven-proof casserole; sprinkle cheese on top; melt cheese in oven or in microwave oven. Serve with sour cream or yogurt; garnish with avocado slices.

COMFORT-FOOD CASSEROLE

I can remember when people made fun of our southern grits, or said "grits, what's that?" or just gagged. No more! Polenta, move over! Innovative, high-brow chefs have discovered grits and are mixing everything with them. But I still love plain grits swimming in a pool of butter.

Makes 6 to 8 Servings

    1 small onion (6-ounce), peeled and diced
    1 tablespoon butter or bacon drippings
    1 7-ounce can Long Green chiles, diced

2 cups chicken broth, fat-skimmed or broth made
  of chicken base like Better than Bouillon'

1 cup instant grits

1½ cups sour cream or yogurt (regular, reduced-fat,
  or nonfat)

Aleppo pepper or cayenne pepper, to taste

Salt and freshly ground black pepper to taste

Paprika for garnish

In a 4 to 5-quart non-reactive saucepan over high heat, melt butter; add onion; cook while stirring until golden, 3 to 4 minutes. Add green chiles, chicken broth, grits and sour cream; stir until boiling; reduce heat and simmer; stir often until mixture is thick, about 5 minutes. Season with salt and peppers. Pour into a shallow 2-quart casserole. Garnish with paprika. When ready to serve, reheat casserole in oven or on turntable in a microwave oven at full power until hot in center, 5–10 minutes.

NOTE: The casserole may be made a day or two ahead and kept covered in the refrigerator. Bring to room temperature before warming.

THE RAJA'S TOMATO CASSEROLE

This luscious casserole from India can be made with peeled fresh or canned whole Roma or plum tomatoes.

Makes 6 to 8 Servings

2 12-ounce cans of peeled whole plum tomatoes
  or 2 pounds fresh peeled Roma tomatoes

1 large red onion, peeled and chopped

1 fresh serrano or jalapeño pepper, seeded and
  chopped; or to taste

1 tablespoon canola oil, in India olive oil is
  not traditional

⅛ teaspoon cardamom seed, crushed

½ teaspoon cumin seed

2 teaspoons fresh ginger, minced

1 tablespoon mustard seed

2 tablespoons fresh lemon, including peel,
  finely chopped

1 teaspoon curry powder

½ teaspoon cayenne pepper

¼ cup fresh lemon juice

2 tablespoons granulated sugar

¾ cup fresh cilantro, chopped

Salt and freshly ground black pepper, to taste

Preheat oven to 375°F. Drain tomatoes, reserving juice. Arrange tomatoes in a single layer in a shallow 9 or 10-inch casserole. Measure 2 cups of reserved tomato juice; if less than 2 cups add water. Reserve any extra juice for other uses. In a 10 to 13-inch frying pan, combine onion, serrano pepper, oil, cardamom seed, cumin seed, ginger, mustard seed, and chopped lemon. Stir over high heat until onion is limp, 3 to 4 minutes. Stir in curry powder and add tomato juice, lemon juice, sugar, and ¼ cup cilantro. Boil, stirring occasionally, until mixture is reduced to 3 cups, about 5 minutes. Pour over tomatoes in casserole. Bake in oven until sauce is slightly reduced and flavors are well blended, about 45 minutes. Baste tomatoes with juices and gently mix in remaining cilantro. Add salt and pepper to taste. Serve hot or at room temperature.

NOTE: In Indian and Pakistani homes, most food is served at room temperature.

RICE AND GREEN CHILE CASSEROLE

David Durham, a private chef in Austin, Texas, claims his dish can be a meal unto itself when served with a favorite salad.

Makes 10 Servings

- ¼ cup butter or margarine
- 2 cloves garlic, peel, mash, and sauté
- 1 cup white onion, sautéd with garlic until soft
- 1 cup small curd, low-fat cottage cheese
- 2 cups low-fat sour cream
- ½ cup fresh parsley, chopped
- 4 cups cooked brown, basmati, or wild rice
- 1 12-ounce can Long Green chiles, chopped
- 2 cups sharp cheddar cheese, grated

Preheat oven to 375° F. Grease a 13 x 9-inch baking dish or casserole. Put butter in a large skillet; melt over medium heat. Add garlic and onions; cook until soft; stir frequently. Remove from heat. To skillet, add cottage cheese, sour cream, parsley, and rice; mix well. In a baking dish, alternate 2 layers of rice mixture, green chiles, and cheddar cheese. Bake for 25 minutes, or until hot and bubbly.

NOTE: Can be prepared day before and refrigerated un-baked. To bake before serving, remove from refrigerator and allow to come to room temperature. Bake as directed above.

SPINACH CASSEROLE

Spinach is not only good for you, but after this casserole you will find it is also tasty.

Makes 4 to 6 Servings

- 2 tablespoons butter
- 1 cup onion, chopped
- 2 garlic clove, peeled and minced
- 2 pounds fresh spinach, washed, stemmed, and chopped
- 2 eggs, beaten
- 1 cup milk or plain non-fat yogurt
- 1½ cups cheddar cheese, grated
- ½ teaspoon nutmeg
- ½ teaspoon cayenne pepper
- ½ teaspoon paprika
- Red Bell Pepper rings for garnish

Preheat oven to 350°F. Melt butter in a 2 quart saucepan with cover. Add onions and garlic; sauté over moderate heat until onions are soft. Add spinach, cover and cook 2 to 4 minutes, stirring occasionally, until spinach wilts. Place eggs in large mixing bowl; beat lightly. Add milk, cheddar cheese, nutmeg, salt and cayenne to eggs; beat to blend. Add spinach mixture; stir to blend. Place entire spinach mixture into buttered 1½–2 quart casserole; sprinkle with paprika. Cover with red Bell Pepper rings. Bake, uncovered, 35 minutes.

Soufflés

TWICE-BAKED GOAT CHEESE SOUFFLÉ

Even amateur cooks can make these soufflés.

Makes 8 Ramekins

- 3 tablespoons butter, plus butter for coating ramekins
- 1 cup dry bread crumbs, or wheat thin cracker crumbs, shredded wheat crumbs
- 3 tablespoons cake flour or sauce and gravy flour (Wondra®)
- 1 cup milk or use a lactose free, low-fat milk, or soy milk
- 10 ounces goat cheese, chèvre, chavrie, or feta, crumbled
- 3 egg yolks
- 1 teaspoon Aleppo pepper or ¼ teaspoon cayenne pepper
    Salt and freshly ground black pepper, to taste
- 7 egg whites

Arrange rack in center of oven; preheat oven to 425°F. Butter eight 5-ounce ramekins, coat well. Fill each ramekin with crumbs; turn them over; tap out excess. Reserve any remaining breadcrumbs. Melt 3 tablespoons of butter in a non-reactive sauce pan over medium-high heat. Whisk in flour; cook for 20 seconds, whisking constantly. Whisk in milk gradually; cook for about 1 minute,

whisking constantly, until mixture has thickened to consistency of a thin, pouring pudding. Crumble 8 ounces of goat cheese into a large mixing bowl. Pour hot milk mixture over goat cheese; mix well. Add egg yolks; mix well. Season with salt and peppers.

Using an electric mixer, beat egg whites in a large bowl until stiff peaks form. Fold half of whites into cheese mixture to lighten it. Then gently fold in remaining whites. Divide half of soufflé mixture among prepared ramekins. Crumble remaining 2 ounces of goat cheese over each ramekin; top each equally with remaining soufflé mixture. Place ramekins in a large baking pan; pour boiling water in pan halfway up sides of ramekins. Bake 25 minutes or until golden. Remove from oven; let stand in water bath 15 minutes. Run a knife around inside rim to loosen; carefully turn each soufflé onto a baking sheet. Soufflés may be held at room temperature for up to 6 hours before final baking.

To Serve: When ready to serve, preheat oven to 425°F; bake soufflés in oven for 5 to 7 minutes, or until deep golden brown. Serve as an appetizer, on a plate of baby salad greens tossed with Bell Pepper Vinaigrette (see Recipe P. 138) with Melba toast or toasted French bread, or serve as a side-dish with the main course.

PECAN, TWICE-BAKED, THREE-CHEESE SOUFFLÉS

These individual soufflés are not the usual fragile soufflé, these are designed to fall and puff up again with the second baking. That means they can be made in advance, even the day before. Serve one on the plate with a salad.

Makes 12 Servings

    Butter for coating ramekins
½ cup pecans, finely chopped. Walnuts may be used
4 tablespoons unsalted butter
¼ cup all-purpose flour
1 cup milk
2½ cups heavy cream or non-fat plain yogurt
4 ounces goat cheese, (chèvre), crumbled, about 1 cup
10 large egg yolks, lightly beaten
2 ounces Roquefort or Bleu cheese, crumbled (about ½ cup)
1½ ounces Gruyere cheese, grated
½ teaspoon cayenne pepper
    Salt and freshly ground white pepper, to taste
8 large egg whites, beaten with a pinch of salt until almost firm

Preheat oven to 350°F. Butter the ramekins. Put chopped pecans in each ramekin; rotate so that pecans adhere to butter. Put excess in next ramekin; continue until all are coated. Set aside. In a medium saucepan, melt butter over moderate heat. Whisk in flour until smooth. Gradually whisk in milk; 1 cup of heavy cream until smooth; bring to a boil, whisking constantly. Reduce heat to low and simmer, whisking, for 5 minutes. Remove from heat; stir in goat cheese. Scrape sauce into a large bowl; let cool, stirring occasionally. Beat egg yolks into cool sauce. Stir in Roquefort and ½ cup of Gruyere. Season with salt and peppers. In a large stainless steel bowl, beat egg whites with a pinch of salt until almost firm. Using a rubber spatula, fold one-third of the beaten whites into cheese sauce; fold in remaining whites until just blended. Gently spoon soufflé mixture into prepared ramekins; fill each three-fourths full. Set ramekins on a baking sheet. Run your thumb around rim of each to clean. Pour 2 tablespoons of remaining cream over each soufflé and sprinkle with remaining Gruyere. Bake soufflés for 8 to 10 minutes, or until puffed and golden brown. Serve immediately or set aside until next day; bake a second time at same temperature before serving. Serve on side of plate of fresh mixed baby greens called mesclun, tossed with Bell Pepper Vinaigrette.

BELL PEPPER VINAIGRETTE

2 tablespoons balsamic vinegar
¼ cup extra-virgin olive oil
¼ cup red Bell Pepper, finely chopped
¼ cup yellow Bell Pepper, finely chopped
    Salt and freshly ground black pepper, to taste

Put vinegar, oil, salt and pepper in a bowl; whip with a fork to mix. Add Bell Peppers and mix well. Serve over salad greens.

CHÈVRE AND GARDEN HERB SOUFFLÉ

When made as an individual soufflé in half-cup sized dishes and served on the side of a tossed salad plate they make a tasty lunch dish.

Makes 4 Servings

- ¼ cup Parmesan cheese, freshly grated
- 4 tablespoons butter, unsalted
- ½ cup all-purpose flour
- 2 cups milk
- 1 bay leaf
- ½ pound fresh Chèvre (goat cheese), crumbled
  Salt and freshly ground black pepper to taste
- 4 large eggs, separated
- 2 tablespoons chives, minced
- 1 tablespoon fresh parsley, minced
- 1 tablespoon fresh dill, minced
- 2 tablespoons fresh tarragon, minced
- 1 tablespoon Aleppo pepper

Preheat oven to 375°F. Butter a 2 quart soufflé dish. Add Parmesan; turn to evenly coat bottom and side of dish.

Shake out any excess. In a medium saucepan, melt butter over moderate heat. Add flour; whisk until a smooth paste forms. Whisk in 1 cup of milk until smooth; gradually whisk in remaining milk; add bay leaf. Bring sauce to a boil, whisking constantly. Reduce heat to low; cook until thick, whisking frequently; about 10 minutes. Transfer to a large bowl. Stir in Chèvre; season with salt and pepper. Add egg yolks and whisk. Cover; let cool; stir in herbs and Aleppo pepper.

In a large stainless steel bowl, beat egg whites with a pinch of salt until firm but not dry. Fold one-third of beaten whites into cheese sauce. Fold in remaining whites, leaving a few white streaks. Scrape mixture into baking dish; bake in the center of oven for 45 minutes, or until browned, puffed and still able to jiggle in center. Serve at once.

NOTE: The soufflé base can be prepared up to point of adding egg yolks, without adding herbs, and refrigerated overnight. Bring it to room temperature; stir in herbs before folding in beaten egg white.

5 SAUCES

SPREADS

DRESSINGS

PESTOS

Sauces

This introduction was in my book *The Pepper Trail* but it bears repeating.

Sauces are described as every kind of liquid or semi-liquid seasoning for food. They may or may not use spices. The ancient Latin word for broths or soups (sauces) was "juices" or *ius* in singular form. The French *sauce* and the Spanish and Italian *salsa* succeeded *ius*. Sauce is derived from the Latin for salted, *saltus*. Humans first seasoned their food with salts, then sauces. During the evolution of sauces only the more-or-less liquid consistency has remained relatively constant, with taste being the limitless element. Obviously there are many categories of sauces that have been incorporated into virtually every cuisine. In medieval European households sauces were mainly served with foods preserved by brining and pickling. These sauces made the foods more palatable, or more tolerable in that period of no refrigeration and slow transportation. In most of the rest of the world they were used as a vehicle for legumes, vegetables, and/or meat that was served with the local starch core—rice, maize, manioc, potatoes, pasta—to make it nutritious and palatable.

When one thinks of French cuisine, sauces are probably the first thing to come to mind. However, the art of sauces only came to France when the Italian Catherine de Medici married the French King Henry II and brought her cooks in her entourage. The French do not have a monopoly on sauces, only a greater variety of them. Some French sauces and techniques have migrated to Latin America where you can be certain peppers have been added. Capsicums are no longer strangers to French type sauces found in *Nouvelle,* Southwestern, or Cajun cuisines.

Gravies are sauces made just before serving to accompany meat. They utilize the fat and browned drippings of cooked meat along with a thickening agent and a liquid—stock, vegetable juices, milk, water. The English type gravy uses flour for the thickener but cookery in other cultures may use vegetable purée, cornstarch, or root-starches such as potato or arrowroot. Several basic gravies serve as the basis for many Indian dishes that use different combinations of chili peppers and spices according to the desired outcome. We call it gravy because the English misspelled the French *grané*. The addition of chili peppers does wonders for your everyday gravy.

Sauces can be cooked or uncooked, hot or cold, sweet or sour, spicy or mild, thick or thin, smooth or lumpy, emulsified or thickened with a starch or gelatin—almost anything goes. A sauce is incorporated into many dishes in Latin America, China, India, Africa, and the Far East; consequently those cuisines do not have a number of separate sauces as do the French. It is in those regions, not France, where we encounter peppery foods. Each country in those areas has some form of chili pepper sauce served as a table sauce to be consumed at the user's discretion.

Elizabeth Lambert Ortiz is probably one of the leading authorities on table sauces throughout the world—certainly those using peppers. With her gracious consent, I have borrowed from her in the sauce section in order to present a representative table sauce from as many countries as possible. She sent me pepper seed and sauce recipes from her travels so that I could grow the peppers to test the sauces.

The sponsor of a *salsa* making contest called me for a list of sauce types to include in the competition so that in fairness to the sauce's creator the jury would not judge one type against another. It is not easy to codify pepper sauces. In her authoritative work on Latin American cookery, Ortiz surmises that if codification could be done it would probably complicate rather than simplify matters. The sauce recipes that follow are divided into two major categories—table sauces and incorporated sauces. Within those two groups are cooked and uncooked sauces. By the way, I did not accept the invitation to judge the contest because I remembered the tears and fits of coughing, gagging, and often pain that accompanied my testing all the peppers I grew during the years I worked on *Peppers: The Domesticated Capsicums.* It did not promise to be a "fun" afternoon.

A word about uncooked sauces: Hand chopping of all uncooked, fresh ingredients is recommended. If a blender or food processor is used it is very easy to over-process the ingredients, thereby destroying the desired texture. Some of the vegetables, especially tomatoes, will become frothy and pale. Well-drained canned tomatoes can be chopped in the food processor because cooking has taken place during the canning process.

Sauces are extremely important to *Capsicum* cookery. I wish I had said what Kathy Gunst said about pepper sauces in her book *Condiments*; "A really good hot sauce takes you by the shoulders, gives you a good shake, and slaps your face to say 'HELLO'." To remove the fear of making sauces, a good understanding of their science is a help. I suggest reading Harold McGee's *On Food and Cooking* and Prosper Montagné's *Larousse Gastronomique.* That old saying "sauce for the goose, is sauce for the gander" ain't necessarily so. These sauces are more specialized than that.

Table Sauces

Table sauces are those served at the table in separate dishes to be spooned onto the food on your plate or for you to dip chips, bread, raw vegetables, etc. into the bowl.

KING RANCH HOT SAUCE

This legendary sauce is adapted from what is possibly the widest known of all sauces made in south Texas. It probably originated on the historic King Ranch, with headquarters in Kleberg County, Texas, near Kingsville, the county seat and my home town. It is served with meats, soups, casserole dishes, vegetables—most everything except desserts. Originally, it was made in a molcajete (mortar and pestle) but today a food processor does a good job.

Makes about 4 Cups

  1 cup chili pequin (chiltepín) peppers, the tiny native chili peppers

1½ cups onion, peeled and chopped

  4 garlic cloves, peeled and chopped

  1 teaspoon salt

  1 14½-ounce can diced tomatoes

 ½ cup vinegar

  1 cup olive oil

Place peppers, onion, and garlic in the bowl of food processor (do not use a blender); process until thoroughly ground. Add other ingredients; mix well. This sauce keeps well under refrigeration in a tightly covered jar. (I think bacteria are afraid of it.) Beat slightly before using. Handle with care!

NOTE: These tiny native chili peppers cost more than twelve dollars a pound. Picking them is very labor intensive and must be done by hand. Most are wild and several bushes are required to produce a cup full.

SALSA CRUDA

This uncooked sauce is the most commonly used condiment/table sauce in Mexico and it goes by many names, Salsa Picante, Ranchero Salsa, Pico de Gallo, but it is mighty good no matter what it is called.

Makes 1 to 2 Cups

  1 medium-size ripe tomato, finely chopped
  2 medium-size onion or 2 to 3 green onions (scallions or leeks), finely chopped
  6 sprigs fresh cilantro (fresh coriander), stemmed and minced
  1 garlic clove, peeled and minced
  3 serranos, finely chopped (or jalapeños, 'Fresnos')
  2 teaspoon salt
  ⅓ teaspoon sugar, a pinch
  1 cup fresh lime juice or half vinegar and half water

Mix all ingredients together in a bowl. Make fresh daily for desired fresh crunchy taste. If you keep uncooked sauce in refrigerator longer than day that is made it is no longer "salsa cruda" (uncooked sauce). You can eat it, but it is not the same. It can, however, be simmered with a little oil in a saucepan over medium heat for a few minutes and used on eggs and meat but please, call it something else.

ROASTED POBLANO CREAM

This sauce is delicious over almost anything wrapped in a warm tortilla—grilled meats, fajitas, burritos, quesadillas, soft tacos, etc.

Makes about 4 Cups

  12 ounces poblano peppers, cut in half lengthways, stemmed, and seeded

  8 ounces fresh Roma tomatoes, whole
  1 onion, cut into ¾-inch slices
  1 teaspoon vegetable oil
  2 cups low-fat sour cream
     Salt and freshly ground black pepper to taste

Place poblanos, whole tomatoes, and onion slices rubbed with oil on a barbeque grill 4 inches above a solid bed of hot coals, or over high heat on a gas grill, or on a broiling pan 4 inches below the broiling heat. Cook vegetables, turning as needed, until well browned on all sides, 8 to 12 minutes. When cooked, transfer to a cutting board. When cool enough to handle, peel, stem, and seed poblanos; core and peel tomatoes. Chop poblanos, tomatoes, and onions. In a 10 to 12-inch frying pan over medium heat, stir chopped vegetables until hot, about 2 minutes. Add 2 cups sour cream and stir just until hot but not boiling, about 2 minutes. Add salt and pepper. Scrape into a bowl and serve.

SMOKY APPLE CHILI PEPPER SALSA

Want to impress your friends? Here is an easy way to make them think you had to work hard to make something that tasted so good. Great on creamed cheese with any type crackers.

Makes 6 to 8 Cups

  5 large green jalapeños, roasted, peeled, and seeded
  2 large green Bell Peppers, roasted, peeled, and seeded
  3 chiltepínes, crushed or 1 teaspoon ground cayenne pepper
  1 cup cider vinegar
  4 garlic cloves, peeled and crushed

1 tablespoons Liquid Smoke Extract

1 teaspoon salt

2 tablespoons corn starch

1 50-ounce jar of prepared apple sauce

1 cup apple juice or water

Place all peppers and the next 5 ingredients in a blender and purée. In a large, 2 to 3-quart saucepan place applesauce; add juice or water, and contents from the blender; mix well. Bring to a boil over high heat, stirring. Reduce heat to medium low; simmer to desired consistency. Store in refrigerator in tightly closed containers up to three weeks. For longer keeping, put boiling salsa into clean jars; seal with scalded lids. Process in a boiling water bath for 15 minutes (Preserving: P. 182). Remove from water bath, tighten lids, cool on racks out of a draft.

GRILLED VEGETABLE SALSA

A tasty accompaniment to grilled meats of any kind, hamburgers, or as a dip.

Makes 7 Cups

4 ears fresh corn (about 1 pound), husked and silk removed

1 onion, peeled and cut crosswise into 2-inch-thick slices

1 red Bell Pepper, rinsed, stemmed, seeded, and halved

8 jalapeños, rinsed, stemmed, seeded, and halved

1 tablespoon olive oil

2 ripe tomatoes (1 pound), rinsed, cored, and chopped

2 garlic cloves, peeled and minced

3 cups fresh cilantro, chopped

3 cups fresh lime juice

2 teaspoons ground cumin

Salt and freshly ground black pepper to taste

Have ready a barbecue grill with a bed of hot coals, or use high heat on a gas grill with lid closed. Rub corn, onion, Bell Pepper, jalapeños with oil. Place vegetables on grill; close lid. Cook, turning corn and other vegetables occasionally, until slightly charred. When done, remove to cutting board; let cool. With a large, sharp knife cut off corn kernels, chop onion and Bell Pepper, and mince jalapeños. In a bowl, place tomatoes, garlic, cilantro, lime juice, and cumin; stir. Add grilled vegetables, salt and pepper to taste; mix gently.

MICROWAVE BROWN ROUX

If you have ever made traditional brown roux, this roux is a shortcut worth trying. The cooking times are only suggestions because microwave ovens vary.

Makes 2 Cups

1 cup vegetable oil

2 cups bread flour

In a 1-quart microwave-safe dish mix together oil and flour until well combined. Microwave mixture, at high power, whisking at 2-minute intervals for 8 minutes. If roux is not a dark reddish-brown color like a chestnut shell, microwave at high power, whisking and checking color at 1-minute intervals, until roux reaches desired color.

NOTE: Roux may be made 1 week ahead, cooled completely, covered, and refrigerated. Reheat before using.

BETTER'N ANYTHING SAUCE

You can't eat vegetables unless they are wallowing in cheese sauce or hollandaise? Now you can! This sauce is not only flavorful but also nutritious, beautiful, full of vitamins and color, and easy. Use it instead of mayonnaise on salads and sandwiches. Pick the color of peppers to compliment the vegetable's color. Try it on baked potatoes; your kids and guests will love it. Also a wonderful dip for vegetables at your next party.

Makes 2 Cups

- 6 medium Bell Peppers, all the same color; roasted, skinned, and seeded
- 2 cups olive oil
- 1 cup plain yogurt, lite or no-fat
- 2 serranos or jalapeños, seeded and chopped
   Salt and freshly ground black pepper to taste

Place all peppers and oil in a blender; process until smooth. Add yogurt and process until just blended. Season with salt and pepper. Serve on hot or cold vegetables; or pour sauce on a plate, arrange vegetables on top. Garnish with fresh greens and/or paprika. Tightly cover and store in refrigerator for up to a week.

NOTE: Roasting not only imparts flavor but also provides necessary cooking. Don't skip the process. This mixture can be thinned down to consistency of soup with milk, water, or broth and served chilled as a refreshing appetizer.

"TO DIE FOR" GARLIC SAUCE

This sauce evolved when I tried to duplicate a Canary Island sauce served in the Tic Tac Restaurant in Puerto De La Cruz, Tenerife—but this is even better. Although I was told the original had a mayonnaise base, this one will not defeat the novice, as making mayonnaise is apt to do. In fact, you may never use mayonnaise again. It is good on almost anything, all you need is a spoon, but don't count calories. Use it like a spread on crusty bread, for a vegetable dip, on almost anything but desserts. Not only does the cilantro make it a delicate green color but it also keeps the oil-egg emulsion from breaking and it takes the garlic odor from your breath.*

Makes 2 Cups

- 1 whole pod of garlic, peeled and finely chopped (yes, entire pod, not just a clove. Smaller pods are more flavorful)
- 2 eggs
- ½ teaspoon salt
- 1 tablespoon fresh lemon juice
- 1 cup fresh cilantro leaves, packed
- 1 green serrano or jalapeño, stemmed and seeded
- 1 slice French type bread, dried, crust removed
- 1 cup canola oil (olive oil is too strongly flavored)
- ½ cup light sour cream or yogurt

Put first 6 ingredients in a blender jar; pulse until puréed and smooth. Add bread; pulse until well mixed. Remove center cup from lid of blender. Using a funnel, slowly drip oil into blender. When sauce thickens, remove funnel; add sour cream. Pulse to blend. Taste to adjust seasonings; add more chili pepper, lemon juice, or salt as desired. If sauce is thicker than desired, stir in a little water to reach desired consistency. Put in a bowl and serve as a table sauce or as a dip on appetizer table.

MOJO ROJO
(RED SAUCE)

I don't believe a meal table on any of the seven Spanish Canary Islands would be complete without a bowl of mojo on it. It is eaten on everything and at every meal. Its consistency and pungency can be adjusted to your liking and it varies from place to place, but the basis is always peppers—both sweet and pungent.

Makes 1 Cup

- 2 tablespoons cider or wine vinegar
- 2 tablespoons olive oil
- 6 garlic cloves, peeled and chopped
- 1 teaspoon cumin seed, toasted
- 1 teaspoon oregano
- 2 cups red Bell Pepper, diced
- 2 teaspoons almonds, blanched, sliced and toasted
- 1 cup dried or toasted French bread or croutons
- 1 teaspoon cayenne pepper, or to taste
- 2 tablespoons sweet paprika

  Sea salt, to taste

  Water as needed for desired consistency

In the jar of a blender, put vinegar, oil, garlic, cumin, and oregano. Pulse until contents are well blended. Add Bell Pepper and almonds; pulse until completely puréed. Add bread, cayenne, and paprika. Add salt to taste. Pulse until well mixed and smooth. Add water and/or oil to thin if desired. Some make this very pungent by adding more chili pepper. Serve it in a bowl with a spoon as a ubiquitous table sauce or as a dip on an appetizer table.

MOJO VERDE
(GREEN SAUCE)

This Canary Island sauce is a variation of the Mojo Rojo, but is equally good on almost anything.

Makes 1 Cup

- 2 tablespoons cider or wine vinegar
- 2 tablespoons olive oil
- 6 garlic cloves, peeled and chopped
- 2 cups yellow Bell Pepper, diced (see note)
- ½ cup fresh cilantro leaves, packed
- 1 cup fresh parsley leaves, packed
- 2 teaspoons almonds, blanched, sliced and toasted
- 1 cup dried or toasted French bread or croutons
- 1 green serrano or green jalapeño, stemmed and seeded

  Green food coloring

  Sea salt, to taste

  Water as needed for desired consistency

In jar of a blender, put vinegar, oil, garlic, cilantro, and parsley. Pulse blender until contents are well blended. Add Bell Pepper and almonds; pulse until completely puréed. Add bread and serrano pepper. Add salt to taste. Pulse until well mixed and smooth. Add water and/or oil to thin if desired. Some make this very pungent by adding more chili pepper. Serve it in a bowl with a spoon as a table sauce or as a dip on an appetizer table. Especially good with seafood.

NOTE: In the Canary Islands the green Bell Pepper is used but I find it extremely indigestible and not too flavorful. Instead, use ripe, yellow Bell Peppers along with a little green food coloring. The flavor and your stomach will be so much better.

EGGPLANT AJVAR

Similar to Baba Ghanouj. In the Balkans, Hungary, and the Central Asian area ajvar is served as an accompaniment to grilled meat. It is also a good topping on cream cheese or chèvre spread on Melba toast as an appetizer.

Makes 2 Cups

- 1 pound eggplant
- 4 Long Green Chile, roasted, peeled, and seeded or canned; chopped
- 1 serrano or jalapeño, seeded and chopped
- 2 garlic cloves peeled and minced
- 2 tablespoons onion, grated
- 2 tablespoons fresh lemon juice
- 6 tablespoons olive oil
  Salt and freshly ground black pepper to taste

Heat oven to 375°F. Pierce eggplant with a fork in 3 or 4 places; bake 20 minutes, turning midway. Remove and hold over a gas flame or hot coals and cook until skin is completely black and blistered. Under cold running water, remove blackened skin. Chop (NOT IN A FOOD PROCESSOR) pulp finely; put in a bowl. Add chili peppers; mix. Add garlic, onion and lemon juice. Stir in oil, slowly. Salt and pepper to taste. Chill before serving

NOTE: In central Asia a woman showed me how to make ajvar. Texture is very important. It should not be slick. She was insistent that eggplant should never be chopped with any thing but a wooden cleaver. I bought one at a market there but if you can't find one, buy a wooden ruler and remove metal edge or use a wooden spatula; chop eggplant on a wooden cutting board. It does make a difference.

ROASTED RED PEPPER AJVAR

This can be purchased in a jar in ethnic food stores specializing in Middle Eastern and/or Mediterranean foods. When I couldn't find it I made this using canned roasted red peppers that have become readily available.

Makes about 1 Cup

- 1 7-ounce jar roasted red peppers; these are a flavorful ethnic type, not Bell Peppers
- 1 serrano or jalapeño, seeded and chopped
- 2 garlic cloves, peeled and minced
- 2 tablespoons onion, grated (important)
- 2 tablespoons Balsamic vinegar
- 3 tablespoons olive oil
  Salt and freshly ground black pepper to taste

Place all ingredients in a food processor; process until well-mixed but not smooth.

Serve with flat bread or Melba toast as an appetizer or put in a bowl and use as a table sauce.

NOTE: It has many uses in preparing appetizers. Use it on top of cheeses, especially goat cheese or cream cheese, or as a filler for cored cherry tomatoes.

BANANA PEPPER SAUCE

This table sauce is not pungent and is excellent served cold with fish, tongue, or veal. When your garden is full of Banana Peppers, try this sauce.

Makes about 2 Cups

- 1 medium-sized onion, chunks
- 1 cup cooked English peas

3 small ripe tomatoes, cut into chunks

2 teaspoon dried oregano

3 teaspoon dried thyme

3 fresh or pickled yellow banana peppers (yellow Bell Pepper, 'Cubanelle' or any sweet ethnic type)

1 tablespoon vegetable oil

3 tablespoons vinegar

1 tablespoon capers, rinsed and drained

12 green olives, pitted and sliced

Combine all ingredients, except capers and olives, in a blender. Process until creamy. Stir in capers and olive slices. Store tightly covered in refrigerator, but use within a week.

BRAZILIAN CHILI PEPPER SAUCE

Inspired by Elizabeth Lambert Ortiz, a widely traveled English woman whose husband was an official of the United Nations. Extended stays in each country allowed her to make in-depth studies of the cuisine. Their first duty station in Mexico resulted in The Complete Book of Mexican Cooking. *That was followed by books on the cuisines of Japan, Latin America, the Caribbean, and the Iberian Peninsula. One of the principal unifying ingredients of the cuisines examined in those works is chili pepper—her work is probably the paramount authority on their usage in foods of the world. The peppers used in Brazil are the small, very, very hot Malaguetas (probably Capsicum frutescens) not usually available here. Any small chili pepper can be substituted. I have found pickled Caribbean peppers, usually from Jamaica or Trinidad to be a good substitute, but you can use chiltepines.*

Makes 2 Cups

6–8 chiltepínes or 3 to 4 hot red or green chili peppers, stemmed

1 medium-size onion, chopped

1 garlic clove, peeled and minced

Salt to taste

2 cup fresh lime or lemon juice

Crush peppers, onion, and garlic with salt using a mortar and pestle; add lime juice little by little; or purée in blender or food processor. Serve in a bowl to accompany meat, poultry and fish, and dried bean dishes. Use with caution.

AFRICAN HOT SAUCE

African countries, like Latin America countries, each have a blistering chili pepper sauce for the table, which will vary from country to country. African chili peppers are especially pungent.

Makes 2 Cups

1 12-ounce can tomato sauce

3 cups chopped onion

1 garlic clove, peeled and minced

Juice of 1 lemon

2–8 small fresh red chili peppers (Thai, chiltepín, cayenne, or jalapeños)

12 teaspoons grated fresh horseradish

Put all ingredients in a blender or food processor and purée. Store in a tightly covered jar in refrigerator. Serve with meats, poultry, or fish.

Variation: Add 1 tablespoon to 1 cup of mayonnaise and use as a dressing for seafood or poultry salads.

ETHIOPIAN AFRIN OR SPICED GROUND PEPPER SEED

Have you ever wondered what you could do with all those pepper seed you removed from dried 'New Mexican Chiles' or Anchos when preparing a dish featuring those chili peppers? Ethiopians have a use for those seed—to spice raw meat before cooking.

Makes about 12 Cups

- 1 cup red pepper seed, dried; 'New Mexican Chile,' Ancho, Pasilla
- ¼ cup fresh ginger root, peeled and chopped
- 3 garlic cloves, peeled and chopped
- 3 cups red onions, peeled and chopped
- 2 teaspoons freshly ground black pepper
  Salt to taste

If pepper seed are not already dry, spread them on a clean cloth to air dry, or place them on a cookie sheet and dry them in a 190°F oven. Mix dried pepper seeds with other ingredients—with exception of salt—in a food processor; process until well ground. Spread mixture out on a cloth or dry in oven as before. Add salt and grind in a blender until mixture is a fine powder. Store in a well covered container. Rub into raw meat before cooking.

JAVANESE SAMBAL

Sambals are pungent chili pepper sauces indigenous to Indonesia but they vary from island to island.

Makes 2 Cups or More

- 3 whole coconuts, peeled
- 2 fresh green chili peppers (Thai, serrano)
- 2 teaspoons shrimp paste or mashed anchovy
- 1 garlic clove
- 3 teaspoons palm sugar (or brown sugar)
- 1 tablespoon tamarind or fresh lime juice
  Salt to taste

Pound all ingredients together into a paste or mix in a blender.

BOLIVIAN LOCOTO SALSA, LLAJWA

"Llajwa" is the ubiquitous, pungent table sauce of Bolivia where the Rocoto, (called Locoto there), is king of all peppers. I went into several kitchens in both homes and hotels where this salsa is made fresh daily to see just how it was made. In most homes it is still made with the batan, or grinding stones. In more modern kitchens a blender is used but this is always recognizable because the sauce is smoother and somewhat frothy.

Makes about 1 Cup

- 3 Roma tomatoes, seeded and quartered
- 1 small red onion, or leek, chopped
- 2 rocotos, seeded and chopped; or 4 serranos or jalapeños, seeded and chopped
  Juice of 1 fresh lime
  Several cilantro (fresh coriander) sprigs
  Salt to taste

Place all ingredients in a food processor; pulse several times until it is almost a purée but still has some texture. Take care not to over-process which makes the sauce frothy.

NOTE: Any sauces made with fresh tomatoes in a blender or food processor become quite frothy or foamy, which is not a desirable texture.

NOTE: A *batan* is similar to a metate but is made of a larger, smoother stone. A grinding stone is much larger and heavier. Most are too large to be moved about.

BOLIVIAN SARZA

Not quite chutney—but a Bolivian sweet-sour sauce that is a real taste teaser and pleaser. This is from "Hacienda Candelario," an old Bolivian cattle ranch I visited.

Makes 2 Cups

- 2 tablespoons vegetable oil
- 1 cup red onion, finely chopped
- 2 red ajís or 3 serranos or jalapeños, finely chopped; or to taste
- 1 Roma tomato, chopped
- 1 cup golden raisins, soaked in hot water to make a cup until softened
- 1 teaspoon ground nutmeg
- 1 teaspoon sugar
  Salt to taste

Heat oil in a medium-size saucepan over medium heat and cook onions and chili peppers until onion is transparent. Add tomatoes; cook, stirring until tender. Add cup of raisins, including soaking water, and nutmeg. Cook until thickened. Season with salt. Pour warm sauce into a bowl. Serve as a condiment with meats.

ECUADORIAN CHILI PEPPER SAUCE

This table sauce is also used in Costa Rican homes today, even though they do not historically use peppers in their food.

Makes 2 Cups or More

- 3–4 fresh red or green serranos or jalapeños, seeded and chopped

- 1 red onion, finely chopped or cut into small, thin strips
- ⅓ cup fresh lime or fresh lemon juice
  Salt to taste

Combine peppers with an equal amount of onion in a glass container with a lid; add lime juice to cover. Season with salt; let stand for 3 to 4 hours before using. Dilute with hot water if desired. Can be stored in refrigerator well-covered for a week or more.

PEPITA SALSA VERDE

Another wonderful sauce for chicken enchiladas but without the acidity of tomatoes or tomatillos.

Makes about 4 Cups

- 2–4 tablespoons pumpkin seeds
- 1 cup green chiles, canned
- 2 fresh serranos, seeded; optional
- ¾ cup fresh parsley, roughly chopped
- 1 garlic clove, peeled
  All-purpose flour, if needed
- 3 cups chicken stock
- 3 cups vegetable oil
  Salt and freshly ground black pepper to taste

Toast pumpkin seeds until browned or use toasted pumpkin seeds (pepitas). Purée pepitas, chiles, garlic, and parsley together in a blender. Add a little flour if a thicker sauce is desired. Add a little chicken stock and process; strain through a sieve. Heat oil in a medium-size sauce pan over medium heat. Add strained mixture and remaining stock to hot oil. Heat thoroughly and serve.

MAGHREB HARISSA

In the Maghreb, a collective term for the countries of Morocco, Tunisia, and Algeria, this indispensable sauce may be called Harissa, Tchermila, or Charmoula. The word harissa comes from the Arabic harissa which means to crush, break, or grind. It is a condiment of pungent red peppers pounded with fresh garlic and spices and topped with olive oil. It is used in cooking as a seasoning for stews (tagines) and couscous, as a table sauce, or as a marinade for fish.

For the Paste
Makes ½ Cup

- 1   ancho
- 4   tablespoons dried cayenne, japonés, de árbol, or any red chili pepper
- 6   garlic cloves, peeled
- 1   teaspoons caraway seed
- 1   teaspoon coriander seed
- 1   teaspoon ground cumin (comino)
      Salt to taste
- 3   cups olive oil, more if necessary to make a smooth paste

Soak chili peppers in hot water to cover for 1 hour; drain; chop. Place in a blender or spice mill with garlic and spices; purée. Season with salt. Place in a tightly covered jar. It will keep in refrigerator for several weeks.

For the Sauce
Makes 1 Cup

- 1   cup olive oil
- 2   cup wine vinegar
- 1   teaspoon Harrisa Paste, or more if desired
- 1   tablespoon sweet paprika
- 1   tablespoon fresh lemon juice
- 1   tablespoon fresh parsley, minced
- 1   tablespoon cilantro (fresh coriander), minced

Place all ingredients in a small saucepan; stir over high heat until warmed through; do not boil. Remove from heat; beat well; pour into small sauce dish. Serve immediately with grilled chicken or meat.

NOTE: In Morocco this sauce is primarily used as an overnight marinade for small white fish, which are then removed and dredged in flour before frying in oil or baking.

SPANISH ROMESCO SAUCE

This cold sauce is used primarily with fish and shellfish but is also good with vegetables and grilled meats. It comes from Tarragona, south of Barcelona and is Catalonia's most famous sauce. In Spain, the peppers used are either the romesco, a long thin, smooth-skinned pepper, or the round, smooth-skinned ñora— nyora in Catalan. Both are dark red and closely resemble the Mexican guajillo, which gives a most beautiful red color to any food with which it is cooked. You can substitute the dried red 'New Mexican Chile.' The sauce should not be fiery, but should be slightly pungent. Dried hot red chili peppers, such as chiltepínes or japonés, seeded, are added to the sauce to add pungency. There are many versions of Romesco sauce. This is a fairly standard one.

Makes about 2 Cups

- 2   cups red wine vinegar
- 2   dried *ñoras* or *romescos* or red 'New Mexican Chile,' seeded
- 1–2 hot dried red chili peppers, seeded (*japonés, de árbol,* Thai, *chiltepín*)
- 1   cup extra virgin olive oil
- 2   slices French-type bread, cut 2-inches thick

2 medium-size ripe tomatoes, peeled, seeded and chopped

4 garlic cloves, peeled and, minced

2 cups almonds, blanched, toasted, and ground

1 ounce hazelnuts or pecans, toasted and ground

Salt to taste

Soak all seeded peppers in warm water until soft, about 30 minutes. Drain; pat dry on paper towels; chop coarsely. Set aside. Heat 1 cup of oil in a small skillet; fry bread until it is golden on both sides. Lift it out to drain on paper towels; chop coarsely. Set aside. Add ripe tomato and garlic to oil remaining in pan; sauté 3 to 4 minutes. Remove from heat; allow cooling. Place tomatoes, parsley, chili peppers, garlic, almonds, and hazelnuts, in a blender with remainder of oil and vinegar; process until well-mixed. Add bread to blender; purée into a smooth, thick sauce. The sauce should have some texture. Season with salt and pepper. If desired, thin with tomato juice or water as more vinegar will make it too sour and more oil separates out. Let sauce sit for at least 2 hours before serving, then stir or beat lightly before using. Tightly covered it will keep in refrigerator for several weeks. No need to limit this thick, red sauce to fish—try it on chicken, veal, pork, or as a spread for bread.

ROASTED PEPPERS IN OLIVE OIL

This is not exactly a sauce but it does go on top of most anything. I was told how to make this by a native Italian, Enzo Domani, of Saint Augustine, Florida, the largest eggplant processor in the world. He said every self-respecting Italian cook always kept these peppers on hand for the family to snack on.

Makes About 1 Quart

6 pounds red, green, and yellow Bell Peppers, Cubanelle, or any ethnic type, roasted

2 sprigs fresh thyme, rosemary, and/or basil

2 garlic cloves, peeled and halved

1 tablespoon red or white wine vinegar

1 cup extra-virgin olive oil, or to cover

Place peeled peppers in a large bowl. Quarter them and remove cores, seeds, and ribs over a bowl to catch juices. Place peppers in a wide-mouth quart jar with herbs and garlic. Strain juices over peppers. Add vinegar and enough oil to cover peppers. Stir to release any air bubbles; cover. These peppers will keep for 2 to 3 weeks in refrigerator or even longer in a container designed so that air can be removed with a pump. Serve with meat dishes, on crusty, warm French bread, or on sandwiches. You can also use the oil for seasoning.

BORNEO SAMBAL

In Kalimantan (Borneo) this sambal is made fresh daily. I learned to make it when I became the sauce maker during days spent on a little houseboat as we floated on the Mahakam River to a Dayak village. Serve as a table sauce with everything.

Makes 2 Cups

5 green chili peppers (Thai, serrano)

1 shallot or green onion

1 garlic clove, peeled and crushed

3 teaspoons shrimp paste or anchovy

2 teaspoons brown sugar

1 small lime, juiced

3 teaspoons salt

Boil whole peppers for 6 minutes; drain. Pound all ingredients together in a *molcajete* (mortar and pestle) to make a creamy paste or purée in a blender.

SALSA VERDE WITH GREEN CHILES AND TOMATILLOS

This versatile sauce is excellent for chicken enchiladas, or to use as a table, or dipping sauce.

Makes 2 Cups

- 1 13-ounce can tomatillos; or use 8 large fresh, husked and washed
- 2 cups fresh green 'New Mexican Chile', peeled and seeded and chopped, or 1 4-ounce can; measure after chopping
- 1–2 serranos, seeded (optional)
- 1–2 garlic cloves, peeled and crushed
- 1 tablespoon cilantro (fresh coriander) leaves, chopped
- 2 teaspoons salt
- 3 teaspoons sugar

If using fresh tomatillos, steam until just tender. Purée tomatillos with chiles, garlic, cilantro and salt in a food processor. This can be used as is, or it may be simmered for a few minutes with a tablespoon of olive or vegetable oil and served hot.

NOTE: When using this sauce for chicken enchiladas, use Monterey Jack cheese instead of cheddar. Top with a dollop of sour cream. Garnish with pepitas (toasted pumpkin seeds). Use the Turkey Enchilada (Recipe: P. 114) for directions for making enchiladas.

Variation 1: Add 1 cup toasted pepitas to mixture in blender before processing.

Variation 2: When used as a dipping sauce, add 1 or 2 avocados, peeled, seeded, and mashed or chopped. Stir in well.

Incorporated Sauces

TEX-MEX ENCHILADA SAUCE

The browned flour is a tasty Texas twist.

Makes 3 to 4 Cups

- 8 anchos, guajillos or dried red 'New Mexican Chiles' or some of each
- 2 tablespoons ground cumin (comino)
- 2 teaspoons dried oregano
- 1 medium-size onion, chopped
- 2 garlic cloves, peeled and minced
- 3 tablespoons vegetable oil
- 2 tablespoons all-purpose flour
- 1 6-ounce can tomato paste
- 2 cups water or beef or chicken stock
   Salt and freshly ground black pepper to taste

Wash peppers. Cover with boiling water; let stand at least an hour but no longer. Drain and reserve water. Remove stems, seeds, and veins. In a blender purée peppers, spices, garlic, and onion with a cup (more if desired for thinner consistency) of strained soaking water. In a skillet, heat oil over medium heat; add flour; stir until smooth and golden brown. Add pepper paste, tomato paste, and remaining water. Simmer about 30 minutes or until thickened. Season with salt and pepper.

NOTE 1: If you have a jar of BASIC RED PEPPER PASTE (see Recipe P. 155); use 2 cups or more, if desired, instead of going through the steps which use first 5 ingredients to make a paste.

NOTE 2: I use already browned flour, which I make and keep on hand in a tightly covered jar in refrigerator. The real Tex-Mex flavor comes from flour that has been browned almost to the point of burning. It is a rather tedious process of constant stirring and watching, so brown at least a cup each time. Or you can save time by cheating on browned flour if you buy a package of brown gravy mix as a substitute.

NOTE 3: To make Tex-Mex enchiladas, use directions for the Turkey Enchilada (see Recipe P. 114) but fill the enchilada with shredded cheddar cheese and chopped onion; or with shredded cooked chicken, shredded cheese, and chopped onion. Garnish with sliced, pickled jalapeños. Serve very hot.

BASIC RED CHILI PEPPER PASTE

This is a paste to keep in the refrigerator to use as a base in many different recipes. It really saves time to have it on hand.

Makes 2 to 3 Cups

    2   cups hot water for soaking peppers, reserve
    4   anchos
    2   guajillos
    2   chipotles
    1   large onion
    4   garlic cloves, peeled
    2   teaspoons ground cumin (comino)
    2   teaspoons ground oregano
    1   teaspoon salt

Soak chili peppers in hot water to cover about 1 hour. Remove from water, reserving 2 cups of soaking water. Remove seeds, stems, and veins from peppers. Place all ingredients in a blender; process until it is a smooth, thick paste; add soaking water as needed. Store in a tightly covered jar in refrigerator for several weeks or freeze. Use to flavor sauces for chilaquiles, enchiladas, and other dishes.

PORTUGUESE STYLE RED PEPPER PASTE FOR MEATS

Iberians—Portuguese and Spaniards—use many more of the big, red, sweet Bell Peppers or pimentóns than pungent ones. However, small pungent ones of the Cayenne type are used to add a little spark to the more flavorful pimentons. They do not grow Serranos and Jalapeños in Iberia at this time. Allow extra sauce so the cook won't eat it all up before the dish is prepared.

Makes 13 Cups

    8   large red Bell Peppers, roasted, seeded, and peeled or canned roasted red peppers
    2   jalapeños or serranos, roasted and seeded
  2–3   large garlic cloves, peeled
    6   tablespoons olive oil
    1   teaspoon salt, or to taste

Place peppers, salt, garlic, and half the olive oil in a blender jar; process until smooth. Slowly add remaining oil; blend until consistency of whipped cream. Place in a jar; seal tightly; store in refrigerator. When ready to use as a dry marinade for poultry, pork, or lamb, allow paste to return to room temperature before rubbing on all sides of meat. Allow rubbed meat to sit several hours or overnight. Scrape off excess before cooking. Use with Portuguese Pork Chops. (Recipe: P. 107)

LONG GREEN/RED CHILE SAUCE

To be used over enchiladas, chiles rellenos, burritos, or similar dishes.

Makes 4 Cups or More

- 2 tablespoons vegetable oil
- 1 tablespoon margarine
- 2 tablespoons all-purpose flour
- 3 teaspoon ground cumin (comino)
- 2 cups fresh ground fresh Long Green/Red Chiles
- 1 cup cold water
- 2–3 cups chicken stock
- 1 garlic clove, peeled and minced
   Salt to taste

Heat oil and margarine; add flour; stir constantly, until it reaches a deep golden color—almost scorched but not quite. Remove from heat. Add cumin. Mix ground chile with cold water until there are no lumps. Whisk chile mixture into flour paste while off the heat. Return to heat; slowly add stock. Simmer for 15 to 20 minutes, stirring frequently. Add garlic; season with salt to taste. Simmer five minutes longer. If lumpy, run in blender for a few seconds. NOTE: This sauce will keep well for a week in refrigerator.

CHIPOTLE BARBEQUE SAUCE

Serve this sauce while warm over grilled or barbecued meats.

Makes 4 Cups

- 2 tablespoons vegetable oil
- 1 medium-size onion, chopped
- 2 garlic cloves, peeled and crushed or pressed
- 1 16-ounce can solid-pack tomatoes, chopped
- 1 12-ounce can tomato sauce
- 1 chipotle, chopped, or to taste.
   Salt to taste

Add oil to a medium-size saucepan over medium heat; heat oil. Add onion; cook, stirring, until clear. Add remaining ingredients and cook 15 to 20 minutes.

Spreads

Butters

LONG GREEN CHILE BUTTER

This pretty butter is a guest pleaser and nice to keep on hand.

Makes 12-ounces

- 1 4-ounce can of Long Green Chiles, diced, drain off excess liquid
- ½ pound (2 sticks) unsalted butter at room temperature; or margarine, well-chilled
  Salt and freshly ground black pepper to taste

Combine all ingredients in a food processor; pulse a few times to get mixture going. Let machine run until all ingredients are well mixed. Butter will be a light green color.

NOTE 1: Remember, margarine is a hydrogenated fat. For fewer calories, try it with a cup of plain, low-fat yogurt.

NOTE 2: For a red butter, use 1 teaspoon crushed red 'New Mexico Chile.'

RED PEPPER BUTTER

This flavorful butter is a great addition to seafood, chicken, pasta, corn-on-the-cob, Melba toast, crusty bread, or almost anything.

Makes about 1¼ Cups

- 2 garlic cloves, peeled and chopped
- 1 tablespoon jalapeño, seeded and chopped
- 1 cup roasted red peppers, canned
- 2 tablespoons unsalted butter, softened
- ½ cup pecans, broken
- ½ teaspoon Aleppo pepper
- ¼ teaspoon salt

In a food processor purée garlic and jalapeño. Add peppers, butter, pecans, Aleppo pepper, and salt; process until smooth. When well-covered this will keep in refrigerator for a week.

RICOTTA WITH ROASTED PEPPERS

Make this flavorful spread several hours, or a day, before it is to be served as a spread for crusty bread or Aztec scones.

Makes 6 Servings

- 1 pound ricotta cheese
- ½ cup extra-virgin olive oil
- 6 tablespoons fresh parsley, chopped
- 7 garlic cloves, peeled and minced
- ½ teaspoon Aleppo pepper
- 1 tablespoon green jalapeño, minced
- 1 tablespoon fresh mint leaves, minced
- 1 teaspoon thyme
- 2 cups roasted red pepper, canned; chopped

In a medium bowl, whisk ricotta until creamy. Whisk in olive oil, parsley, garlic, Aleppo pepper, jalapeño, mint, and thyme. Stir in peppers. Season with salt and pepper. Mound red pepper ricotta in center of a plate and serve with crusty bread, preferably whole grain.

Salad Dressings

ROASTED RED PEPPER DRESSING

This is as easy as it is tasty because bottled roasted peppers are used. The most flavorful are put up in Bulgaria from a long, mild, thick-fleshed pepper that has more flavor than a red Bell Pepper.

Makes 4 Servings

- ¾ cup vegetable broth or a vegetable base such as Better Than Bouillon®
- 1 tablespoon red wine vinegar
- 4 tablespoons olive oil
- 2 teaspoon salt
- 2 teaspoon Dijon mustard
- 2 teaspoon dried thyme
- 3 teaspoon freshly ground black pepper
- 2 7-ounce bottles roasted red peppers, drained

Place all ingredients in a blender; process until smooth. Refrigerate dressing in an airtight container for up to 1 week. Serving size: 3 tablespoons. Very good on a cobb salad made using turkey or chicken.

ZESTY POPPY SEED DRESSING

This is delicious on fruit salads of any kind, but has a special affinity for grapefruit and in combinations where grapefruit is present.

Makes about 4 Cups

- 1 cups sugar
- 2 teaspoons dry mustard
- 1 teaspoon salt
- 3 cups white or cider vinegar
- 1 thick slice of onion
- 1 serrano, seeded or 1 teaspoon ground cayenne pepper
- 2 cups vegetable oil (do not use olive oil)
- 3 tablespoons poppy seeds

Mix sugar, mustard, salt, and vinegar in a blender. Add onion and serrano; purée thoroughly. Add oil slowly, processing constantly at medium speed; continue to beat until thick. Add poppy seeds; process for a few minutes. Store in refrigerator. Stir before using.

CREAMY SERRANO DRESSING

This is a fairly thick dressing. Not only is it great for salads but also is also delicious with boiled shrimp. It is a favorite.

Makes 2 ½ Cups

    1   teaspoon Dijon mustard
    3   teaspoon dried tarragon
    1   garlic clove, peeled
    3   teaspoon sugar
  1–2   serranos, or 3–4 green chiltepínes or jalapeños
    3   tablespoons fresh lime juice (never bottled)
    1   egg yolk, uncooked
  2–3   parsley sprigs
    2   cup olive oil

In a blender, combine mustard, tarragon, garlic, sugar, chili peppers, salt, and black pepper. Process. Blend in egg yolk, parsley, and lime juice. Pour oil in very slowly. Keep well covered in refrigerator. Use within a week.

CHIPOTLE MAYONNAISE

Rather than go through the tedious process of making "home made" mayonnaise I use "store bought" low fat mayonnaise as the base for this habit-forming dressing.

Makes 1 Pint

    1   pint jar of your favorite lite mayonnaise, regular or low-fat
    2   tablespoons chipotle adobado, canned and puréed, or to taste

Remove 2 tablespoons mayonnaise from jar; add chipotle; stir to mix well. Seal and store in refrigerator.

NOTE: Or you can use your favorite recipe and make the mayonnaise.

TOMATILLO SALAD DRESSING

A very simple dressing but very good.

Makes ¾ Cup

    ½   cup sour cream, regular, lite or no-fat
    ¼   cup salsa verde (see Recipe P. 154)

Place ingredients in a blender; whirl until well blended. Toss enough dressing with a mixed lettuce and tomato salad to lightly cover leaves. Top with shredded Monterey Jack cheese, if desired.

NOTE: Recipe is easily doubled.

Pestos

Pesto is a thick, uncooked, sauce that originated in Genoa, Italy. Italians use it primarily on pasta or fish but it makes a delicious spread for canapes, or on celery and endive for appetizers. Olive oil and fresh basil are key ingredients.

LONG GREEN/RED CHILE PESTO

A Southwestern answer to Italian pesto. Use in any recipe calling for pesto or serve as an appetizer on French bread or crackers.

Makes 10 to 12 Cups

  6 fresh Long Green Chiles peeled, seeded, and chopped

  2 cups olive oil

  2 cups packed well-washed fresh spinach, chopped

  2 cups chopped fresh parsley

  2 garlic cloves, peeled

  2 teaspoons chopped fresh or dried basil

  2 tablespoons pine nuts or sunflower seeds

     Salt to taste

In a blender, purée all ingredients to make a smooth sauce. Thin with water if necessary.

RACY PESTO SAUCE

A south Texas answer to Italian pesto. Use in any recipe calling for pesto. Make it when your garden's basil is rampant.

Makes 6 Servings

  2 cups fresh basil leaves, washed

  2 garlic cloves, peeled and minced

  2 cups olive oil

  2 cups Parmesan cheese, freshly grated

  3 cups sunflower seed, toasted or pumpkin seeds (pepitas)

  1 serrano, seeded, or to taste

  2 cups water

  3 cups heavy cream

     Salt and freshly ground black pepper to taste

Blanch basil leaves and garlic in boiling water for a few seconds. Roll in a towel to remove water. Place basil, olive oil, Parmesan, serrano, sunflower seed, garlic, and olive oil in a blender. Purée until very smooth. Season with salt and pepper to taste. Pour sauce into a saucepan; stir in cream. Heat without boiling. Serve sauce over freshly cooked pasta. Toss to mix and serve with grated Parmesan.

NOTE: Omit cream and serve as a dip with raw vegetables, on sliced tomatoes, or on crusty Italian bread. It will keep in a tightly sealed container in refrigerator for a couple of weeks.

SUN-DRIED TOMATO AND CALAMATA OLIVE PESTO

This pesto makes a tasty spread for thin, toasted bread rounds.

Makes 1 Cup

- ¾ cup sun-dried tomatoes, packed in oil or red wine; drain
- 8 calamata olives, pitted
- 2 garlic cloves, peeled
- 4 tablespoons fresh parsley leaves
- 4 tablespoons fresh basil leaves
- ½ cup pumpkins seed (pepitas), toasted
- ¼ cup extra-virgin olive oil
- 2 tablespoons balsamic vinegar
- 1 tablespoon Aleppo pepper or ½ teaspoon cayenne, or to taste

Place all ingredients except oil and vinegar in bowl of a food processor. Process, scraping sides of bowl as necessary, until coarsely chopped. With machine is running, pour oil and vinegar through feeder tube in a thin stream. Process until a coarse paste is formed. Serve with hot or cold pasta or with toasted bread rounds.

SUN-DRIED TOMATO PESTO

Try this on melba toast that has been spread with a soft goat cheese

Makes 2½ Cups

- 1 cup sun-dried tomatoes, soaked in ¼ cup red wine until soft
- 9 calamata olives or other black olives, pitted
- 2 garlic cloves, peeled and chopped
- 1 serrano, stemmed, seeded
- 3 tablespoons fresh basil leaves
- ½ cup pepitas (squash seed), toasted; or pine nuts, toasted
- ½ cup Parmesan cheese, shredded
- ½ cup olive oil
  Salt to taste

Drain the tomatoes; place in a food processor. Add olives, garlic, serrano, basil; process until coarsely chopped. Add pepitas and cheese; pulse. Scrape sides as necessary. With machine running, gradually add oil through feeder tube; process until mixture forms a thick paste. Add salt to taste. Serve with hot or cold pasta or thin, toasted bread rounds (crostini or melba toast).

NOTE: For a thinner sauce, more oil may be added.

SPICY BEER BATTER

This batter is a delightful light, puffy coating for fish, chile rel-lenos, shrimp, or anything that needs to be batter-fried. I like it better than tempura batter.

Makes 8 to 10 Servings

- 1 cup all-purpose flour
- 1 teaspoon baking powder
- 1–2 teaspoon ground cayenne pepper
- 1 teaspoon paprika
- 2 teaspoons salt
- 1 8-ounce can of light beer
  Vegetable oil

Sift all of dry ingredients together in a large mixing bowl. Just before you are ready to fry the food, add the beer and mix well but do not beat. Dip pieces of food to be fried into batter one at a time. Heat enough vegetable oil to cover food pieces in a deep skillet over high heat until a little sample of batter sizzles. Lower food into oil a few pieces at a time—too many at one time will lower temperature below optimum for frying—and cook until golden on all sides turning as necessary. Remove the food from fat with a slotted spoon or pancake turner and drain on paper toweling. Serve at once.

POBLANO PESTO

Roasting poblano peppers in order to remove the cellophane-like skins is a troublesome must. Prepare more of them than the recipe calls for and freeze the extra ones to use at another time.

Makes 1 Cup

- 2 poblano peppers, roasted and peeled.
- ½ cup pumpkin seeds (pepitas), toasted
- ¼ cup fresh cilantro with stems, chopped
- 1 green serrano or jalapeño, seeded and chopped, or to taste
- ¾ tablespoon lime juice, freshly squeezed
- ¼ teaspoon salt
- 2 teaspoons extra-virgin olive oil

Place poblanos, seeds, cilantro, green chili peppers, lime juice, and salt in work-bowl of food processor; pulse until puréed. Add oil in steady stream while processor is running. Adjust seasonings.

6 DESSERTS!

DESSERTS!

DESSERTS!

Desserts! Desserts! Desserts!

Just Desserts

Desserts and chocolate with chili peppers? That is nothing new. It all began with the Pre-Columbian Olmec Indians of Mesoamerica who left records of their use of chili peppers and cacao as early as 1,000 B.C. They and their neighboring Mayans drank a stimulating, unsweetened, frothy drink made of the roasted and ground cacao beans combined with chili peppers, and often with native spices such as annato, allspice, and vanilla, three of the many comestible New World plants that were unknown to the Old World before the Columbian Exchange that began in 1492.

Mesoamerica is the constricted area of the Americas that separates the larger masses of North and South America. It includes southern Mexico with the Valley of Mexico and the Yucatan Peninsula, Guatemala, British Honduras (now Belize), El Salvador, and the northern part of Honduras. Further south in Ecuador, Peru, and Bolivia was the Andean Area where the great Inca Empire reigned in its final glory. The indigenous people of those areas of diverse geography were agriculturists who domesticated and cultivated many plants including chili peppers of different species in both areas. On the other hand, the only domesticated animals were the turkey and the dog, both used for meat. There were no wild animal species in the New World suitable for milk and cheese production or as draught animals, although the Andean llama was used as a pack animal.

When the Spaniards invaded Mexico in 1519 they found the Mayans in the east and Aztecs in the area where Mexico City is now located, drinking a frothy, stimulating beverage, either cold or hot, made of cacao (*Theobroma bicolor*), chili peppers (*Capsicum annuum*), and water with spices such as annato (*Bixa orellana*), which is called *achiote* in Mexico, vanilla (*Vanilla planiflora*), and/or allspice (*pimenta dioica*) ground into a paste. This beverage was stimulating because it was made with cacao, which contains both theobromine and caffeine, and it was drunk many times a day, especially by the nobles. The desired froth was produced by pouring the concoction from one pot to another. The Spanish developed a *molinillo,* a type of swizzle stick, to take the place of that operation. When sugar from sugar cane arrived, it became a popular flavoring for the beverage. The drink reached the Old World by 1544 and a trade in cacao began in 1585. There it later became known as chocolate. As late as the nineteenth century the French still sometimes flavored their chocolate with chili peppers.

Although sugar cane (*Saccharum officinarum*) is a perennial grass native to humid, tropical lands, those early native Americans in similar climates had no sugar cane. It was not known in the Americas until the Portuguese and Spaniards introduced it after their conquests in the late fifteenth and early sixteenth centuries. Prior to that, the only sources of sweets in the Americas were honey, fruits, and some tree saps. Sugar cane is thought to have originated in New Guinea or some place in Indonesia and was introduced through trade to northern India where unrefined sugar had been produced since 2992 B.C. and written about in Sanscrit texts during 500 B.C. The Asian Indians were the first to refine the cane into sugar. From India it went to China and Persia. Its usage did not become widespread in China but from the Middle East it was spread by the seafaring Arabs throughout the Mediterranean. From there it went to the Iberian Peninsula and Madeira, thence, in the late 19th century, to the Portuguese islands of Sao Tomé and Principe where it flourished. The Ottoman Turks refined white sugar in the fourteenth century; however honey remained the principal sweetener in Europe until after 1500 due to the high cost of sugar. The discovery of the New World provided Europeans with the tropical, humid land required to grow sugar cane thereby making it affordable. On his second voyage in 1493, Columbus took it to the Caribbean islands where it prospered.

Once Europeans acquired sugar in quantities, they could have desserts other than fruits, cheese, and honey-flavored dishes which were presented in magnificent displays at the end of the meal. The French word *desservir,* meaning to clear the table or remove the dishes, is the origin of the word dessert. In England a course of sweetmeats was served on a separate table or placed on the table. It was in North America that this course became a miscellany of sweet "desserts" with a wider meaning.

Cacao produces cocoa and chocolate, two of the world's favorite dessert ingredients. It was first recorded by the Olmec of Mesoamerica before 1,000 B.C. and discovered in 1502 by Columbus in Nicaragua during his fourth voyage. From there the hard-to-grow nibs of the cacao plant, an understory tree, moved to Venezuela. The Spanish entered Mexico in 1519 where they found the Mayas and Aztecs drinking a stimulating, unsweetened beverage made of ground cacao beans, annato, vanilla, and chili peppers, which was beaten to a froth. They drank it either hot or cold several times a day. It was drunk by all classes of Native Americans throughout Mesoamerica. Those ingredients were also used for soups and sauces similar to moles. The cacao beans or seeds, which are found in large pods growing on the trunks of small, tropical, understudy trees, were also used for money. It was that usage that gave us the expression "money grows on trees." On one of my trips to Guatemala I found dried chili peppers similar to the dried guajillo that were called "Chile Chocolate."

The cacao beans are roasted, which develops the chocolate flavor. Then they are cracked to release the large cotyledons (seed leaves) called **nibs** which is the part of the fruit used to make chocolate. The nibs are ground to a paste by rollers that generate enough heat to melt the fat in the nibs and produce a thick, dark liquid called **chocolate liquor**, which was always the final product until the middle of the nineteenth century. The small squares made from the liquor produce baking chocolate, now used to make chocolate candy.

The Spaniard and Portuguese taste for cacao developed very slowly. It was not until it was combined with sugar that Europeans began consuming the beverage now called chocolate. After the drink arrived in London in 1657, chocolate houses sprang up there. It still remained a drink until the end of the eighteenth century. A screw press was patented by the Dutch in 1828 and the excess cocoa butter was made into molded cake with sugar, and often a dairy product. The Dutch also produced the first cocoa, a dry powder, by pressing out much of the fat. These two processes made chocolate confections possible. Today chocolate is used in Europe and North America as an important flavoring for desserts.

There is good news for chocoholics who fear chocolate products because of the fat content. Laboratory studies have shown that the stearic acid in chocolate lowers total cholesterol and it also contains compounds that act as antioxidants in the body. In fact, a single candy bar contains the same quantity of polyphenols as all the fruits and vegetables normally eaten each day. So, don't feel too guilty.

Chili peppers cut the cloying sweetness of preserves, chutneys, and desserts. Use an amount that suits your taste. In most cases I prefer the ground, dried pods of Ancho,

Guajillo, Chile Chocolate, Pasilla, or some cayenne, paprika, or Aleppo pepper. Others use dried, ground red 'New Mexican Chile.' Fresh chili peppers like serranos, jalapeños, and habaneros can be used also. A little chili pepper makes chocolate sing. Other common ingredients found in recipes with chili peppers are: citrus fruits, coconut, melons, and pecans.

FROZEN FRUIT DESSERT

For your sweet tooth! A dessert that will not put you completely over the top on calories—that is, if you can eat just one small (half-cup) serving.

Makes 12 or More Small Servings

> 1 8-ounce package cream cheese or lite no-fat yogurt, dripped (see P. 44)
> ½ cup sugar or use artificial sweetener to taste
> 3½ cups fruit; canned or fresh mango, fresh peaches or nectarines, puréed in blender
> 2 serranos, seeded and chopped
> 1 teaspoon red pepper flakes, seedless type
> 1 8-ounce carton frozen lite-whipped topping, thawed

Place cream cheese and sugar in bowl of food processor with plastic blade; process until smooth. Gradually add fruit purée and peppers; pulse until blended. Add heaping spoonfuls of whipped topping, beating with a spoon, or whip after each addition to combine. Pour mixture into a 10 x 15-inch pan. Freeze until firm, about 3 hours or overnight. To serve, cut into rectangles; remove with spatula. Garnish with fresh fruit or edible flowers.

Alternate: Spoon mixture into individual ½-cup size paper cups; freeze until firm. Run under warm water to remove; serve on a plate with puréed fruit over or under each serving. Garnish with a mint sprig. Cover unused frozen cups with plastic wrap; keep frozen until needed.

CITRUS-RUBIO SORBET

This refreshing pale, yellow sorbet is a real crowd pleaser, as are most blondes.

Makes 8 Servings

> 4 Hungarian Wax or any yellow chili pepper, seeded and chopped (for flavor with less heat use Banana peppers, yellow bell, or half sweet and half pungent peppers—but no Habaneros).
> 2½ cups sugar
> 5½ cups hot water
> 8 large oranges, peeled and chopped
> ¼ cup tequila, cointreau, or mixed
> ½ cup fresh lemon or fresh lime juice to taste
> 6 tablespoons light corn syrup

Combine 4 cups of water with sugar in a sauce pan; heat until sugar dissolves; then bring to a boil. Cool to room temperature; refrigerate for 2 hours. Purée remaining ingredients with 1½ cups water; refrigerate until well chilled, at least 2 hours. Stir sugar mixture into fruit. Pour mixture into an ice cream maker; follow directions for making ice cream. Serve sorbet as a dessert or as a refresher between the courses of a large meal.

Variation: Use 4 white grapefruit and a drop or two of green food coloring instead of oranges, and jalapeños instead of Hungarian Wax. Jalapeños have a flavor very different from the yellow chili peppers.

HONEYDEW COMPOTE WITH LIME, GINGER, AND SERRANO

A delightful combination of fresh flavors that does not involve cooking. Try sprinkling chili pepper on your morning honeydew or cantaloupe; it makes them sing.

Makes 6 Servings

- ½ cup fresh lime juice
- 2 teaspoons grated lime peel
- ½ cup water
- ⅓ cup sugar
- 1 tablespoon fresh ginger, peeled and minced
- ½ teaspoon serrano, seeded and finely slivered
- 1 teaspoon fresh mint, finely slivered
- 1 large honeydew melon (3 pounds or so), seeded and cut from the rind in uniform shapes
  fresh figs and mint sprigs for garnish

Combine fresh lime juice, rind, water, sugar, ginger and serrano slivers in a small saucepan. Bring to a boil, reduce heat; simmer for 5 minutes until sugar is dissolved. Cool. Strain before using. To serve, pour syrup over melon and, if possible; allow to marinate refrigerated for at least 1 hour. Garnish with slices of fresh fig and fresh mint sprigs. Also very nice garnished with a thin slice or two of good proscuitto or Bayonne ham.

ANCHO FUDGE

This is my adaptation of a smooth, rich fudge recipe from the innovative kitchens of Sunset Magazine.

Makes 3 Pounds

- 2 tablespoons butter or margarine, softened
- 2 cups half-and-half cream
- 4 cups sugar
- ½ cup light corn syrup
- 1 teaspoon salt
- ½–1 tablespoon ground ancho
- 8 ounces semisweet chocolate, chopped
- 4 ounces unsweetened chocolate, chopped
- 1 tablespoon vanilla or rum extract
- 2 tablespoons butter
- 1½ cup pecan halves, broken

Line a 9-inch square pan with foil. Butter foil lightly. In a 3 to 4-quart sauce pan, mix cream, sugar, corn syrup, salt, and ancho. Place over high heat; boil about 3 minutes, stirring occasionally. Reduce heat to medium; add chocolates; stir gently until melted and mixture begins to simmer. Insert a candy thermometer and bring the mixture to a boil; stir occasionally until thermometer reads 235°F, or a drop of candy spooned into cold water forms a soft ball; about 30 to 40 minutes. Remove from heat; add butter and vanilla; place pan with candy in another pan containing cold water to aid cooling. Let mixture stand undisturbed until it is cool enough to touch. Stir and beat until the candy becomes smooth and glossy and begins to thicken but is still soft and workable. Add nuts and mix. Scrape fudge into foil-lined pan. Let stand until firm. Remove from pan; remove foil. Cut fudge into 1-inch squares and serve. Can be wrapped stored at room temperature up to 1 week.

NEW WORLD PIE: CHILIES TO CHOCOLATE PLUS PECANS

The pecans, chocolate, and chili peppers that make this dessert fit for the gods, are all products of the New World. How the Old World must have suffered without them.

Makes 8 Servings

- 1 cup semi-sweet chocolate chips
- 6 tablespoons (¾ stick) butter or margarine cut into pieces
- 2 large eggs, slightly beaten
- ¼ cup plus 1½ teaspoons granulated sugar
- ¼ cup all-purpose flour
- 1 tablespoon of freshly ground ancho, mulato, or pasilla
- ¼ teaspoon salt
- 1 teaspoon instant coffee granules
- ½ cup milk-chocolate chips
- 1 cup pecans, coarsely chopped
- 1 9-inch, deep, pie crust, lightly baked and cooled
- ½ cup sour cream
- Paprika

Preheat oven to 325°F. Melt the cup of semi-sweet chocolate chips and butter in a heavy medium saucepan over boiling water or in a microwave oven; stir until smooth; cool to room temperature. In a mixing bowl, whisk eggs and sugar until well blended. Whisk in melted chocolate-butter mixture; gently fold in flour, chili peppers, salt, and coffee until well mixed. Add half of the milk-chocolate chips along with pecans; stir until evenly distributed.

Spread batter over cooled crust; bake in oven for about 25 minutes until a toothpick inserted in center comes out clean; take care to not overcook the pie.

The pie is best served while still warm. Sprinkle remainder of milk-chocolate chips on top of warm pie; cover it tightly with foil. Allow to stand on a rack until ready to serve. Remove foil; cut into wedges. Serve slightly warm pie with a dollop of sour cream; garnish with paprika.

NOTE: If the pie is baked ahead of time don't put remaining chocolate chips on until it is rewarmed. Warm it in a preheated 200°F oven until just warm, then sprinkle with the chocolate chips, wrap, and serve as directed above. Leftovers should be heated before serving.

APPLE PIE WITH GREEN 'NEW MEXICAN CHILE'

Another great green 'New Mexican Chile'(Long Green/Red Chile) recipe to surprise your guests.

Makes One 9-inch Pie

- 5 cups tart apples, peeled and sliced (do not use 'Delicious' apples)
- ¾ cup sugar
- 2 tablespoon butter or margarine
- 1 teaspoon ground cinnamon
- ½ teaspoon ground nutmeg
- 2 teaspoons pure red 'New Mexican Chile,' ground
- 1 cup water
- salt to taste
- 2 9-inch, deep pie crusts

Preheat oven to 375°F. Combine all ingredients except crust in a large sauce pan; cook over medium heat (this can be done in microwave) until apples are slightly tender and juice is thick, 20 to 25 minutes. Pour into un-baked pie shell; dot with additional butter or margarine, cover with top crust and cut vents into it (or cover the top with lattice strips of crust); sprinkle with additional sugar. Bake 30 to 40 minutes.

CHOCOLATE SHORT-CAKE WITH BERRIES

A shortcake better than Mother used to make. Although fresh strawberries and blueberries are delicious on this shortcake, the fruit soul-mate of chocolate is raspberry.

Makes 6 Servings

> 2 cups all-purpose flour
> ⅔ cup plus 2 tablespoons granulated sugar
> ⅔ cup unsweetened cocoa
> 2 teaspoons baking powder
> ½ teaspoon baking soda
> ½ teaspoon salt
> 1 tablespoon Aleppo pepper flakes or ground ancho pepper
> ½ cup butter, cold
> 2 large egg yolks
> 4 cup buttermilk or fat free yogurt
> 4 cups fresh raspberries, blueberries, or sliced strawberries
>   Vanilla yogurt or lightly sweetened whipped cream
>   Powdered sugar

Preheat oven to 375°F. In a food processor or bowl, combine 2 cups flour, ⅔ cup granulated sugar, cocoa, baking powder, baking soda, salt, and Aleppo or ancho pepper. Process or mix until blended. Cut butter into small chunks and add to flour mixture. Process by rubbing with fingers, or cut in with a pastry blender until mixture forms fine crumbs; put into a small bowl.

In another bowl, whisk egg yolks with buttermilk or yogurt to blend; add to flour mixture; stir just until evenly moistened. Turn dough out onto a floured board; knead lightly with floured hands; knead just until it comes together. Pat out to about 1¼-inches thick. Using a 3-inch round cutter, cut out shortcakes; gather dough scraps and pat out again as necessary to make six. Place 2 inches apart on a 14 x 17-inch baking sheet. Place on middle oven rack; bake until tops feel firm when pressed, about 25 minutes. Transfer shortcakes to a rack; cool completely. Meanwhile, rinse berries. In a processor, or blender, put half the berries with remaining 2 tablespoons granulated sugar; whirl until smooth. Press through a fine strainer into a bowl; discard residue. To assemble shortcakes, slice each in half, horizontally; set bottoms on plates. Spoon yogurt or whipped cream over bottoms; top with remaining berries; drizzle with berry sauce. Place shortcake tops over berries; sprinkle with powdered sugar.

NO HASSLE BROWNIES

Really impress your guests, family, and yourself with these effort-less chocolate-chili pepper morsels.

Makes 16 2-inch Brownies

> 1 box or pouch of Ghiradelli® Double Chocolate Brownie Mix
> 2 tablespoons ground or powdered ancho peppers
> 1 cup pecan halves, coarsely broken

Preheat oven to 325°F. Follow directions on the box, but add ancho powder to dry ingredients. Add pecans; stir until just mixed. Follow manufacturer's baking instructions, taking care not to over cook. Served warm with a dollop of sour cream and a dash of paprika makes an outstanding, but simple dessert.

MONTEZUMA'S BROWNIES

The New World chili peppers and chocolate were combined in native food and drinks in pre-Columbian Mesoamerica, where chocolate originated, and later by the Aztecs. Some dishes added honey and vanilla but there was no sugar until it was introduced by Spaniards after Columbus. The combination is wonderful. The addition of dried red chili flakes, especially Anchos or Guajillos, to sweet chocolate desserts makes what would have been a cloying sweetness into a mellow richness. My long-time friend, Carol Kilgore, created this recipe to prove it. Try it!

Makes 12 to 16 Servings

    2   anchos, dried and microwave toasted (see below)
    6   ounces (squares) unsweetened baking chocolate, chopped
  1½   cups pecans, toasted
    ½   cup butter
    ½   cup (1 stick) margarine, unsalted
    5   eggs
  2¾   cups sugar
  1½   teaspoons vanilla
  1½   cups flour

Preheat oven to 375°F. Select pliable anchos; do not wash. With scissors stem, seed, and cut lengthwise. Microwave cut anchos for 2 minutes on high; stir. Continue cooking and stirring at 1 minute intervals until anchos are crisp, about 5 minutes. Crumble them gradually into an electric spice grinder or blender; reduce to a fine powder. Use 2 tablespoons of powder in recipe. Prepare at least 2 dozen anchos at a time; put what are not used in a tightly closed container in refrigerator for future use. Microwave pecans on high power for 8 to 10 minutes or until they are crisp but not browned; stir occasionally. Chop toasted pecans coarsely.

In a large bowl, microwave chocolate, butter, and margarine at 1 minute intervals until just melted; stir occasionally. Remove; continue stirring until chocolate mixture is well blended. Stir in 2 tablespoons of powdered ancho. In a large mixer bowl, beat eggs until light; add sugar gradually. Add vanilla. Stir in chocolate mixture. Add flour, beating just to blend; stir in pecans. Pour batter into a 9 x 13-inch pan sprayed with non-stick cooking spray. Bake for about 35 to 40 minutes until a toothpick inserted into cake center will come out with moist crumbs. Take care not to over-bake (very important). Cool in pan, then cut in rectangles. Serve warm.

ESPRESSO CAKE WITH BUTTER CREAM

Chocolate and peppers—two plants of New World origin. How had the Old World lived without them? Before 1492, Pre-Columbian natives of southern Mexico and Central America used them together. Today, Guatemalans still grow a chili pepper they call Chile Chocolate. Add to these that habit-forming Egyptian coffee bean and you are certain to have a winner. Both chocolate and coffee have caffeine.

Makes 8 to 10 Servings

    1   cup pecans, toasted
    ½   cup butter, cut into chunks
    6   ounces unsweetened chocolate, Ghiradelli® Double Chocolate, chopped fine
  2¼   cups granulated sugar
    ¼   cup instant espresso coffee powder, (Megdaglia d'Oro® preferred)
    2   tablespoons ancho ground or Aleppo peppers

4 large eggs

1 teaspoon vanilla

1¼ cups White Lily® or cake flour

¾ teaspoon baking powder

Preheat oven to 350°F. In a 2 to 3-quart sauce pan, add butter and unsweetened chocolate. Place on low heat or microwave; stir often until melted and smooth. Remove from heat; cool slightly; beat in granulated sugar, espresso powder, ancho powder; whisk in eggs 1 at a time; add vanilla; whisk until well blended. Mix baking powder into flour. Whisk in flour in 3 additions just until mixed; add pecans; whisk until mixed. Pour batter into a lightly buttered or cooking sprayed tart pan with removable rim or a 9 x 13-inch foil lined and sprayed baking dish. Bake until toothpick comes out of center clean, about 30 minutes. Cool completely on a rack, about 1 hour. Cut into wedges.

Alternative: Top with butter cream before cutting, if desired.

BUTTER CREAM

2 tablespoons butter

1 tablespoon espresso powder

¼ powdered sugar

2–3 tablespoons of coffee-flavored liquor, such as Kahlua

⅓ cup semi-sweet chocolate chips

In a bowl combine butter, espresso powder, powdered sugar, and liquor. With an electric mixer on medium speed, beat until smooth and fluffy, adding up to 1 more tablespoons liquor if necessary to make mixture smooth and spreadable. Spread evenly over top of cool cake. Place chocolate chips in a 1-quart unpleated, plastic bag. Heat in microwave at full power at 15-second intervals, squeezing

between intervals, until melted and smooth. Squeeze chocolate to one corner of bag, then cut off about ¼-inch of that corner. Pipe chocolate decoratively over buttercream. Chill until chocolate is firm. Remove pan rim. Cut cake into wedges and serve. A dollop of sour cream, Crema Mexicana or Centro Americana (see P. 28), on each serving is a tasteful addition.

PERUVIAN FLAN

While visiting in the home of Peruvian friends in Lima, Peru, I learned to make their traditional flan.

Makes 6 Servings

1 cup granulated sugar

¼ cup water

1 can sweetened condensed milk

1 cup evaporated milk

4 eggs

In a small saucepan over low heat sugar; stir constantly until sugar melts and turns a deep brown, taking care not to scorch. Add water; stir as you bring to a boil. Remove from burner; allow to cool. In a bowl, mix both of the milks and the eggs; whisk until blended. Pour cooled sugar mixture into a small ring mold. Over this pour milk and egg mixture. Cover tightly. Pour water in a very large sauce pan and place mold inside sauce pan. Over high heat, bring water in saucepan to a boil. Turn down to a medium heat and cook for 1 hour. Remove from heat and cool for 30 minutes. Turn mold onto serving dish and garnish with fresh edible flowers or fresh fruit, such as mango slices.

NOTE: A dash of cayenne pepper modifies the excess sweetness that Latinos love so much.

THE PEPPER LADY'S VERSION OF LAURA BUSH'S TEXAS COWBOY COOKIES

When Laura's husband, George W. was governor of Texas, this recipe was one of the crowd-pleasers at the Governor's Mansion. I've doctored it a bit to level out some of the sweetness.

Makes 6 Dozen

 3 cups all-purpose flour
 1 tablespoon baking powder
 1 tablespoon baking soda
 1 tablespoon ground cinnamon
 2 tablespoons ground Ancho chili peppers
 1½ cups butter or low-fat margarine or mixed, at room temperature
 1½ cups granulated sugar
 1½ cups light-brown sugar, packed
 3 eggs
 2 tablespoons vanilla
 3 cups semisweet chocolate chips, Tropical Source®, Guittard®, Ghirardelli®, or Nestle's Toll House®, are my preferences, in that order
 3 cups old-fashioned rolled oats
 2 cups coconut, sweetened flakes
 2 cups pecans, coarsely chopped

Preheat oven to 350°F. In a bowl, mix flour, baking powder, baking soda, cinnamon, ancho, and salt; mix well. In a 8-quart bowl, beat butter on medium speed until smooth and creamy; gradually add sugars while beating. Add eggs, one at a time, beating after each. Beat in vanilla. Stir in flour mixture until just combined. Add chocolate chips, oats, coconut and pecans; mix well. For each cookie, drop a heaping tablespoon dough onto ungreased baking sheets, spacing 2 inches apart. Bake 17 to 20 minutes, until edges are barely brown, being careful not to get too brown; rotate sheets halfway through. Remove cookies to a rack to cool.

NOTE: In a chocolate chip tasting contest conducted by *Cook's Illustrated Magazine,* the winning chocolate chips were ranked as I have listed in the recipe. No others were recommended.

SERRANO-LIME TARTS WITH COCONUT CREAM

This recipe has but a small amount of chili pepper in it but it is a very nice compliment to a highly spiced meal. Most of it can be made a day or more ahead of time.

Makes 6 Servings

LIME CURD:

Makes 2½ Cups

 1¼ pounds limes, rinsed and juiced
 1 Serrano, seeded (more, to taste, if desired)
 1 cup granulated sugar
 5 large eggs
 ½ cup butter or margarine, cut into pieces

With a vegetable peeler, pare green part of peel from 4 limes. Put peel, serrano, and sugar in a food processor; process until peel is minced; let stand, covered, 30 minutes or up to 6 hours. Add 1 cup lime juice (save remainder for other uses) to sugar and peel mixture; process until sugar dissolves. Pour mixture through a fine strainer into a 2 to 3-quart sauce pan, pressing liquid from peel; discard peel. Add eggs and whisk to blend; add butter. Stir over medium-low heat until mixture thickly coats a metal spoon, about 15 minutes. Scrape into a bowl, cover, and chill until cold, at least 1 hour, or up to 3 days. Stir before using.

COCONUT CREAM

⅓ cup coconut flakes, sweetened
⅔ cup whipping cream
⅓ cup coconut milk, stirred before measuring
2–3 tablespoons powdered sugar
6 4-inch tart crusts, (see Recipe P. 84)

In a 8 to 10-inch frying over medium-high heat, stir coconut until lightly browned, 1 to 2 minutes; pour into a small bowl. Cover; let stand at room temperature up to 2 hours. In another bowl, combine whipping cream, coconut milk, and powdered sugar. Beat with a mixer on high speed until coconut cream holds soft peaks. Cover; chill up to 2 hours. Blend in browned coconut.

To Serve: Divide cold curd between 6 tart shells; top each filled tart shell with coconut cream. Place filled tarts on individual dessert plates; serve. Plates may be garnished with fresh flowers such as pansies or violets.

MARGARITA PIE

Although this recipe contains no peppers, I have included it in this collection. There is nothing better before or with a spicy dinner than a tangy margarita. This pie is a good follow up that can be made the day before.

Makes 8 Servings

1½ cups pretzels, crushed
¼ cup granulated sugar
⅔ cup butter or margarine, melted
1 can sweetened condensed milk
¼ cup fresh lime juice
¼ cup tequila
4 tablespoons Triple Sec
2 cups whipping cream or frozen light Kool Whip® type topping, or equal parts of each
8 lime slices, thinly cut

In a bowl mix crushed pretzels, butter and sugar. Press into bottom of a 9-inch pie pan; also coat sides. In another bowl mix tequila, Triple Sec, condensed milk, and lime juice. Fold in whipped cream. Spoon into crust. Freeze until firm; wrap in plastic wrap and freeze for 4 hours until solid, or overnight. Remove from freezer about mid-way during meal; slice into 8 wedges. Garnish with a lime slice.

CHOCOLATE BERRY TART

This is so simple a child could do it, but it is GOOD!

Makes—depends on the number of shells in the package you purchase, usually 6 to 8

1 package pre-baked phyllo tart shells (available in frozen food case)
¾ cup heavy cream
1 teaspoon ancho powder (ground ancho chili pepper)
   Sugar to taste
1 6-ounce package semisweet chocolate chips
1 cup fresh berries; raspberries, blueberries, or strawberries

Put cream and ancho powder in a small saucepan over medium heat; bring to almost boiling. Add sugar to taste. Stir in chocolate chips until smooth. Fill tart shells with chocolate sauce; top with berries. A dollop of whipped cream would add to appearance, taste, and calories.

BANANAS FOSTER AL MEXICANA

Rich and delicious. Look for the cajeta, a caramelized condensed milk, in a jar in ethnic food stores that carry foods from Mexico. Don't try to make the cajeta yourself.

Makes 4 to 6 Servings

- 10 ounces cajeta, in jar or can; no substitute
- 2 teaspoons Aleppo pepper or ½ teaspoon cayenne
- ¼ cup tequila
- 3 bananas, not over ripe
- 1 tablespoon butter
- 1 pint vanilla ice cream or frozen yogurt; use low-fat if desired
- ¼ cup pecans, toasted and chopped

Put cajeta in a microwave safe bowl; warm in microwave oven or set bowl over boiling water. Stir in tequila. Slice bananas in half lengthwise and crosswise. Melt butter in a nonstick skillet, add bananas; saute lightly. In each serving dish put a scoop of ice cream or frozen yogurt; top with banana pieces. Spoon warm cajeta over top. Sprinkle with pecan pieces. Serve immediately.

NEW WORLD TRUFFLES

These rich morsels evolved from my New World Pie. Don't eat if calorie counting.

Makes 24 Truffles

- 1½ cups milk chocolate chips

- ¼ cup (½ stick) butter or margarine
- 1 tablespoon finely ground ancho, see note below
- ½ teaspoon finely ground cayenne pepper
- ½ cup no cholesterol egg product
- 2 tablespoons Kaluha liqueur or brandy
  Ground pecans or other nuts

Place chocolate and butter in top of a double boiler over barely simmering water. Cover; let stand until partially melted; remove cover; stir until completely melted. Remove top pan of double boiler, keeping water in lower pan heated. Add ground chili peppers; mix well. Stir egg product into chocolate mixture; return it to pan of fully simmering water. Stir mixture continuously until it is quite hot but not boiling. Continue cooking and stirring for 3 minutes. Remove boiler top from heat; add liqueur gradually while stirring. Set pan in a large bowl of ice water. Add ice as necessary to keep water very cold. Stir constantly until entire mixture forms a fairly firm, non-sticky ball.

Place slightly rounded teaspoonfuls of candy on a sheet of waxed paper; let them dry for 1 to 2 hours, or until firm enough to handle. Put ground nuts on a sheet of waxed paper and roll each truffle in nuts. Allow truffles to dry for 30 minutes to 1 hour; shake off excess nuts. These truffles will keep for 2 to 3 days at room temperature, but they are best fresh. To keep them up to a week, they may be refrigerated in a tightly closed container but they should be allowed to return to room temperature before serving.

NOTE: To grind the ancho, remove stem, seeds, and veins from dry pod. Break pod into pieces; place it in a spice mill, blender, or mortar. Grind ancho to a very fine powder. Store in a tightly closed jar or Ziplock plastic bag. It is best to do several at a time because the properly sealed powder will keep almost indefinitely in a refrigerator.

7

RELISHES

CHUTNEYS

PRESERVES

CONDIMENTS

Relishes, Chutneys, Preserves, and Condiments

Introduction to Preserving

We can thank the Arabs for preserves, marmalades, jellies, jams, and those sweet condiments that grace our tables and rot our teeth. The Arabs took over the Greco-Roman practice of conserving fruits in honey, and extended or improved the process when they acquired sugar. Sugar had come to Arabia via Persia. The Persians had obtained it from India where the technology of making "raw" sugar originated around 500 B.C., following the introduction of sugarcane (*Saccharum officinarum*), probably from New Guinea. As early as 325 B.C. the Greek geographer Strabo reported that sugarcane was present in India. The Persians carried sugar westward in the sixth century A.D. The Arabs got it from them and introduced it to Syria, North Africa, and Spain. However, at that time the Far East was the only known area of the Old World where the climatic conditions permitted the cultivation of sugar. Consequently, only a small amount made its way to Europe via the Middle East and Venice before 1500. Throughout that period, honey was the primary sweetener, while the costly imported sugar was reserved for medicinal purposes. The English words sugar and candy are derived from the Arabic version of the Sanskrit *sharkar* and *khandh,* both of which mean "sugar."

Columbus brought tropical sugarcane to the West Indies on his second voyage. Sugarcane cultivation was carried farther and farther west as settlers followed the early explorers to the New World. The sweltering, tropical New World sugar plantations were established in order to satisfy the European yearning for sweets, and millions of Africans were enslaved to appease that craving. With the new production, the price of that luxury item became somewhat lower, making it possible for people other than the wealthy to enjoy sugar. The amount and range of sugar usage increased as worldwide sugar production grew. Then it became possible to afford the sweetener for other than medicinal purposes, and sugar-preserved fruits began appearing as a final dessert course.

Not only did sugar affect a culinary change, but it also produced the fortunes that made the Industrial Revolution possible. A considerable addition to those fortunes came from rum, a by-product of the sugar industry, which became the official liquor of the English navy. For a single plant species that offers no special benefit to the health or well-being of humankind, sugar has had an extraordinarily broad influence on Western history.

Sugar-preserved fruits and syrups had dual roles, first as healing (or therapeutic) potions and later as table delicacies. The knowledge of the making of these fruit confections migrated from the Middle East to medieval Europe, thence from Europe to America. The arrival of the art of making preserves and sweetmeats was the most outstanding addition to gastronomy in Renaissance Europe. Italians were the basic revolutionaries in the realm of preserves, and a significant book on preserving was *Bastiment de Recettes,* an Italian publication that introduced the completely unknown art of making preserves, jams, and jellies into France. To me, the arid desert seems an unlikely place, but during that same period, in sixteenth century Egypt, there was a minor industry in preserves and sweetmeats. In my travels I have observed that speaking Arabic and eating sweets go hand-in-hand—obviously a very long standing tradition.

During the sixteenth century the job of sweetmeat cooks, called *confituriers,* was to make not only jellies and preserves but also liqueurs and cordials. The Western world was in its formative stage of preserve-making when the French physician Michel de Nostradamus separated preserved fruit into two categories—dry and liquid—for his *Opuscule* in 1555. His liquid preserves included fruit based jellies, jams, and preserves in syrups similar to those we make today. Anything that could be eaten with the fingers—candied fruits, nuts, seeds, and vegetables—comprised dry preserves. His recipes used both sugar and honey as sweeteners for the liquid kind, but only sugar for the dry type.

During the period of European expansion, sugar was still a luxury. Europeans, who took their recipes for preserves and marmalades with them to their colonies in the New World, found that cane sugar was expensive in the North American colonies, so most early colonial cooks followed the Native American practice of using maple sugar, although white sugar was the ideal. At the end of the nineteenth century cane sugar became affordable and plentiful as a result of the Spanish-American War, when the sugar-growing territories of Cuba and the Philippines came under American control. Sugar consumption in America soared following that event, and Americans also began adding it to pickled vegetables and fruits such as cucumbers, radishes, purslane, gherkins, peppers, and peaches. In the United States cooks began treating pickles as more than just a "salad" (served mixed with olive oil, as in the eighteenth century) or as a condiment eaten with meat. Pickles became something to be eaten alone or as a side dish.

Before you can have pickles you must have vinegar, and before you can have vinegar you must have alcohol, because vinegar is the product of a bacterial-implemented (what's known as the "mother") fermentation of an alcoholic liquid. Consequently humans have had vinegar as long as they have had wine. If the start-up liquid has been pasteurized, or if the percentage of alcohol is high enough, no "mother" will form, hence no vinegar. No one knows for certain when wine making began, but it is estimated to have been between 8000 B.C. and 3000 B.C. As a condiment, vinegar has long been held in high regard, as testified by a reference to it in the Book of Ruth (2:14). "And Boaz said unto her, at mealtime come thou hither, and eat of the bread, and dip thy morsel in the vinegar (wine)." Pickles were known in Mesopotamia, ancient Egypt, Greek and Roman antiquity, and China as well as in India. Pickles, in general, were made in European cultures as early as vinegars became available to preserve them and that has been a very long time. The ancient Celts used cider vinegar, the Romans used wine vinegar.

Chutney is a sweet and sour fruit condiment that originated in India and was introduced to Europe by early British or Dutch trading ships and later through England's colonization of India. The word chutney may come from the Hindi *chatna,* meaning "taste." Making chutney was a means of preserving fruits in a tropical climate. Indian cooks favor very hot, spicy pickles, achaar. Mixed vegetable pickles, also called *achaars,* which we call chow chows, are another Indian specialty. I wondered whether the term chow chow could have come from India along with the relish, as a corruption of *achaar*—chaar or char, so I asked food historian William Woys Weaver, whose specialty is relishes and preserves, for an opinion. He deduced that it was entirely possible that Dutch traders and colonists in southern India and Ceylon picked up the term along with the relish because he had learned that early Pennsylvania Dutch used a corrupted form, *jar jar,* as their initial way of writing chow chow. Continuing, he said that the term can be traced to the U.S. Centennial in 1876, since a great many commercial foods were sold there, among them packaged pickles from India. Also, many Philadelphia hotels and food specialty shops offered goods from India—they were quite chic in the 1870s. Today, chutney is having a well-deserved resurgence on our tables.

The British came to favor another type of pickle—pickled, stuffed mangoes—after they began trading with the Portuguese along the Malabar coast of India early in the seventeenth century. Since tropical mangoes were not available in the British Isles, small melons and cucumbers were substituted and stuffed with a mixture of six or seven spices, garlic, and horseradish mixed with olive oil before they were pickled in a crock filled with vinegar. In fact, British cooks took to "mangoing" various other substitutes. When the English colonized America, they brought the recipe for "mangoes" with them but had to use small muskmelons and green Bell Peppers. Pepper mangoes were so popular that Bell Peppers were and still are called mangoes in several parts of the United States.

Not only in the art of making relishes, chutneys, and pickles are peppers a marvelous addition, but I also find their acridity a perfect complement to the sometimes cloying sweetness of preserves, marmalades, and jellies. There is a physiological basis for this. When foods with different taste characteristics are mixed, these characteristics do not meld to produce a new taste but rather suppress or enhance one another; for example, salt added to sweet enhances the latter, while pungent, acid, and acrid things mitigate sweetness. Don't be afraid to try them in your favorite plum or peach jam. Serranos or chiltepínes add zest without changing the fruity flavor.

Putting Peppers By

Methods

It was through my hobby of pickling and preserving that I met and fell in love with *Capsicum* peppers in the early 1970s. Peppers were indispensable to pickles and relishes, and now, I find them equally vital to my preserves. The addition of capsicums to a sweet fruit enhances and compliments the cloying sweetness of sugar. The pickle and relish book that I had begun, along with recipes I had developed, went in the closet during my pursuit of peppers. Now, years later, I have rescued those tasty recipes from oblivion by including them in this book.

One hot Texas summer, while I was peeling and preserving a bumper crop, an old timer dropped by and drawled to me, "Honey, you better put up enough for two or three years, *'cause* you might not make a crop next year." He was right! However, if your colorful, tasty products are to last more than a few weeks, care must be taken to insure the homemade condiments and preserves are sterile before they are put in the pantry. There is so much hard work involved in preserving that it is a shame to risk losing all those ingredients and such effort through careless procedures. Unless you have ideal storage—30° to 50°F. and dry and dark—giving the product of your labors a boiling water bath according to directions will insure that you and your friends will enjoy the fruits of your garden. The four things that cause spoilage in preserved food—bacteria, enzymes, molds, and yeast—can be controlled by heat, hence the hot water bath. You will need a six to seven-quart, non-reactive pot to cook in (too many boil-overs occur in anything smaller), a large preserving kettle with a lid, a jar rack for the water bath, and a pair of tongs designed to lift jars from hot water.

Pickling

Canning relishes and sauces that have been acidified with vinegar can be a very satisfying experience, and family and friends will be provided with taste treats throughout the year. For pickles the fruit and/or vegetables are left whole or cut to a specific size, while in relishes they are chopped. Only the very freshest, firmest fruits and vegetables, and whole spices (ground spices will cause darkening during storage) should be used and the recipe directions followed exactly. They are sealed and stored as are other canned foods, but they require a wait of at least six weeks before eating for the flavors to meld. A boiling-water bath will guarantee a safe relish or pickle that will keep for several years at 50° to 70° F in a dark, dry place, although the contents may darken if kept too long. After opening they will keep in a tightly closed container in the refrigerator almost indefinitely.

Preserving

Preserving is an ancient procedure for safeguarding fruits and vegetables by increasing their sugar content to a concentration in which microbes are dehydrated by osmotic pressure, and are thereby destroyed. Sugar, fruit, pectin, and acid are the common denominators of jelly (made from juice), preserves (whole or large pieces of fruit in syrup), jam (made from ground or crushed fruit), and marmalade (a soft jelly with bits of citrus throughout).

Sugar This acts as a preservative and aids the formation of gels. Honey or corn sirup can be used for half the sugar in jams and marmalades but only a quarter in jellies.

Fruit Select full-flavored, slightly under-ripe fruits to overcome the sweetness of sugar.

Pectin This is what makes jelly gel. Pectin occurs to some extent in all fruits and decreases with maturity. Commercial pectin—liquid or crystalline—take the guesswork out of jams and jellies without affecting color or flavor. Capsicums require the addition of such supplemental pectin.

Acid Without acid, no fruit will thicken or gel. Under-ripe fruit is higher in acid than fully ripe fruit. Lemon juice is frequently added to low acid fruits.

In the process of preserving, the fruit to be preserved—whole or cut up—is simmered for 10 to 20 minutes in a small amount of water to extract pectin. If the fruit is deficient in either pectin or acid, then add commercial pectin or pared lemon slices. Follow the printed directions from the pectin package exactly. Additional or excessive cooking will break down pectin molecules. The correct amount of sugar is added and the mixture is kept at a rolling boil until the desired consistency is reached. If a sample of the preserves fails to gel when cooled in a spoon, additional lemon juice or pectin can be added to stabilize the ingredients. Measure carefully and **NEVER** double a recipe because the additional cooking required not only darkens the fruit but also lessens the flavor. Experience, or an experienced friend, is a big help until you get the hang of preserving.

Properly sealed preserves stored in a dark, dry place at 50 to 70°F should keep indefinitely; however, it will darken. Once opened jars of preserves should be tightly closed and stored in the refrigerator where they will keep up to a year.

Canning

The *Capsicum* is a low-acid fruit/vegetable, which must be canned in a pressure canner for safety. The risk of botulism makes it unwise to can peppers as a vegetable at home.

Jars, lids, and sterilizing them

Use modern, self-sealing jars, unused flat lids, and reusable rings/bands that can be purchased at supermarkets, hardware stores, or feed stores. If you have saved jars from previous years, be certain the rims are intact. Use only new lids. The jars and lids must be washed thoroughly before use. If a boiling-water bath is to be used they will not need to be sterilized prior to filling; however, the jars should be hot when they receive the boiling fruit. Before you start cooking, fill clean jars one quarter full of very hot water and place them in a flat pan in a 225° F oven so they will be the right temperature when the fruit is ready to be poured. Do not boil the self-sealing lids; instead put them in a glass or metal container, scald them by covering them with boiling water and let them rest until you are ready for them.

Filling the jars

Fill hot, clean jars to within ½ inch of the rim. If air bubbles appear, run a sterile knife down the inside of each jar to release the air. Wipe rims clean and seal with scalded lids. Put the band on, then tighten it completely before hot jars are placed in a boiling-water bath. Do not tighten lids after the bath or you will break the seal.

Boiling-water bath

After sealing the hot jars of goodies, place them on a rack in a canning kettle. Add enough steaming hot water—never cold water—to cover jars an inch or two. Cover the kettle; turn the heat up. When the water reaches a rolling boil, start timing—20 minutes for quart jars of whole dill or sour pickles, 5 minutes for jars of sweet pickles and rel-

ishes such as chutney, piccalilli, relish, chow chow, pickled jalapeños, and preserves. Be certain the water boils steadily throughout the processing period. If necessary, add boiling water to replace any that evaporated. When the processing time is up, remove jars from the canner at once. Place on racks to cool, out of any breeze. After jars are cool check the seal by pressing the lids. If the lid pops back, the jar is not sealed; store in the refrigerator. If lid stays down, store in cool (50° to 70°F), dry place.

NOTE: Jellies should not receive a boiling water bath but should be put up in sterilized jars (boiled for 15 minutes at 212° F.) to within ½-inch of the rim and sealed immediately with a ¼-inch layer of melted paraffin in order to prevent surface mold. Cover with scalded lids.

NOTE: To melt paraffin place it in a clean can that has been bent at the rim to form a pouring spout. Place can in a saucepan of boiling water to melt. Never place it over the flame as it catches fire easily. Be very careful when melting paraffin.

Relishes

CHOW CHOW

Chow chow, according to the dictionary, is a mixed pickle in mustard. The name comes from achaar (see P. 26), which is a Indian condiment flavored with mustard seed. After studying numerous chow chow and mustard pickle recipes I came to the conclusion that there is little, if any, difference between the two. In my parents home, we always had a jar labeled Crosse and Blackwell Mustard Pickle on our table and my Yankee father called it chow chow, in spite of its label. The main difference appears to be the size of the vegetable—smaller in chow chow. I prefer the smaller bits. The combination of vegetables is variable. A lot of folks call any vegetable relish chow chow.

Makes 4 Quarts

- 2 small (2-inch to 3-inch) green cucumbers, sliced
- 1 red Bell Pepper, seeded and chopped
- 1 green Bell Pepper, seeded and chopped
- 1 pint pearl onions, peeled (canned cocktail onions may be substituted)
- 1 head cauliflower, cut into florets
- 1 pint tiny green tomatoes, cut in half if too large
- 1 pint whole tiny snap beans
- 1 pint lima beans, shelled
- 1 pint tiny pickled gherkins (buy these bottled)

NOTE: Amounts are estimates. Prepare at least 4 or 4 ½ quarts of vegetables.

For the Brine
- 1 cup salt
- 4 cups boiling water

For the Sauce
- 1½ cups all-purpose flour
- 1 teaspoon ground cayenne pepper
- 6 tablespoons dry mustard
- 1½ tablespoons turmeric
- 2 quarts cider vinegar
- 2½ cups sugar
- 3 tablespoons celery seeds
- 1 tablespoon mustard seeds

Combine vegetables in a crock. In a bowl, stir brine ingredients together until salt is dissolved; pour over vegetables to cover. Let stand overnight. In a large non-reactive saucepan bring vegetables and brine to a boil. Let stand 10 minutes. Rinse thoroughly in cold water. Drain. Combine vegetables in a large non-reactive kettle. Make a paste of flour and ground spices with a small amount of the vinegar. In a non-reactive saucepan, bring remaining vinegar, sugar, and seeds to a boil. Slowly stir in flour mixture; cook until smooth; thickened. Combine with vegetables. Simmer over medium heat until vegetables are just barely tender. Pour into hot, clean jars and process in a boiling-water bath for 15 minutes as described on page 182.

Variation: For a snappier chow chow, add 1 tablespoon or more canned nacho-sliced jalapeños to the vegetables.

CREOLE CHOW CHOW OR MUSTARD PICKLE

What follows is an adaptation of an old Creole recipe from New Orleans. In this country, Creoles are descendants of French, Spanish, or Portuguese settlers of Louisiana and the Gulf States who retained their special speech or culture, which includes food preparation.

Makes 10 to 12 Pints

3	quarts cider vinegar
2	tablespoons mustard seeds
½	cup celery seeds
1	tablespoon horseradish, grated
1	garlic clove, peeled and minced
2–3	fresh chili peppers, (serrano, jalapeño, Fresno), seeded and chopped
1	cup brown sugar, firmly packed
1	teaspoon turmeric
1	cup dry mustard
½	cup vegetable oil

Put vinegar in a non-reactive saucepan; bring to a boil. Add mustard seeds, mustard, celery seeds, horseradish, garlic, and chili peppers. Boil 5 minutes, stirring constantly, then add the sugar. Make a paste of the turmeric, dry mustard, and oil with a little cold vinegar. Slowly pour into hot vinegar mixture. Stir well; pour over chilli and spice mixture. Pour into hot, clean jars, seal; process in a boiling water bath according to directions on page 182. A small, bright red chilli pushed down the inside of filled jars so that it can be seen against the glass is an attractive addition. Refrigerate once opened.

HAYDEN'S RELISH

I have never known who Hayden was but when I was a child a neighbor gave this recipe to my mother and it has always been our very favorite relish. We made it every summer. Thank you Hayden, whoever you were!

Makes 12 to 18 Pints

1	gallon firm, ripe tomatoes, cored and coarse-ground (about 4 pounds)
1	gallon green and red Bell Peppers, seeded and coarse-ground (about 5 pounds)
1	gallon cabbage, medium-chopped (about 6 pounds)
1	quart red onions, chopped (about 4 pounds)
1	cup non-iodized salt
6	jalapeños, seeded and chopped
8	cups five percent cider vinegar
6	cups granulated sugar
2	tablespoons mustard seeds
2	tablespoons celery seeds
2	teaspoons turmeric
2	teaspoons ground cinnamon
1	teaspoon ground clove
1	teaspoon ground ginger

Place vegetables in a large container such as a plastic dishpan; mix with salt. Let stand for 2 hours. Lift from juice, drain. Put in a large non-reactive pan (6 to 7-quarts or larger); add the remaining ingredients. Boil vegetables and spices for 30 minutes; stirring frequently. Pack into hot, clean jars, seal; process in a boiling water bath for 10 minutes according to directions on page 182. Refrigerate in a tightly closed jar once opened. Relish will keep for several months. Delicious with meats, ham, mixed in mayonnaise for salad dressing, in deviled eggs, tuna salad, or on hamburgers.

OLD FASHIONED PEPPER RELISH

Remember the old county fair? This relish was always there. It is a gardener's delight. Serve it with grilled meats, barbecue, in tuna or chicken salad, or on sandwiches and hamburgers.

Makes about 10 Pints

- 8 cups Bell Peppers of all colors, seeded and coarse ground (or a garden mix of Poblano, Banana, 'Cubanelle,' 'New Mexican Chile,') about 15 large; measure after grinding
- 4 jalapeños or serranos, or your garden chili peppers, seeded and coarse-ground
- 8 cups red onions, coarse ground (about 8 to 10 large)
- 4 cups five percent white vinegar
- 1 cup water
- 3 cups sugar
- 2 tablespoons salt
- 3 tablespoons mustard seeds
- 2 tablespoons celery seeds
- 1 teaspoon fresh ginger, peeled and minced

Place ground peppers, chili peppers, and onion in a large container (plastic dishpan will do); cover with boiling water; let stand for 10 to 15 minutes. Drain; return to container. Mix 1 cup vinegar and 1 cup water; heat to boiling; pour over drained vegetables. Let stand 15 minutes. Drain again. Place vegetables in a large (6 to 7-quart) non-reactive pot; add remaining ingredients; place over high heat. Bring to a rolling boil. Pour mixture into clean, hot jars. Process in hot water bath according to directions on page 182. Remove from water; place on racks out of a draft. Check your seal by tapping the metal cap. It should ring. If the sound is dull, use in next 6 weeks. Tighten lids. Allow to mellow for a month before using.

MEDITERRANEAN RELISH (UNCOOKED)

This easy eggplant and Long Green Chile relish is reminiscent of the Mediterranean flavors, but with alien peppers.

Makes 2 Cups

- 1 1-pound eggplant
- 4 mild, Long Green or sweet banana pepper, seeded and finely chopped
- 1 fresh jalapeño, seeded and finely chopped
- 2 garlic cloves, peeled and crushed
- 2 tablespoons onion, grated
- 3 tablespoons fresh lemon juice or white wine vinegar
- 1 tablespoon fresh basil, chopped
- 6 tablespoons olive oil
  Salt and freshly ground black pepper to taste

Preheat oven to 375°F. Pierce the eggplant with a fork in two or three places. For good flavor, bake in oven for 20 minutes, turning once. Place baked eggplant over a gas flame, hot charcoal, or under a broiler; roast until soft and blackened. Remove blackened skin under cold running water; then press gently to remove any bitter juices. Chop pulp fine; mix with peppers. Add garlic, onion, and lemon juice; gradually stir in oil. Season with salt and pepper to taste. Chill before serving. Keep in refrigerator, covered, for up to a week.

Chutneys

RED PEPPER AND TOMATO CHUTNEY

This is an easy chutney for the novice—but good!

Makes 10 Cups

- 6 cups ripe tomatoes, peeled and quartered
- 1 cup red Bell Pepper or any sweet red pepper, seeded and sliced lengthwise
- 2 red chilli peppers, jalapeños, serranos, or Fresno
- 2 Granny Smith apples, cored and sliced into narrow wedges
- 2 red onions, sliced and separated into rings
- 3 tablespoons mustard seed
- 1 tablespoon salt
- 4 cups cider vinegar
- 1 6-ounce pouch liquid pectin (Certo®), See: note 1 below

For the Spice Bag:

- 1 tablespoon cloves, whole
- 1 tablespoon allspice, whole
- 2 tablespoon fresh ginger, peeled and sliced
- 2 tablespoon celery seed
- ½ teaspoon cumin seeds, bruised
- 3 tamarind pulp from seed pods; remove shell and seed (see Note 2 below)
- 3 cups brown sugar

Place tomatoes in a 6 to 7-quart non-reactive kettle. Add Bell Pepper, chili peppers, apples, onions, mustard seed, and salt. Simmer over medium-low heat gently for 30 minutes. Put all other spices, pulp and seeds of tamarinds in a spice bag or piece of muslin secured with a rubber band. Place spice bag and vinegar in a 2 quart non-reactive pan; bring to a boil; reduce heat to medium; simmer for 30 minutes. Remove spice bag; strain vinegar into tomato mixture. Add sugar and bring to a rolling boil. Reduce heat to medium-low; simmer for 1 hour. Turn off; cover. Let chutney sit over night. Next day bring chutney to a rolling boil; add pectin (see Note below). When mixture comes to a rolling boil again, boil for 1 minute. Remove from heat; pour into hot, sterilized jars. Wipe rims with wet paper toweling, seal with a thin layer of melted paraffin and cap. Wait three weeks to allow the chutney to mellow before using.

NOTE: Chutney can be made without commercial pectin by boiling much longer, until it has thickened. This reduces volume considerably and produces a darker product.

JEAN'S OWN CHUTNEY

Making this is a lot of work, but well worth the trouble. I came up with this recipe after analyzing over 50 chutney recipes. Always use any two different firm fruits that are in season. Granny Smith apples or dried Turkish apricots are a good stand-by for one, then use others such as: green tomatoes, figs, loquats, peaches, etc., for the second. Tamarind is the "secret weapon."

Makes About 9 Pints

- 4 cups brown sugar, firmly packed
- 2 cups granulated sugar
- 1 quart cider vinegar
- 1 pound golden raisins, ground in blender
- 1 cup fresh lime juice
- 1 cup tamarind juice and purée; or a purée of ½ cup dried apricots, soaked in water to make 1 cup, plus 2 tablespoons Worcestershire sauce
- 1 cup red onion, chopped
- 2 garlic cloves, peeled and, minced
- 1 teaspoon salt
- 12 Kieffer or hard, green canning pears (not Bartlett); or Granny Smith apples, pared, diced (8 pounds before peeling)
- 3 tablespoons preserved ginger
- 4 tablespoons fresh ginger, peeled and sliced thin
- 4 cups red Bell Peppers, or mixed sweet peppers, seeded and 1-inch diced; or mango, slightly under-ripe; or 4 cups peaches, peeled, seeded, and chopped or sliced; or other such fruit as citron melon; or green tomatoes
- 2–4 serranos or jalapeños, seeded and sliced
- 1 cup fresh lime juice

For the Spice Bag

- 2 cinnamon sticks
- 20 whole cloves
- 2 dried red chili peppers or ½ teaspoon ground cayenne pepper
- 1 teaspoon ground nutmeg
- 2 teaspoons ground allspice
- 1 teaspoon turmeric
- 1 teaspoon ground mace

Place sugars, spice bag, and vinegar in large 6 to 7-quart non-reactive pan; cook until clear, stirring to dissolve sugar. Add dried fruit purée, onions, garlic, and salt; cook until thickened over a low-medium heat. Add sliced fresh fruits, ginger, and peppers; boil gently for 15 minutes, no more, stirring frequently. Cover immediately; let sit overnight. Next day, adjust seasonings; cook chutney down by simmering 15 to 20 minutes. This final cooking down may take more or less time but must be watched very carefully to prevent scorching. Remove spice bag and pour boiling chutney into hot, clean jars. Seal; process in a boiling water bath according to the directions on page 182. Remove and place on racks out of draft to cool. Allow flavors to meld for 3 weeks before serving.

This fairly dark-colored chutney is great with meats, curries, over cream cheese as an hors d'oeuvre, or in sour cream on fruit salad. Cover tightly and refrigerate once opened. It will keep almost indefinitely in the refrigerator.

CRANBERRY CHUTNEY

Although this is cooked, do not can this chutney, it is better as a fresh accompaniment to meat, especially poultry. A delightful change from the traditional cranberry sauce.

Makes 3 to 4 Cups

- 2 cups fresh cranberries
- ½ cup water
- ½ cup golden raisins
- 1 small onion, thinly sliced and separated into rings
- 1–2 serranos or fresh jalapeños, seeded and thinly sliced
- 1 cup sugar
- ¼ teaspoon ground ginger
- ¼ teaspoon ground cinnamon
- ⅛ teaspoon ground allspice
- ⅛ teaspoon salt
- 1 cup fresh pineapple, diced, or 8-ounce can pineapple tidbits, drained

Combine all ingredients except pineapple in a non-reactive Dutch oven or similar deep pan; stir well. Cook over medium heat, uncovered, until reduced and thickened, 10 to 15 minutes. Add pineapple, bring to a boil, remove from heat, let sit covered, until cool. Serve with turkey, ham, lamb, or in baked acorn squash halves. Cover and keep refrigerated for 7 to 10 days.

PAKISTANI MANGO CHUTNEY

I found this delectable chutney during my numerous visits with my friend Noodie Khan at her home in Lahore, as well as in hotels throughout Pakistan. I fell in love with it.

Makes 12 to 13 Cups

- 8 pounds under-ripe mangos, peeled, seeded and thinly sliced, then weighed
- 3 cups cider vinegar
- 5 pounds granulated sugar
- 10 garlic cloves, peeled and minced
- 1 cup candied ginger, chopped and lightly packed
- 3 tablespoons Aleppo pepper or 2 tablespoons Cayenne pepper
- Salt to taste
- 1 envelope of liquid pectin (Certo®)

In a 8 quart or larger, non-reactive kettle place all ingredients except pectin; mix well. Bring uncovered mixture to a rolling boil. Reduce heat to maintain a very low boil for 15 minutes, stirring frequently. Cover kettle; turn off heat. allow mixture to sit overnight. The following day bring uncovered mixture to a rolling boil again for 15 minutes; add pectin. When mixture returns to a boil, allow it to boil for one minute; turn off heat. Fill hot, sterile jars to within one-half inch of rim. Cover chutney with a thin layer of melted paraffin and seal. Allow it to mellow for at least three weeks before serving with chicken, curries, ham, or as an appetizer on a block of cream cheese.

RED BELL PEPPER AND APPLE CHUTNEY

Be sure to use a tart, firm apples like Granny Smith or Gala for this tasty but simple bottled chutney.

Makes about 10 Cups

- 12 red Bell Peppers, stem, veins and seeds removed; chopped
- 1 pound red onions, peeled and finely chopped
- 4 garlic cloves, peeled and finely chopped
- 8 pounds Granny Smith apples, pared, and chopped (weight before peeling)
- 5 cups brown malt vinegar, five percent acetic
- 8 cups dark brown sugar
- 1 cup ginger, crystalized or sugared
- 1 tablespoon celery seed, whole
- 2 teaspoons salt
- 1 teaspoon cayenne pepper

Place peppers, onion, and garlic in a large non-reactive kettle; add enough water to cover; bring to a boil then reduce heat; simmer gently uncovered for about 15 minutes. Drain and return to cooking pan. Add apples, vinegar, sugar, ginger, celery seed, salt, and cayenne pepper; stir to mix well. Bring to a boil, stirring until sugar is dissolved; reduce heat; simmer gently; stir occasionally; cook for 15 to 20 minutes. Move to a cool burner, cover immediately; let stand overnight. Next day, adjust seasonings; cook chutney down by simmering 15 to 20 minutes more. Watch very carefully to prevent scorching. Pour boiling chutney into hot, clean jars; seal. Process in a boiling water bath according to directions on page 182. Let cool on racks out of a draft. The flavors should mellow for at least 3 weeks before serving. Cover tightly; refrigerate once opened.

INDIAN STYLE MINT CHUTNEY (UNCOOKED)

It is worth growing a big mint bed to insure a source of mint for this habit-forming uncooked chutney from the sub-continent.

Makes 1 Cup

- 1 cup fresh cilantro (fresh coriander) leaves
- 1 cup fresh mint leaves
- 1 large garlic clove, peeled
- 3 tablespoons red onion, roughly chopped
- 1 small green tomato, cored or 2 tomatillos, husked
- 4–6 fresh green chili peppers, seeded (serrano, Thai, 'Fresno,' 'Santa Fe Grande')
- 2 tablespoons fresh lime juice
- 2 tablespoons olive oil
- 1 teaspoon salt

Put all ingredients in a blender; process until coarsely puréed. Serve with curry dishes, any meats, or as a dip with unsalted chips.

Variation: The timid may mix several spoonfuls of this in plain yogurt or sour cream, to taste. Use as a dip with chips, cold chicken, lamb, or vegetables.

NOTE: Do not use New Mexican type Long Green Chiles.

Pickles

PICKLED JALAPEÑOS OR HUNGARIAN WAX PEPPERS

These pickled peppers are the pickled peppers that Peter Piper probably wanted to pick.

Makes about 8 Pints

  1 gallon 'Hungarian Wax' peppers, jalapeños, serranos, left whole, or your garden chili pepper mix; or sweet peppers, if you must.

  1 gallon water, plus 1 cup

  2 cups salt

  5 cups five percent white vinegar

  2 tablespoons sugar

  1 tablespoon pickling spice

  2 small onions, quartered

  2 carrots, parboiled and sliced

  8 cloves of garlic, not peeled, parboiled 2 minutes

  8 tablespoons olive or vegetable oil

Thoroughly wash peppers. Prick with a fork or make several small slits in each. Bring the gallon of water to a boil; dissolve salt in it to make a brine solution. Let cool. Put peppers in the cool brine solution in a crock (do not use a metal container). Place a clean plate on top of peppers with a quart jar full of water on it to hold them down in brine. Leave in brine for 12 to 18 hours. Rinse peppers thoroughly to remove all salt. Drain. Combine the 1 cup of water, vinegar, sugar, and pickling spice in a stockpot; bring to a boil. Reduce heat; simmer 10 minutes. In each hot, clean jar place ¼ onion, 1 tablespoon oil, several carrot slices, 1 garlic clove; pack peppers into jars. Pour in hot liquid; seal jars. Process in a boiling water bath according to directions on page 182 for 20 minutes. Store 3 weeks before using. Refrigerate tightly closed once opened. These pickled peppers will keep several months in the refrigerator.

EASY PEPPER SAUCE PICKLES (UNCOOKED)

These will surprise you. These simple, very crisp pickles keep well and make great hostess gifts.

Makes 8 Pints

- 1 gallon sliced "hamburger" dill pickles
- 5 pounds sugar
- 12 ounce bottle chili pepper sauce
- 3 tablespoons pickling spice
- 4 teaspoons mustard seeds

Drain pickles well. Use the glass gallon pickle jar; return sliced pickles to it in alternate layers with sugar and pepper sauce. Screw lid on tightly. Allow to sit for 1 week. Each day turn jar of pickles upside down so that one day they sit with top up; next day bottom is up. After a week, remove pickles; pack them into sterile jars to which have been added 1 teaspoon of pickling spice and ½ teaspoon mustard seed. Put scalded lids on tightly. Refrigerate tightly closed once opened; they keep almost indefinitely.

NOTE: A small, dried or fresh red chilli pepper added to pickles so that it can be seen through jar adds a bright touch.

Preserves

Preserves include Marmalades, Jellies, and Jams. Remember, you should never double a recipe of preserves.

Marmalades

LEMON AJÌ MARMALADE

A refreshing flavor change from the original orange marmalade.

Makes 10 cups

  6 large, yellow and or orange Bell Peppers, seeded and chopped

 12 Lemon Ají peppers or small yellow chili peppers, minced

  8 lemons, peeled and juiced

  2 cups water

 ½ teaspoon baking soda

 10 cups of granulated sugar

 ¼ teaspoon salt

  2 6-ounce pouches of liquid fruit pectin (Certo®) Paraffin

Score citrus skin in quarters and remove; cut skinned fruit in half and juice. Set juice aside. Cut excess white from peel; thinly slice peel in food processor. Place lemon peel and soda, with enough water to cover in a covered saucepan; bring to a boil and simmer until rinds are tender (20 to 30 minutes). Remove from heat, drain and rinse. Place lemon pulp in a food processor; puree. Place fruit, peel, and peppers in a large bowl and mix—there should be 6 cups. Divide mixture into two 3-cup portions to be cooked separately. Better results are obtained when making preserves by keeping your "batches" small.

Place 3 cups of mixture in a 6 to 7-quart non-reactive pot; add 5 cups of sugar. Add 1 cup of water, salt, and lemon juice to citrus peel and pepper mixture. Bring to a boil over high heat; reduce heat; simmer for 5 to 10 minutes. Raise heat to high; bring to a rolling boil that won't stir down; continue boiling and stirring for 2 to 3 minutes. Add 6 ounces of pectin. Let marmalade return to a boil; boil for exactly 1 minute. Remove from heat. Skim foam, if necessary. Pour hot marmalade to within ½-inch of rim of hot sterilized jelly jars. Wipe rims with damp paper toweling. While still very hot pour on a ¼-inch layer of melted paraffin (see P. 182). Put scalded lids on jars; tighten; place on a rack to cool. Repeat process using other half of fruit, sugar, and pectin. Keep tightly closed in refrigerator once opened. Use it up so that it won't turn to sugar, but if it does, melt marmalade in a saucepan over low heat or in microwave; use it for a glaze with meats. Additional chili peppers can be used for a more pungent marmalade.

JEAN'S CAPSICUM MARMALADE

Have you ever wondered what to do with all those grapefruit or tangerine rinds? Wonder no more—save them in the freezer and use them for this spirited marmalade, and don't think you can just eat it on toast—chicken and ham are a delight with this treat.

Makes 10 cups

  2 lemons, peeled and juiced

  2 cups grapefruit rind, coarsely grated

 ½ teaspoon baking soda

  6 large, red Bell Peppers, roasted, peeled, seeded and chopped or canned roasted red peppers, chopped

4–6 chiltepínes or small red chili peppers, minced (use additional for a more pungent marmalade; see note 2)

 10 cups of sugar

  2 cups water

 16 ounce can orange juice concentrate

 ¼ teaspoon salt

  2 pouches liquid fruit pectin (Certo®)
     Paraffin

Score citrus skin in quarters; remove; cut skinned fruit in half and juice. Set juice aside. Cut excess white from skin; then coarsely grate lemon and grapefruit peel in food processor. Measure 2 cups and place grated citrus peel, soda, and enough water to cover in a covered non-reactive sauce pan; bring to a boil; simmer until rinds are tender (20 to 30 minutes). Remove from heat; drain and rinse well.

Coarsely grind or process citrus pulp, reserving juice. Mix pulp, tenderized peel, and peppers together in a 6 to 7-quart non-reactive kettle; there should be about six cups of mixture. Divide in half; set one half of it aside. Place 3 cups of fruit mixture in preserving kettle with 5 cups of sugar. Add 1 cup of water, ½ can orange juice concentrate, and ½ of the reserved juice to the citrus and pepper mixture. At this point, there should be two equal batches of the fruit mixture. Bring first batch to a boil over high heat; then reduce heat; simmer for 5 to 10 minutes. Raise heat to high; bring to a rolling boil that won't stir down; continue boiling; stir for 2 to 3 minutes. Add one pouch of liquid pectin; let mixture return to a boil; boil for 1 minute. Remove from heat. Skim foam, if necessary. Pour hot marmalade in hot, sterilized small jelly jars. Wipe rims with damp paper towel. While still very hot, pour on a thin layer of melted paraffin (see P. 182). Put scalded lids on jars and tighten; place on a rack to cool. Repeat process using other half of fruit, sugar, and pectin.

NOTE 1: In winter when citrus fruits are at their best, freeze the rinds of your breakfast grapefruit until late Summer or Fall when peppers are prime to make the marmalade.

NOTE 2: When using chiltepínes, don't try to remove seed. Mash chili peppers in a small amount of hot water; let stand for a few minutes. Use only the infused liquid so those eating the jelly won't get a killer bite.

NOTE 3: Once the jar of preserves has been opened, keep tightly closed in refrigerator. If it turns to sugar, melt marmalade in a saucepan over low heat, or in the microwave; use it for a sauce or a glaze with meats.

TEXAS RUBY RED GRAPEFRUIT MARMALADE

The beautiful Ruby Red grapefruit of Texas, the state fruit, has no equal, do not substitute.

Makes about 10 Cups

- 3 pounds Ruby Red grapefruit, about 4, washed and cut in half
- 3 lemons, washed and cut in half
- 3 quarts water
- 12 cups granulated sugar
- ½ teaspoon cayenne pepper
- ½ cup roasted red pepper, chopped (now available canned)
- 1 pouch liquid fruit pection (Certo®)
  Parafin

Squeeze juice from grapefruit halves, save seed, remove pulp; set aside. Remove excess pith from skins; set skins aside. Cut skins into very thin strips, set aside. Squeeze juice from lemon halves; save seed; remove pulp; set aside. Cut lemon skins thinly. In a muslin bag, place grapefruit pulp and seeds, lemon pulp, seeds, and lemon skin strips; tie loosely. In a large non-reactive kettle place strips of grapefruit skin, grapefruit and lemon juice, filled muslin bag, and water. Bring to a boil; reduce heat; simmer until grapefruit peel is tender, about 2 hours. Remove muslin bag; squeeze out any liquid. Add sugar and cayenne pepper; bring to a boil, stirring until sugar is dissolved. Boil rapidly over high heat; reduce heat; simmer for 5 to 10 minutes. Add roasted red pepper; stir to mix. Raise heat to high; bring to a rolling boil that won't stir down; continue boiling; stir for 2 to 3 minutes. Add 1 pouch of liquid pectin; let return to a boil; boil for 1 minute. Remove from heat. Skim foam if necessary. Pour hot marmalade in hot, sterilized small jelly jars. Wipe rims with damp paper toweling. While still very hot, pour on a thin layer of melted paraffin (see P. 182). Put scalded lids on jars; tighten; place on a rack to cool. Keep tightly closed in refrigerator once opened.

Jellies

CHILLI PEPPER JELLY

Tasty, savory, tangy, piquant, appetizing—this jelly is all these things. Once you have introduced it to your repertoire of delectable treats you'll find you must have it to serve with chicken and meats, as well as on hot breads, waffles, and pancakes.

Makes 7 Cups

- ¼ cup fresh chili peppers; chiltepínes, jalapeños, or habaneros, seeded and chopped
- ¾ cup Bell Peppers, use same color as the chili peppers
- 6½ cups sugar
- 1½ cups white vinegar
- 6 ounce pouch liquid pectin (Certo®)
  Food coloring, same color as peppers (optional)
  Paraffin

Peppers can be chopped in a food processor if care is taken to not get them too fine. Mix peppers, sugar, and vinegar together in a 6 to 7-quart non-reactive pan; boil for 2 minutes. Let cool 5 minutes. Add pectin; 1 or 2 drops of food coloring, then bring to a rolling boil and boil for 1 minute (do not exceed recommended time).

Pour into hot, sterilized jelly jars to ½ inch from the rim. Wipe rims with a clean damp cloth; seal immediately with melted paraffin (see P. 182). Place scalded lids on the jars and tighten. Place on a rack to cool. Store in refrigerator once opened. If jelly turns to sugar, melt it and use it to baste fowl or as a sauce or glaze for meats or in salad dressing.

The flecks of pepper are attractive, but for a clear jelly, strain mixture after it has boiled for 2 minutes; return to pan; bring to a boil; continue as directed.

Any chili pepper—jalapeños, habanero, datil, serrano, chiltepínes—can be used, but don't mix them if you want a distinct flavor typical of that variety.

Alternative: Try a chili pepper jelly that is not from scratch.

- 2 habanero or Scotch bonnet chili peppers; or 4 jalapeños, 4 serranos, or 8 chiltepines, or to taste; stemmed, seeded, and chopped
- 1 cup white vinegar
- 1 cup sugar
- 4 10-ounce jars apple or current jelly

Mix chili peppers, vinegar, sugar in a 4 to 5-quart non-reactive sauce pan. Bring to a boil over high heat and boil; stir until mixture is reduced to about ⅓ cup, about 7 minutes. Remove jelly from jars with a sterile spoon; stir it into pepper mixture. Boil, stirring, until jelly melts. Ladle hot jelly back into unwashed apple jelly jars to within ¼ inch of the rims. Wipe rims clean with damp paper towel; tighten lids onto jars. If there is any jelly left over, put it into a covered dish for immediate use. After 1–2 hours, agitate jars to redistribute pepper pieces. When jelly is cool, store it in the refrigerator up to 4 months.

Condiments

ZESTY JALAPEÑO VINEGAR (UNCOOKED)

An easily made vinegar to have on hand to spice-up vegetables and salads.

Makes 3 Cups

- 6 or more jalapeños
- 1 cup water
- 2 cups apple cider or white vinegar
- 2 tablespoons olive oil
- 3 garlic cloves, peeled and, crushed
- ½ teaspoon oregano, fresh or dried
- 1 slice of onion
- 1 teaspoon peppercorns, crushed

Cut the jalapeños in several places with a knife. Place all ingredients in a saucepan; bring to a boil. Reduce heat and simmer for five minutes. Cool; place in a glass jar or bottle; store in refrigerator. Use on vegetables, cooked greens, in salad dressings, or substitute for vinegar or lime juice in sauce recipes.

"SUN-DRIED" TOMATOES

When visiting Austin, chef and restaurant owner Mark Miller showed me how to dry tomatoes in this manner which retains more flavor than by long sun drying. Go to a farmer's market or wait for a special on Roma tomatoes (it takes quite a few).

Makes 2 to 3 Cups

4–5 pounds ripe Roma tomatoes (no other kind)
     cayenne pepper

Preheat oven to 190°F. Select tomatoes approximately all the same size; otherwise some will dry quicker than others causing you to have to watch them more closely. Buy enough to do several broiler pans full at a time or what ever your oven will hold. Oil broiler racks; place racks in broiler pans. Cut tomatoes in half; place cut side down on racks. Fill pan; place it in oven. The length of cooking time will depend on tomatoes. Turn them once about mid-drying time. It will take from 16 to 24 hours, or a little more depending on the size of the tomatoes. If some "dry" before others, remove them; return pan to oven. Don't let them get crisp. When tomatoes are as "dry" as you desire, remove them from pan; cool. They can be seasoned with cayenne pepper, salt, or whatever. I put them in a closed container unseasoned but they keep longer packed with olive oil and marjoram. Having them on hand plain, you are free to use them in many ways. They will keep several weeks in refrigerator or longer if you freeze them.

NOTE: Try serving them as appetizers with a good bleu-cheese or mozzarella chunks, a side dish of olive oil with crushed parsley and basil, and pieces of fresh, crusty French bread to dip.

DRIED RED PEPPERS

Attention gardeners! Try drying Bell Peppers, 'Cubanelles,' 'Sweet Bananas,' or your garden's surplus. Also dry your surplus thin-walled peppers.

Makes about one percent of the fresh weight, so do as many as your oven will hold.

12 unblemished red Bell Peppers, quartered or cut in ¾ inch strips, cored, and ribs removed. Do at least 12 at a time.

Preheat oven to 140°F. In a large steam basket, steam the peppers for 10 minutes. Drain, then dry on paper towels. Place peppers, cut-side down, on cheese cloth-covered racks. Set racks on baking sheets. Dry peppers in oven for 8 to 10 hours, or until just short of being crisp; or crisp if desired. Turn pepper pieces once about mid-way during drying time. Keep oven door slightly open to allow moisture to escape. Let peppers cool completely before packing in airtight containers. Marinated in olive oil with herbs and garlic the pepper strips make a nice appetizer, or use plain in salads and casseroles.

HERBED CHILLI VINEGAR (UNCOOKED)

Herb growers will love this. I make it every year because my non-herb growing friends have come to look forward to it.

Makes 3 Gallons

- 1½ gallons fresh herbs: salad burnet, lemon balm, marjoram; lemon thyme, chives, tarragon; or rosemary, thyme, basil, oregano
- 6–8 garlic cloves, peeled and crushed
- 2–3 jalapeños or serranos, slashed (any garden chili peppers will work)
- 1 small onion, sliced
- 3 gallons cider vinegar
  Dried small red chili peppers
  Sprigs of rosemary or other herbs

Place herbs and vegetables in a very large pickling crock or non-reactive container (3-gallon); press with a wooden spoon to bruise. Pour container full of vinegar. Cover container with plastic wrap. Mark with date. Three to four weeks later, remove cover; strain vinegar through muslin, coffee filters, or 2 layers of paper towels. Sterilize enough bottles to hold 3 gallons. Place a dried red chili pepper and a sprig of rosemary (other herbs will serve) in each bottle. Using a funnel, fill each bottle to within 1 inch of top. Add cork; use a wooden mallet to insert cork firmly. Store as you would pickles, etc. Use this vinegar in salads, on vegetables, in salad dressings, or to marinate meats.

CAYENNE PEPPER CATSUP

This famous Louisiana Creole preparation is very pungent but is excellent with oysters. It makes a great gift.

Makes 4 to 5 Cups

- 4 dozen ripe cayenne peppers
- 4 cups best-quality white or cider vinegar, or sherry (very mellow)
- 3 tablespoons grated fresh horseradish
- 5 onions, sliced
- 1 teaspoon sugar
- 1 garlic clove, peeled and minced
- 1 cup hot water

Place all ingredients in a non-reactive stockpot; boil together, uncovered, until onions become soft. Remove from the heat; place in a blender, purée well. Return purée to pot and bring to a boil. Pour into hot, clean jars, seal; process in a 5-minute boiling water bath as described on page 182. Refrigerate once opened.

NOTE: Ripe red 'New Mexican Chile,' 'Santa Fe Grandes,' jalapeños, 'Hungarian Wax,' or serranos can be used, but the flavor will be a little different with each.

CURRY POWDER OR MASALA (UNCOOKED)

A visit to the huge Indian market in Durban, South Africa, and markets of all sizes throughout India made me realize that the spices used to make curries are very variable. Almost anything goes, except the commercially prepared standardized product called curry powder in American supermarkets. Those colorful, aromatic piles of ground spices might vary in composition but not in freshness. They were all recently ground. If you want to grind your own, try one of the following combinations. You can also use them as a base to compose your own.

CURRY POWDER NO. 1

Makes about ¾ Cup

- 4½ teaspoons freshly ground black pepper
- 1½ teaspoons cardamom seeds
- 2 teaspoons ground cayenne pepper
- 1½ teaspoons ground cinnamon
- 1½ teaspoons cumin (comino) seeds
- 2 tablespoons plus 1½ teaspoons ground ginger
- 4½ teaspoons mustard seeds
- 1 teaspoon sweet paprika
- ¼ cup turmeric
- ½ teaspoon crushed dried red chili peppers, (de árbol, Thai, japonés, or chiltepínes)

CURRY POWDER NO. 2

Makes about 6 Tablespoons

- 2 teaspoons freshly ground black pepper
- ½ teaspoon cardamom seeds
- 6–8 whole cloves
- 4 teaspoons ground coriander
- 4 teaspoons ground cumin (comino)
- 2 teaspoons ground ginger
- ½ teaspoon ground mace
- ½ teaspoon mustard seeds
- 4 teaspoons turmeric
- ½ teaspoon crushed dried red chili peppers (de árbol, japonés, chiltepínes)

CURRY POWDER NO 3

Makes about ¼ Cup

- 1 teaspoon freshly ground black pepper
- ½ teaspoon cardamom seeds
- ¼ teaspoon ground cinnamon
- 3 teaspoons coriander seeds
- ½ teaspoon ground cumin (comino)
- ½ teaspoon fenugreek seeds
- 1 teaspoon ground ginger
- 1 teaspoon mustard seeds
- 3 teaspoons turmeric
- ¼ teaspoon crushed dried red chili peppers, (de Árbol, Thai, japonés)

NOTE: Use whole spices and either crush them in a mortar, or whirl them in a blender. You can also grind them in an electric spice or coffee mill until fine, then sift and return any large particles for further powdering. Experiment! Tightly covered and stored in the refrigerator curry powder will keep a year. Better yet are the plastic containers with the type of rubber stoppers that allow the air to be pumped out like those used on wine bottles.

Notes on Nutrition

Anyone preparing food needs to know something about the nutritional value of what they are "cooking up" if only to be able to read the labels on food packages, but most have not had the opportunity, time, or desire to acquire that information. To begin with, the process of nutrition is the sum total of all processes by which food is assimilated, growth promoted, and injuries repaired in living organisms. The Senate of the United States has a Select Committee on Nutrition and Human Needs that recommends:

1. Eat a variety of foods
2. Maintain desirable weight
3. Avoid too much fat, saturated fat, and cholesterol
4. Eat foods with adequate protein, starch (a carbohydrate), and fiber (a carbohydrate)
5. Avoid too much sugar (a carbohydrate)
6. Avoid too much sodium (a mineral)
7. If you drink alcohol, do so in moderation

Calories are not nutrients but are the measure of nutritional energy, which originates as solar energy caught and stored by green plants. Animals eat plants or other animals that eat plants, thereby getting the solar energy they cannot capture directly as plants are able to do. Protein, fats, carbohydrates, vitamins, water, and minerals are the nutrients that make up the food we eat. Recommended Dietary Allowances of these nutrients have been made and published by the National Academy of Sciences and can be obtained from the Human Information Service, U.S. Department of Agriculture, Federal Building Room 325A, Rockville, Maryland 20782. Additional information can be found with your computer. See:

1. Food Pyramids and other nutrition information from the Harvard School of Public Health at: http://www.hsph.harvard.edu/nutritionsource/pyramids.html.
2. Department of Health and Human Services (HHS) and the Department of Agriculture (USDA) at: http://www.health.gov/dietaryguidelines.
3. University of Texas Southwestern Medical Center at: http://www8.utsouthwestern.edu/utsw/cda/dept27712/files/40245.html.

The Basic Nutrients

Water and food—macro-nutrients and micro-nutrients—are the basic building blocks of a good diet that enable your body to function optimally.

WATER

Our bodies are two-thirds water and water is involved in every bodily function, as well as maintaining the proper body temperature. Drinking at least eight 8-ounce glasses daily will ensure that your body has what is needed to maintain good health.

FOOD

MACRONUTRIENTS AND MICRONUTRIENTS

Macronutrients

The three macronutrients—protein, carbohydrates, fats—that supply all the body's caloric (energy) and structural needs.

1. PROTEIN

Pronunciation Key: "pro teen" or "pro te in." Both are correct but the one you use probably depends on how your nutrition professor pronounced it.

Proteins are the fundamental components of all living cells. They are essential for the proper functioning of an organism—its growth and repair of tissue. They contain carbon, hydrogen, oxygen, nitrogen, and usually sulfur and are composed of one or more chains of amino acids, which are the raw material for all protein. Because the body does not store amino acids, as it does fats or carbohydrates, it needs a daily supply to make new protein. Some of the protein you eat contains all the amino acids needed to construct new protein. These are complete proteins and are supplied by animal sources. Other proteins lack one or more amino acids that the body cannot make or create by modifying another amino acid. Those incomplete proteins usually come from fruits, vegetables, legumes, whole grains, and nuts. To get all the amino acids needed to make new protein, people who do not eat meat, seafood, poultry, eggs, or dairy products should eat a variety of other protein-containing foods each day because protein can only be had from protein or its component substances.

Adults need a minimum of 1 gram of protein for every kilogram of body weight per day to keep from breaking down their own tissues. That comes to about 9 grams of protein for every 20 pounds of body weight. In the US getting enough is no problem, but getting too much is. Digesting protein releases acids that the body usually neutralizes with calcium and other buffering agents in the blood. Eating lots of protein as recommended in the "no-carb" diets requires lots of calcium, some of which may be pulled from bone. A few weeks of this diet probably will not weaken bone strength but extended periods on this diet will do so. High-protein diets should be used with caution, if at all.

You rarely eat straight protein. Some comes with considerable unhealthy (but tasty) fat, such as marbled beef or whole milk. When eating red meats, steer yourself toward the leanest cuts whether it is beef, venison, bison, lamb, or whatever. Fowl and seafood are excellent alternatives. With dairy products, skim or low-fat versions are healthier choices. Vegetable sources such as legume (beans and peas), nuts (peanuts and almonds are included with nuts, but are not true nuts), and whole grains offer protein with plenty of healthful fiber and micro-nutrients and without much saturated fat. Almost any reasonable diet will give you enough protein each day: 10 to 20 percent of your daily calories or one egg is sufficient. Eating a variety of foods will ensure that you get all the amino acids you need.

2. CARBOHYDRATES

Carbohydrates are of vegetable origin and enter our bodies in three forms: sugar, starch, and fiber (mostly cellulose). Those carbohydrate compounds are composed of hydrogen, carbon, and water, and provide fuel for the body—they keep us going. Sugar molecules are the basic building blocks of carbohydrates. Starches and fibers are composed of chains of sugar molecules.

The digestive system handles all carbohydrates in much the same way. It breaks them down into single sugar molecules, which are the only ones small enough to be absorbed into the bloodstream. It also converts most digestible carbohydrates into glucose/blood sugar because cells are designed to use this form of sugar as a universal source of energy. Sugars are the simplest carbohydrates. The monosaccharides are: glucose, fructose (fruit sugar), galactose (a milk sugar). The disaccharides are: maltose (grains), sucrose (sugar-cane and sugar beets), lactose (milk). Plants often turn sugars into starches that store energy (roots, underground stems, seeds). When we eat starchy foods our bodies turn those carbohydrates back into glucose and use it for fuel.

Fiber is an exception. It cannot be broken down into sugar molecules. Consequently it passes through the body mostly undigested. It is present in all plants that are eaten for food; however, all fiber is not the same. The important difference is that some fibers partially dissolve in water but others do not. Oats, nuts, some seeds, legumes, apples, pears, strawberries, and blueberries have water soluble fiber. Insoluble fiber is found in whole grains, wheat bran, some seeds, carrots, celery, zucchini, and cucumbers. Fiber is an important part of a healthy diet because it reduces the risk of developing various conditions such as constipation, heart disease, diabetes, and diverticulitis. It should be consumed daily.

The glycemic index is a new system for classifying carbohydrates and measures how fast and how far blood sugar rises after you eat a food that contains carbohydrates. An important factor determining a food's glycemic index is how highly processed its carbohydrates are. The refining process to produce white flour removes the fiber-rich outer bran and the vitamin-and mineral-rich inner germ from the wheat grain, leaving mostly starch. White flour products are one of the unhealthiest creations of food technology.

Factors Influencing How Quickly Carbohydrates in Food Raise Blood Sugar Include:

- **Fiber content.** Fiber shields the starchy carbohydrates in food from immediate and rapid attack by digestive enzymes, slowing the release of sugar molecules into the bloodstream.
- **Ripeness.** Ripe fruits and vegetables tend to have more sugar than unripe ones, and therefore, have a higher glycemic index.
- **Physical form.** Finely ground grain is more rapidly digested than coarsely ground grain, therefore has a higher glycemic index.
- **Type of starch.** Starch has many configurations. Some are easier to break into sugar molecules than others. Potato starch is digested and absorbed in the bloodstream relatively quickly.
- **Fat content and acid content.** The more fat or acid a food contains, the more slowly its carbohydrates are converted to sugar and absorbed into the bloodstream.

Whenever possible, replace highly processed grains, cereals, and sugars with minimally processed whole-grain products. Carbohydrates from vitamin-, mineral-, and fiber-rich vegetables, fruits, legumes, and grains should provide the bulk of your calories. For optimal health, eat your grains intact from foods such as brown rice, whole grain bread, whole grain pasta, and other less familiar grains like quinoa, whole oats, barley, bulgar wheat, and semolina/durum wheat. **FORGET WHITE POTATOES WITHOUT THE PEELING, WHITE FLOUR, AND POLISHED WHITE RICE!**

3. FATS

Fats, including liquid fats or oils—*lipids*—are concentrated sources of energy. Weight for weight they provide twice the number of calories as protein or carbohydrates. Most often fats are stored in the seed of plants and only rarely in the fruits, and virtually never in other parts. The human body makes fat from glucose and stores it under the skin. When its caloric intake exceeds that spent, the body stores the excess fat. When more calories are used than taken in, fat reserves are used for metabolism. Your basic metabolism is the number of calories needed just to keep you alive without moving or exerting any energy. Add to that the number of calories needed to furnish energy for any bodily movement to determine the calories a person can consume before the body begins storing calories in the form of fat. Additional bodily movement or exercise to burn the stored fat or the reduction of caloric intake will cause the body to use the fat calories that have been stored. Although our bodies can turn glucose into fat, they cannot turn that fat back into glucose. They can, however, turn protein into glucose if they have no other source. A little fat is necessary each day to carry the necessary vitamins A, D, E, and K which are soluble in fat but not in water.

There are different types of fat. Bad fats increase the risk of certain diseases, and good fats reduce the risk. Cholesterol is a hard, waxy substance that occurs in many animal foods: whole milk, egg yolks, meat. It is important to many body functions but dietary excess or deficiency cause its normal functions to go awry causing arterial plaque, which is the basis of circulatory disasters. The mix of fats—not total fat—in the diet is the biggest influence on blood cholesterol levels.

Bad Fats

Saturated fats: mainly animal fats found in meat, whole-milk dairy products, butter, seafood, poultry skin, and egg yolks. Some plant fats, such as coconut oil, palm oil, and palm kernel, oil are also included. They raise both good and bad cholesterol levels.

Trans Fats: Hydrogenation or the heating of liquid vegetable oils in the presence of hydrogen produces fats that are hard at room temperature like oleo and shortening. Most are found in commercially prepared baked goods, snack foods including fried potatoes and onion rings, and processed foods. They are worse than saturated fats because they not only raise bad cholesterol but also lower good cholesterol.

Good Fats

Unsaturated Fats: Poly-unsaturated and Mono-unsaturated. These are found in products derived from plant sources such as vegetable oils, nuts, and seeds.

Polyunsaturated fats: sunflower, soybean, safflower, flaxseed, sesame, cottonseed, grapeseed, walnut, and corn oils.

Mono-unsaturated fats: peanut, olive, avocado, and canola oils.

Tips on fat intake

Choose liquid vegetable oils or a soft tub margarine containing little or no trans fats.

Reduce intake of commercially prepared baked goods, snack foods, and processed foods, including fast foods.

When food containing hydrogenated or partially hydrogenated oils can't be avoided, choose products that list hydrogenated oils near the end of the ingredient list.

Micronutrients

The micronutrients are needed in lesser amounts than the macronutrients but are essential for optimum bodily health. The four classes are: vitamins, minerals, fiber, and phytochemicals (nonnutrient plant chemicals that contain protective, disease-preventing compounds).

1. VITAMINS

A diverse group of organic chemical compounds discovered in the early twentieth century that make it possible for our bodies to use the food they take in. They are required only in tiny amounts to do their work. Some are found primarily in plants, others in animal tissue, and some in both. Today, the Harvard School of Public Health advises there is sufficient evidence to justify taking a daily multivitamin supplement for most adults.

Vitamins fall into two groups: water-soluble (B complex and C) and fat-soluble (A, D, E, and K). Recommended daily allowances (RDAs) set by governmental agencies only prevent deficiencies. It is important to get the right amounts of vitamins because either too much or too little can be problematic. Vitamin needs are increased by smoking and drinking alcohol.

Vitamin A (Retinol): Current recommended intake: 1,000 RAE for men and 800 RAE for women. An oil-soluble vitamin stored in the liver. Necessary for new cell growth, healthy tissues, and essential for good vision. Found in the beta-carotene of dark-green and yellow vegetables and when eaten by animals it is in such things as eggs, liver, and dairy products.

Vitamin B complex:

B-1 (Thiamine): Current recommended intake: 1.2 mg for adult men and 1.1 mg for adult women. Water soluble, therefore not stored in the body. Necessary for good digestion, growth, nervous system functioning, and carbohydrate metabolism. Found in legumes, pork, whole wheat, brewer's yeast, and blackstrap molasses.

B-2 (Riboflavin): Current recommended intake: 1.3 mg for adult men and 1.1 mg for adult women. Water soluble, therefore not stored in the body. Necessary primarily for good digestion where it is essential for efficient metabolism of carbohydrates and proteins. Found in green leafy vegetables, legumes, pork, whole grains, liver, dairy products, eggs, blackstrap molasses and some nuts.

B-3 (Niacin): Recommended intake: 16 mg. for men and 14 mg.for women. Water soluble. Stable and easy to obtain. Necessary to maintain a healthy condition in all tissue cells. Found in liver, meats, legumes, whole grain cereal products, and fish.

B-6: Recommended intake: 1.3 mg. for men and 1.3 mgs. for women. Water soluble and not stored in the body. Essential for proper growth and the me-

tabolism of protein. Found in liver, grains, and whole grain cereals, lean meats, green vegetables, corn, and potatoes.

Folic Acid (Folacin): Recommended intake: Only minute amounts of this member of the B-complex are needed for good health. Necessary for the conversion of food into energy and in the manufacture of red blood cells. Found in foliage of green leafy vegetables (hence the name) legumes, nuts, fresh orange juice, whole wheat products, and brewer's yeast.

B-12: Recommended intake: Only minuscule amounts are required. Lack causes a distinctive form of anemia and nerve damage. Found only in foods of animal origin.

The other minor members of the B-complex will be supplied by the same diet that provides those six named above.

Vitamin C (Ascorbic Acid): Discovered in 1932, by the Hungarian Albert Szent-Györgyi (Andrews 1995, 79–81), water-soluble ascorbic acid is essential to health. Long before its discovery experts realized that there was something in citrus fruits that prevented scurvy, a deadly disease that was common in sailors between 1500 and 1800. Not only does vitamin C have a role in controlling infections but it also is a strong antioxidant. Cooking, storage, and exposure to oxygen (air) readily destroy this unstable vitamin. Recommended intake: 90 mg for men; 70 mg for women. Found in fresh, raw citrus fruits and juices, berries, green and red peppers, tomatoes, broccoli, and spinach. Peppers have 3 times more vitamin C per ounce than citrus fruit. Many cereals are fortified with vitamin C.

Vitamin D: If you are not outside in the sun for at least 15 minutes each day you probably don't get sufficient fat-soluble vitamin D. Recommended intake: 10 micrograms for males and females, and 15 after age seventy. Found in fish liver oils, fortified milk, and cereals. Very few foods naturally contain vitamin D. A daily multivitamin is recommended.

Vitamin E: A fat-soluble vitamin that can be accumulated in the body and acts as an antioxidant. Early studies saw it as a heart disease preventive but continued trials have lessened enthusiasm. Ongoing studies will reveal more about its benefits. Recommended intake: 15 mg for men; 5 mg for women. Found in vegetable oils, legumes, eggs, wheat and other grain germ, liver, vegetables, and fruits.

Vitamin K: A fat-soluble vitamin that helps make 6 of the 13 proteins needed for blood clotting and is involved in building bone. Recommended intake: 120 mg for men; 90 mg for women. Most American adults get enough but children and young adults need a supplement. Found in many foods, especially green leafy vegetables. The Nurses' Health Study suggests eating a serving of leafy vegetables a day cuts risk of hip fracture in half when compared to one serving a week.

2. MINERALS:

inorganic chemical elements needed by the body for growth and maintenance. The key to getting enough minerals: **eat more fruits and vegetables.** The most important to general health are calcium, iron, sodium, potassium, selenium, and zinc.

Calcium: the most abundant mineral element in the body. It is primarily responsible for the density of bones and teeth. Milk and dairy products are its best source, also dark-green leafy vegetables and the bones found in canned fish.

Iron: only small amounts of iron are required in order for the body to produce hemoglobin, which carries oxygen from the lungs to the cells and carbon dioxide from the cells back to the lungs in exchange. Sources: Liver, organ meats, red meat, shellfish, dry beans and peas, egg yolk, dried fruits, and blackstrap molasses.

Sodium: found naturally in foods and is the major element in table salt. Some is needed for body water balance. When your kidneys lose the ability to regulate sodium and water you may experience thirst, fluid gain, high blood pressure, or discomfort while urinating. Use less sodium to control these.

To Reduce Sodium Intake:

a. Cook with herbs and spices such as chili pepper instead of salt.
b. Read food labels: if salt is listed in the first five ingredients, the item is too high in sodium.
c. Avoid salt substitutes because they are high in potassium.
d. When eating out, ask for meat and fish without salt, and gravy or sauce on the side.
e. Limit use of canned, processed, and frozen foods.

Potassium: Is involved in growth, and muscle and nerve functioning. Found in seafood, bananas, dates, figs, raisins, peaches, tomatoes, citrus fruits, peanuts, and blackstrap molasses. Those taking diuretics should be aware that potassium can be lost through urination, which makes a supplement necessary.

Selenium: Only minute amounts are required as an antioxidant. Excessive amounts can be toxic. Found in whole grains, nuts, fruit, and some vegetables.

Zinc: Small amounts are needed by the immune system to respond to infections, in tissue repair, in the detoxification of certain elements, and in our senses of smell and taste.

Found in pumpkin, sunflower seeds, yeast, eggs, red meat, and grains grown in zinc-rich soil.

3. FIBER
(see Carbohydrates) Is the roughage or the indigestible part of food furnished mostly by plant foods and contributes to health in several ways. There are two types. Insoluble fiber occurs in wheat bran, whole grains, nuts, seeds, fruits, and vegetables increases stool bulk and speeds the passage of food through the digestive system. Pectins and gums are the two kinds of soluble fiber that bind cholesterol and bile acids in the intestinal tract, preventing their reabsorption thus helping to lower serum cholesterol. Get at least 40 grams a day by eating more fruits and vegetables daily.

4. PHYTOCHEMICALS
Brightly colored compounds found in plant foods that bolster the body's defenses and reduce the risks of serious illnesses such as cancer. They include antioxidant polyphenols that protect the heart and arteries from oxidative damage. There are several types of polyphenols such as EGCG, or condensed tannins found in green tea and apples; and anthocyanin, the red and purple pigments in grapes and berries that provide cardiovascular benefits. Carotenoids, that give color to carrots, tomatoes, and squash are another group of antioxidants. There are many other protective phytochemicals in fruits and vegetables—EAT MORE!

Annotated Bibliography

The growing curiosity of Americans about culinary matters is of relatively recent origin and is a very encouraging sign. To help satisfy that culinary curiosity I offer this small, very personal bibliography of the references I keep on my kitchen bookshelves (Yes, kitchen bookshelves that house not only food and culinary related books but at least 150 cookbooks full of recipes from around the world.) I have an insatiable curiosity and my culinary questions concern more than the recipe for the pie in my oven. Who made the first pie and why? Did they have an oven like mine? If not, why not and what did they have? Where did sugar, flour, shortening come from and why are they needed? Does the pie have any nutritional value? Who made the ingredients and where and why? How should I serve it? Why do we eat it with a fork and who used the first fork in the world? In America? These are only a few of the questions that fill my mind when I handle food. Consequently, I like to be able to look for the answers and I see a growing concern for similar information among others who like to prepare and serve food as well as eat it. May I suggest these books as a beginning and their bibliographies as further sources. Eating is so much more than just survival. These books will add to your culinary pleasure. They are also the primary sources of the information found in the ingredient section of this book (see: P. 26).

ANDREWS, J.

1984. *Peppers: The Domesticated Capsicums.* Revised 1995. Austin: University of Texas Press. More than you ever wanted to know about peppers with paintings of 34 species. 186 pp.

1998. *The Pepper Lady's Pocket Pepper Primer.* Austin: University of Texas Press. 184 pp. A small book filled with color photographs of peppers and descriptions designed to take into the market, garden store, kitchen, or desk drawer like a field guide.

2000. *The Pepper Trail: History and Recipes from Around the World.* Denton: University of North Texas Press. 261 pp. A companion to *Peppers,* taking up where it left off. It discusses how peppers moved from the New World after the Discovery, how they traveled around the Old World, and how the cuisines of those peoples were affected by them. This is followed with instructions on how to cook with peppers and about 200 recipes from famous chefs to try your hand with.

CARSON, B. G.

1990. *Ambitious Appetites: Dining, Behavior, and Patterns of Consumption in Federal Washington.* Washington DC: the American Inst. of Architects Press. 212 pp. A culinary history of early Washington DC during the Federal period. Such facts as "the single most significant characteristic of old-fashioned dining was the lack of knives and forks and the use of spoons." And "reasons why" abound in this most informative book.

CHANG, K. C. (Ed.)

1977. *Food in Chinese Culture: Anthropological and Historical Perspectives.* New Haven: Yale University Press. 429 pp. This is one of the only anthropological and historical studies of a culture that I have ever found that covers the culinary aspects of a people, even though every group in the world eats daily and spends most of their time in either the acquisition, preparation, or serving of food. It should be a model for other such studies.

COE, S. D.

1994. *America's First Cuisines.* Austin: University of Texas Press. 276 pp. One of my favorite books. Sophie, an anthropologist, and her husband Michel, an authority on Mexican archaeology and the ancient peoples of Mexico, make quite a pair. Together they mastered ancient Mexico. This work gives the details of the cuisines of the Aztecs, Mayas, and South American Incas. She not only gives the history of the basic New World foodstuffs, but also describes how these foods were prepared, served, and preserved, with insights into the cultural and ritual practices surrounding their consumption.

CROSBY, A. W., Jr.

1972. *The Columbian Exchange: Biological and Cultural Consequences of 1492.* Westport, CT: Greenwood Press. 268 pp. This is my bible on what happened with the New World foods after Columbus discovered America in 1492. Among scholars, the title—*Columbian Exchange*—has become synonymous with that event which changed the world for ever more. It will open a new world for you!

DAVIDSON, A. (Ed.)

1999. *The Oxford Companion to Food.* Oxford: Oxford University Press. 892 pp. The British Davidson was one of the world's great authorities on the history and use of food. He packed his magnum opus with 2,650 entries from A to Z. Subjects include: culinary terms, food science, food preservation, diet, cookbooks and their authors, the role of food in culture and religion, plus articles by fifty guest specialists from around the world. For many years Davidson edited *The Proceedings of the Oxford Symposium of Food and Cookery.* He died in 2003 and I shall miss him.

EGERTON, J.

1993. *Southern Food: At Home, on the Road, in History.* Chapel Hill: University of North Carolins Press. 408 pp. Egerton is a real southerner whose book is for reading, cooking from, and referring to. Most cookbook writers are so intent on getting their recipes right that they have given little time or thought in determining where the dishes came from or how and why some have been favored over others. It took culinary magicians to deliver miracles out of the kitchens of the south before electricity and refrigeration and it is all described here with much more: bibliographies, sources and resources, recipes—a treasure trove.

FISCHER, D. H.

1989. *Albion's Seed: Four British Folkways in America.* New York: Oxford University Press. 946 pp. This book is a cultural history of America including so much more than just foodways and foodstuffs. A real treat for the culinary historian, especially one who is also a serious genealogist with colonial ancestors.

FISHER, M. F. K.

1971. *The Art of Eating.* New York: Macmillan. 749 pp. Fisher was considered to be the poet laureate of food and wine writing, but did not consider herself a food writer. This one is actually several books in one. My favorite segment is her alphabet for gourmets. Delightful reading.

HALPERN, D.

1993. *Not by Bread Alone: Writers on Food, Wine and the Art of Eating.* Hopewell, NJ: The Ecco Press. 186 pp. A collection of delightful essays about food, eating, appetites, etc., written by people who are well-recognized in the culinary world. Fun to read while something is baking.

HAWKE, D. F.

1989. *Everyday Life in Early America.* New York: Harper & Row. 195 pp. A clearly written description of life in early Colonial America. It lays the groundwork for the understanding of what, why, and how the settlers ate what they ate. It includes excellent descriptions of the home and sections on what they ate and drank, manners and morals and much, much more.

HEISER, C. B.

1973. *Seed to Civilization: The Story of Man's Food.* San Francisco: W. H. Freeman and Co. 243 pp. Written by a prominent botanist and a personal friend and advisor who describes the origin of agriculture, the nature of man's basic food plants and animals, and the essentials of our current and future food problems. "We are what we eat." He suggests that palatability—taste, texture, odor, and color—played an important role in early man's food choices. Did they have the nutrients he needed? Obviously had he not eaten what he needed he would have been eliminated by natural selection long, long ago. These were our fascinating culinary beginnings.

1985. *Of Plants and People.* Norman, OK: University of Oklahoma Press. 237 pp. A collection of informal essays that investigate questions raised by the interactions of plants and people. Good coverage of my favorite new food, the protein-rich Andean quinoa and much, much more. In 1978, Heiser, who pioneered Capsicum taxonomy, shared his personal pepper bibliography with me, which opened the world of capsicums to me making my first pepper book possible.

HILL, B.

1987. *The Cook's Book of Essential Information: A Kitchen Handbook.* New York: Dell Publishing Group, Inc. 321 pp. A one-stop information center on selecting, storing, cooking, and eating food. The first chapter is a "Cook's Dictionary" and the book moves to selecting foods, how much to use, food and food preparation tools, storage, nutrition, measurements, and much, much more. ESSENTIAL!

KIPLE, K. F. and ORNELAS, K. C., (Eds.)

2000. *Cambridge World History of Food.* 2 vols. Cambridge: Cambridge University Press. Vol. I, 1120 pp. Vol. II, 1121 pp. As stated on the dust jacket, "This monumental two volume work encapsulates the history of food and nutrition through the span of human life on earth covering the full spectrum of foods that have been hunted, gathered, cultivated, and domesticated." Each chapter has its own bibliography. It is the work of 224 experts from 15 countries, including me. Example: 140-page section on Dietary Liquids from breast milk to wine. A table book, too heavy to hold.

McGEE, H.

1984. *On Food and Cooking: The Science and Lore of the Kitchen.* New York: Collier Books. 684 pp. This explains it all! An absolute must for any serious cook's book shelf. It combines culinary lore and clear scientific explanations into a readable whole. Not only science but also the history of his subject. Heavily illustrated. Indispensable! Revised and updated edition published in 2004. New York: Charles Scribner's Sons. 896 pp. More than 200 pages of additional valuable information!!!

1990. *The Curious Cook: More Kitchen Science and Lore.* San Francisco: North Point Press. 339 pp. The first book for the home cook that translates into plain English what scientists have discovered about foods. The findings presented put to rest many long-held myths of diet and health. He even takes the fear out of making and eating "home made" mayonnaise.

MONTAGNÉ, P.

1968. *Larousse Gastronomique.* New York: Crown Publishing, Inc. 1100 pp. A history of French Culinary Art from prehistoric times to present presented in the form of a handy 1000-plus page dictionary from A to Z. It gives the evolution of the table through the ages. There is no better source for the etymology of certain words, the definition of culinary terms, the origin of foods in every day use, and the many recipes for each dish. I have had my copy for nearly 40 years and it is still timely and handy to use—my ever ready reference.

MORTON, J. F.

2000. *Fruits of Warm Climates.* Miami, FL: Julia F. Morton. 505 pp. "This book is a guide and tool for those who need to choose fruits that are of real value in the home garden or are intended to be commercial crops for domestic consumption or export." It includes such hard to find tropical fruits as lychee, calamondin, naranjillo, rambutan, mangosteen, passion fruit, tamarillo, and many, many more. Wonder no more about those exotics that you savor on your tropical travels.

NABHAN, G. P.

1985. *Gathering the Desert.* Tucson: University of Arizona Press. 209 pp. This is but one of my friend Gary's many beautifully written books. This recipient of the MacArthur "genius" fellowship, who is more at home in the desert than in cities, has a solution to the planet's environmental problem: eat locally and think globally. This book includes more than 425 edible wild species found in the Sonoran Desert—of course, chiltepíncs.

PELLEGRINI, A.

1984. *The Unprejudiced Palate.* San Francisco: North Point Press. (Afterword by M. F. K. Fisher.) 242 pp. This book suggests ingredients and how to use them in a manner that inspires experimentation by an author who considers cuisine a part of a people's culture.

ROMBAUER, I. S. and BECKER, M. R.

1971. *The Joy of Cooking.* Indianapolis, Indiana: Bobs-Merrill Co. Inc. 849 pp. Here is another "oldie but goodie." I got my first copy as a student in Home Economics at the University of Texas, Austin in 1942 and replaced it in 1971. If you can't find what you want to cook or how to cook it in one of your fancy nouvelle cuisine cookbooks, you can find it here. There is a 70-page chapter on ingredients, measurements, and seasoning. The meat section has 10 pages of diagrams showing and naming the cuts of beef, pork, lamb, and veal. Revised and updated edition, *The all new, all purpose joy of cooking,* was published in 1997. New York: Scribner and Sons. 1152 pp. Every kitchen should have one; it is indeed a real joy.

ROSENGARTEN, F., Jr.

1973. *The Book of Spices.* New York: Pyramid Books. 475 pp. This paperback is the most comprehensive book on spices ever produced. Forty-one are discussed in non-technical terms. Chilli peppers were the first spice to be used by humans. Black and white illustrations and a few recipes.

ROZIN, E.

1983. *Ethnic Cuisine: The Flavor Principle Cookbook.* Brattleboro, VT: Stephen Green Press. 267 pp.

1992. *Ethnic Cuisine: How to Create the Authentic Flavors of 30 International Cuisines.* New York: Penguin Books. 267 pp. A fascinating collection of background information that shows how various ethnic cuisines are shaped according to basic foods, cooking techniques, and (most importantly) flavor principles. A flavor principle abstracts what is absolutely fundamental about a cuisine. It contains recipes that allow the reader-cook to explore a vast range of ethnic cuisines from around the world.

SCHNEIDER, E.

1986. *Uncommon Fruits and Vegetables: A Commonsense Guide.* New York: Harper & Row Publishers. 546 pp. This is the book that tells you how to cook, serve, and store all those uncommon fruits and vegetables that you didn't know what to do with. With each entry she gives the names, both common and scientific, description, selection and storage, use, preparation, nutritional highlights, and several recipes. Now you can be an informed shopper and cook or food fan.

2002. *Vegetables from Amaranth to Zucchini.* New York: Morrow. 777 pp. Schneider has given us another food bible. This time it covers vegetables in a way that should leave you without anymore questions.

SIMPSON, B. B., and CONNER-OGORZALY, M.

2001. *Economic Botany.* New York: McGraw Hill. 640 pp. Designed as a college textbook this very readable book, first printed in 1986, contains history and complete botanical descriptions—morphology, chemistry, and modern usage—of fruits and vegetables with myriads of detailed, explanatory illustrations, photographs, and tables. A true fountainhead of information about all plants of major economic importance in the United States, most of which feed people. I could not function without it.

SOKOLOV, R.

1991. *Why We Eat What We Eat: How the Encounter Between the New World and the Old Changed the Way Everyone on the Planet Eats.* New York: Summit Books. 254 pp. This is an informative history of the world as seen from a gourmet's table. Sokolov explains how the people of the earth—Asians, Europeans, Americans—came to eat what we eat today, and it all began with Columbus. Not only a cultural history of food but a delight to read.

SWAHN, J.O.

1991. *The Lore of Spices: Their History, Nature and Uses Around the World.* New York: Crescent Books. 208 pp. The art work, illustrations, and maps in this Swedish book (covering forty spices) are excellent. It explores their cultural history in addition to describing the plants and their origins. You can really see what they look like in this book.

TYREE, M. C., (Ed.)

1879. *Housekeeping in Old Virginia.* Louisville, KY: John P. Morton & Co. 528 pp. This classic, published about 125 years ago, was written by Patrick Henry's granddaughter. It will make you wonder how anything turned out, with such lack of detail in the elaborate recipes—or when it was cooked in kitchens without gas, electricity, refrigeration, and often no hot water. There are at least 40 recipes for cooking oysters, and even turtle, calf's head, and various organ meats. A rare treat to read and a testimony to how fortunate American cooks are today.

VISSER, M.

1986. *Much Depends on Dinner: The Extraordinary History and Mythology, Allure and Obsessions, Perils and Taboos of an Ordinary Meal.* New York: Collier Books. 351 pp. Byron wrote: "Since Eve ate apples, much depends on dinner." This book proves he was right. It corrects our lack of knowledge of the most ubiquitous of foods—lemons, corn, ice cream, chicken, butter, to name a few—and lays before us a captivating register of facts, myths, fetishes, and rituals that stretch back into the early history of humans.

WEAVER, W.W.

1983. *Sauerkraut Yankees: Pennsylvania-German Foods & Food Ways.* Philadelphia: University of Pennsylvania Press. 218 pp. A factual guide and a first-person tour through the cookery of the Pennsylvania Germans, who were first knows as "Sauerkraut Yankees" during the American Civil War. Weaver should know because he is not only one of them but also a highly regarded food historian, who has written a history of the foods with which he is most familiar. this is but one of his informative food books.

WEIL, A., M.D.

2000. *Eating Well for Optimum Health: The Essential Guide to Food, Diet, and Nutrition.* New York: Alfred A. Knopf.

307 pp. This is a must for your food library if you want to know all you can about what to eat and why. When I was writing my first book on peppers, Weil and I corresponded at length and he introduced me to "Mouth Surfing," whereby one who likes the burning sensation of capsaicin from eating a very pungent chili pepper, gets his kicks by keeping that sensation or the capsaicin high going by eating another pepper or pepper sauce just before the burn of the previous one can no longer be felt. Thus he "surfs" into each burning sensation as long as he wants to keep it going. But seriously, Weil knows whereof he speaks about nutrition.

Subject Index

Note: Page numbers in *italics* indicate illustrations or tables.

A

achaars, 26, 179–80
achiote, 32–33, 166
achoteras, 33
acid, 181, 201
Acini di Pepe, 90
adobo, 26
adobo style pickling, 31
African peppers, 27
ajís, 5, 151
ajvar, 26
al dente, 44
Albion's Seed: Four British Folkways in America
    (Fischer), 208
alcohol, 9, 179
Aleppo pepper, 26–27, 33, 168
allspice (Pimenta dioica), 3, 5, 166
Alzheimer's disease, 43
Ambitious Appetites: Dining, Behavior, and Patterns of
    Consumption in Federal Washington (Carson), 207
America's First Cuisines (Coe), 208
amino acids, 200
ammonia, 9, 21
Anaheims, 5, 16
anatomy of peppers, 7–8, 8
anchos, 18, 25, 27, 167
Andrews, J., 205
anise, 41
annatto, 32–33, 166
antioxidants, 205
apex, 8
Arabs, 178–79
Arawaks, 4
arborio rice, 40
Arequipa, Peru, 106–7
"armadillo eggs," 32
aroma, 9, 26
aromatic rice, 40
The Art of Eating (Fisher), 208
arterial plaque, 202
ascorbic acid, 203
Associated Pimento Canners of Georgia, 39
attachment sites, 8
avocado, 33

B

bad fats, 202
balsamic vinegar, 43
banana peppers, 11
barley, 76, 78
bases, 44
Bastiment de Recettes, 178
batters, 77
Becker, M. R., 210
Bell Peppers
    described, 11–12
    freezing, 25
    fresh, 32
    jellies, 30
    pepper mangoes, 180
    selection and use, 21, 22
Bible, 179
birds, 8
Bixa orellana, 32–33
black mustard, 37–38
black pepper (Piper nigrum), 3, 4, 5, 8
blanching, 43, 44
bleached flours, 78
"blistering" peppers, 23–24
blood sugar, 77, 201
blossoms, 8
Book of Ruth, 179
The Book of Spices (Rosengarten), 210
botulism, 182
bow tie pasta, 90
brining, 142
broiling, 24
brown flour, 44
brown rice, 40, 78
bulgar wheat, 33, 78
Bush, George W., 61, 174
Bush, Laura, 61, 174
butter, clarifying, 45

C

cacao, 166–67
cactus, 38
Cajun cuisine, 27, 142
cake flour, 78

Aztecs, 119, 166, 172

calcium, 78, 204
calyx, 8
calyx margin, 8
Cambridge World History of Food (Kiple
    and Ornelias), 209
canned peppers, 31
canning, 182
canola oil, 33
capellini, 90
capones, 23
capsaicin (CAPS), 6, 7–9
capsaicin glands, 8
capsanthin, 9
Capsicum, 3–4
carbohydrates, 78, 200–201
cardamom, 3, 33
carotenoid, 9
Carson, B. G., 207
cascabels, 25
casein, 63
cayenne pepper
    and chocolate, 168
    described, 12, 27
    dietary information, 7
    names, 5
cereal grains, 76
Chang, K. C., 207–8
cheeses, 37, 44
cherry peppers, 12–13
Chilacas, 16–17
Child, Julia, 46
chile, 5
"Chile Chocolate," 167, 168
chile Colorado, 16
chile de árbol, 13
chili, 5
chili oil, 27
chili peppers, 25, 30
chili powder, 27, 28
chili queens, 98
chili sauce, 28
chiltepínes, 13–14, 32, 180
Chinese pepper mix, 28
chipotle adobado, 28
Chipotle capons, 23
chipotles, 21, 25, 28
chives, 38
chlorine, 9, 21

Recipe Index